# ABANDONMENT IN DIXIE

*Endowed by*
**TOM WATSON BROWN**
*and*
**THE WATSON-BROWN FOUNDATION, INC.**

# ABANDONMENT IN DIXIE

*Underdevelopment in the Black Belt*

Veronica L. Womack

MERCER UNIVERSITY PRESS
MACON, GEORGIA

MUP / P461

© 2013 Mercer University Press
1400 Coleman Avenue
Macon, Georgia 31207
All rights reserved

First Edition

Books published by Mercer University Press are printed on acid-free paper that meets the requirements of the American National Standard for Information Sciences—Permanence of Paper for Printed Library Materials.

Mercer University Press is a member of Green Press Initiative (greenpressinitiative.org), a nonprofit organization working to help publishers and printers increase their use of recycled paper and decrease their use of fiber derived from endangered forests. This book is printed on recycled paper.

Library of Congress Cataloging-in-Publication Data

Womack, Veronica L.
   Abandonment in Dixie : underdevelopment in the Black Belt / Veronica L. Womack. -- First edition.
      pages cm. -- (MUP/P461)
   Includes bibliographical references and index.
   ISBN 978-0-88146-440-5 (pbk. : acid-free paper) -- ISBN 0-88146-440-6 (pbk. : acid-free paper)
   1. African Americans--Southern States--History--21st century. 2. African Americans--Southern States--Social conditions--21st century. 3. Southern States--Politics and government--21st century. 4. Southern States--Rural conditions. 5. Southern States--Race relations. 6. Black Belt (Ala. and Miss.) I. Title.
   E185.92.W66 2013
   305.896'073075--dc23
                           2013030160

# CONTENTS

| | |
|---|---|
| Tables | vii |
| Preface | ix |
| Chapter 1: The Black Belt Region Defined | 1 |
| Chapter 2: How Slavery Shaped the History of the Black Belt | 18 |
| Chapter 3: The Unique Political Culture of the Region | 42 |
| Chapter 4: Modern Racialized Politics in the Black Belt | 85 |
| Chapter 5: Rural African Americans and Persistent Poverty | 115 |
| Chapter 6: Development Policy and the Region's Political Economy | 159 |
| Chapter 7: Recent Developments in the Black Belt | 191 |
| Chapter 8: Conclusions | 208 |
| Sources | 217 |
| Index | 231 |

# TABLES

Table 1.0 Percentage of Race in Region, 1910
Table 1.1 Population, 1790–1910
Table 1.2 Black Population Percentages within Southern States, 1910
Table 2.0 Slave and Slave Owner Population in Hancock County, Georgia
Table 2.1 US Slave Population, 1820 and 1860
Table 3.0 Partisan Lineups in House and Senate Votes on Civil Rights Laws, 1866–1890
Table 3.1 African Americans in Congress During Reconstruction
Table 3.2 Farm Operators in the South in 1910
Table 3.3 Black Farm Owners in 1910
Table 4.0 Partisanship in the House of Civil Rights Law Passage
Table 4.1 Partisanship in the Senate of Civil Rights Law Passage
Table 4.2 Estimated Black Voter Registration in the Southern States
Table 4.3 Black Elected Officials as a Percentage of Total Officials in Southern State Covered by the Voting Rights Act. July 1980: Specific Categories
Table 4.4 The Number of African American Elected Officials in 1980
Table 4.5 Black Belt 2000 Voting and Registration Information
Table 4.6 2002 Black Elected Officials in the South
Table 4.7 111th Congress African American Congressional Leadership
Table 4.8 Alabama's Black Belt 2008 Presidential Vote
Table 5.0 Percent of Rural Families below Poverty
Table 5.1 African American High Population Counties in Georgia in 2000
Table 5.2 Quality of Life in Georgia Black Belt in 2000
Table 5.3 Alabama's Black Belt Region
Table 5.4 Arkansas's Black Belt
Table 5.5 Florida's Black Belt
Table 5.6 Georgia's Black Belt
Table 5.7 Louisiana's Black Belt
Table 5.8 Mississippi's Black Belt
Table 5.9 North Carolina's Black Belt
Table 5.10 South Carolina's Black Belt
Table 5.11 Tennessee's Black Belt
Table 5.12 Virginia's Black Belt
Table 5.13 Alabama's Black Belt Education and Unemployment in 2000

Table 5.14 Arkansas's Black Belt Education and Unemployment
Table 5.15 Florida's Black Belt Education and Unemployment
Table 5.16 Georgia's Black Belt Education and Unemployment
Table 5.17 Louisiana's Black Belt Education and Unemployment
Table 5.18 Mississippi's Black Belt Education and Unemployment
Table 5.19 North Carolina's Black Belt Education and Unemployment
Table 5.20 South Carolina's Black Belt Education and Unemployment
Table 5.21 Tennessee's Black Belt Education and Unemployment
Table 5.22 Virginia's Black Belt Education and Unemployment
Table 5.23 Black Cooperatives and Credit Unions in the South
Table 6.0 Overall Unemployment Rate by State and Quarter, 2007–2010
Table 6.1 Quarterly African American Unemployment Rates by State,* 2007–
Table 6.2 Labor Union Membership as a Percentage of Nonagricultural Workers
Table 6.3 Selected Development Incentives Available in Eleven Southern States
Table 6.4 BHI State Competitiveness Rankings for Southern States
Table 6.5 Southern State Competitiveness Subindexes Rank 2010
Table 6.6 Appalachian Regional Commission Model
Table 6.7 Governmental Models of Development
Table 7.0 Governmental Structure Models

Inserts

Insert 6-1 Demographics of African American Farmers
Insert 6-2 A Tale of Working with the USDA

# PREFACE

The collapse of the Black Belt plantation system is a perfect preface to American peasantry. The Black Belt South was the Jeffersonian republican's worst nightmare come true.

The Black Belt region, like the phoenix, has experienced death and reincarnation many times, and its connection to the black population within has always been contradictory, highlighting episodes of loathing and fear while at the same time exhibiting divergent adoration and dependence. Beginning with the arrival of 100 Africans in South Carolina, in 1526, when Luis Vasquez de Ayllon used them in the establishment of a Spanish colony, the black American existence predated the republic and its republican values and was central to its development in all things social, political and economic. And ninety-three years later, in 1619, twenty African settlers were recorded in the annals of history as residents of Jamestown, Virginia, once again documenting the interconnection between blacks and the founding of this country, particularly the rural, Black Belt South.

Yet there would be a transformation of the status of blacks from indentured servants to enslavement through the use of law, violence, and coercion. This conversion ironically developed simultaneously with the deliberations of freedom and equality that were taking place in colonial America. These Africans were excluded from the fabrication of the ideals espoused by the new nation and were conceived only as toilers of the rich, fertile land, the very foundation on which a successful plantation economy would emerge. This fertile land encompassed a powerful geographic region of enormous economic wealth and political strength, birthing several of the first presidents and statesmen who shaped the founding political and economic system. This region, the Black Belt region, stretched from Texas to Virginia and encompassed hundreds of counties that were blessed with rich, black soil. The term "Black Belt" was derived from the description of the land and later the

---

[1] Louis Mazzari, *Southern Modernist: Arthur Raper from the New Deal to the Cold War* (Baton Rouge: Louisiana State University Press, 2006) 111.

black people. This unique place made Southern planter aristocrats politically powerful and rich. In turn, they created a prosperous plantation system unrivaled anywhere in North America. Although the institution of slavery arose throughout the country, only the Black Belt region solely depended on this institution for its economic survival. With little or no additional economic diversity, this region relied exclusively on agriculture and was underdeveloped. Although deemed merely subjects, the large population of Africans influenced the Black Belt region economically, culturally, socially, and politically.

This region founded a distinct traditional sociopolitical culture that not only shaped the Black Belt region, but the Southern region as a whole along with its border states. This traditional political culture promoted strong individualism and espoused limited government, with its primary role being the protection of private property and defense. In addition, it developed a hierarchically structured society with a privileged few as the only deserving political actors, while allowing very limited political participation among the masses. This political ideology was also reflected in very limited social policy, such as public education or welfare, as well as a lack of physical infrastructural development that would have encouraged additional modes of enterprise beyond agriculture. Because of their development of a complementary economic and political system that benefitted them exclusively, the wealth and influence of Black Belt aristocrats grew with their flourishing crops, all propagated in the rich, black soil of the region. The slave economy that emerged from this arrangement lasted more than 240 years, and the lives of all Southerners and the peoples of the nation continue to be affected by it. None were influenced as much as the blacks within the region, though, as they were central to its economic and social success. Due to the size of their population and the implications of their history, blacks played an instrumental role in the future of the Black Belt. Yet historically, the leaders of this region were averse to any concessions to the group because they viewed these actions as unprofitable and not beneficial to them. So, desperate for the preservation and sustainability of slavery, the leaders of the Black Belt were willing to violently create a new nation in order to maintain it. They were well aware that black labor was the most vital part of the Black Belt region's economy before the

Civil War, and a fundamental element after the war, and the region could not afford to lose it. The Black Belt was not willing to restructure itself to allow blacks the opportunity to enjoy any fruits of the harvest they produced.

Blacks yearned for freedom in all of its forms—social, political, and economic—and they craved the one thing most essential to life in the Black Belt: land. Recognizing the significance of land to political and economic power and social standing, its pursuit became a major part of the life experience of blacks in the Black Belt. They also did like most aggrieved groups in an effort to change their circumstance: they fought for their freedom early on by running away, participating in work stoppages, arson, and other malevolent actions. Black people also linked their protest to faith. The historical roots of protest bonded with religious conviction can be found in early Southern rebellions, such as those led by Denmark Vesey, Nat Turner, and Gabriel Prosser, all connected to black faith and expectations of deliverance. Daring attempts at freedom came from black people of the South, such as Henry "Box" Brown of Virginia, who mailed himself North in a wooden crate, or Josiah Henson of Maryland, who escaped slavery and developed a settlement for other runaways in Canada, or Araminta Ross, best known as Harriet Tubman of Maryland, who not only assisted thousands of enslaved black people in their quest for freedom but also served her country as a cook for the Union army and as a spy. All of these noteworthy black activists had a common Southern experience, only afforded those of a darker hue, which helped shape their expression of resistance. Blacks residing outside of the Black Belt South resisted their second-class status through the assemblage of various gatherings and organizations for change. However, the exclusion of blacks from the workings of Black Belt society did not negate their desire for a remedy to their condition. One popular tool of activism was the Negro conventions, with the first convention being held on 15 September 1830, in Philadelphia. According to Herbert Aptheker, W. E. B. Du Bois found "the Meetings and petitions of Southern Negroes [during and immediately following the Civil War] were significant and can not be discounted. This…offer[s] excellent evidence of the desire and political level of the native southern Negro as expressed by himself in his own gatherings."[2]

The great catastrophe of war eventually provided the opportunity of freedom for blacks within the Black Belt, and for a brief moment, the prospect of serving as citizens. After centuries of degradation, brutality, and exclusion, blacks were allowed to participate politically in the South. As both voter and elected official, they proved counter to the traditional political themes of conservatism through their promotion of governmental activism. Dedicated to social reform, they advocated for universal secondary public education and free textbooks, the acquisition of land for newly freed blacks, as well as the development of higher education and skills development. However, the South and the Black Belt within proved formidable opponents of change and the reconstruction efforts sweeping the country after the war. Forces in the Black Belt were quickly at work to restore the traditions and norms of the Old South, and with a weak reconstruction effort and the quick reinstatement of the political rights of the former rebels, by the 1880s, most progressive efforts were impeded. Redeemer governments had set in motion efforts to restore the Old South sociopolitical system through intimidation, violence, and the passage of discriminatory public policy, with blacks again positioned at the bottom of Black Belt society. Yet from the ashes of hopes set ablaze by revulsion and detestation, like a phoenix, the faith and determination of blacks in the Black Belt helped to nurture and grow a civil rights movement that would not only reshape the Black Belt and the larger South but the entire country and, to a larger extent, the world.

These efforts were piecemeal at times and strategic during others, but they always focused on developing an equitable citizenship status for blacks. Blacks looked to approaches for change that were unique to their circumstances, and in the process, they redefined politics within the country. The fight over segregation and white supremacy sometimes aligned blacks with unlikely allies, such as socialist and communist groups, who provided opportunities not afforded them by the traditional Southern political system. They also developed political ideologies that

---

[2] Herbert Aptheker, "South Carolina Negro Conventions, 1865," *The Journal of Negro History* 31/1 (January 1946): 91.

proved akin to their lives, such as the Black Power ideology developed in Lowndes County, Alabama, through the work of Lemon Johnson and Stokely Carmichael. They also continued their quest for educational opportunities, and education proponents such as W. E. B. Du Bois, Booker T. Washington, and William James Edwards promoted diverse ideas for educating the masses of blacks within the region.[3] Others promoted economic independence by participating in efforts such as the development of cooperatives and activities related to land acquisition. Blacks within the region also influenced the cultural development of the country before and after the war. Cultural promoters such as Lead Belly, Ma Rainey, and Robert Johnson displayed the culture of the Black Belt by highlighting the language of oppression, love, and life of the Black Belt people for all the world to hear. Advertised in the work of Paul Laurence Dunbar and his promotion of the dialect of the Black Belt, or through the depictions of Black Belt folk in the works of Zora Neale Hurston, or as seen in the influential work *Cane,* which Jean Toomer based on his time in the Black Belt of Georgia, the region was critical in the development of American culture, and these artistic expressions helped to capture and portray the unique life experiences of rural blacks.

Recognizing the power of religion, blacks within the region relied on its strongest institution, the black church, tapping its leaders and members for social change. Leaders such as the Revs. Martin Luther King, Jr., Ralph Abernathy, Wyatt T. Walker, and Fred Shuttlesworth were instrumental in facilitating social and political change within the Black Belt. The fight against segregation and for voting rights in the South developed a unity among various political organizations throughout the country. The Black Belt and its organizations proved critical as most violent battles for civil rights were located in the region, such as those that occurred in Selma, Alabama; Lowndes County, Alabama, the delta of Mississippi, Arkansas, and southwest Georgia. Fighting for the

---

[3] Lemon Johnson was a tenant who worked on a Lowndes County, Alabama, plantation and was instrumental in Communist efforts in Alabama during the 1930s and served as a mentor to Carmichael and SNCC members in the 1960s. Edwards founded an institute in the Alabama Black Belt for blacks in Snow Hill, Alabama.

last remnants of the Old South, white resistance became a major part of life in the Black Belt, and brutality, inhumanity, and murder were used constantly as tools of white protest. However, the thought of black liberation inspired millions and created world-renowned activists such as Stokely Carmichael and Malcolm X, who linked with an international black liberation movement and connected it to the movement of blacks in America and in the Black Belt. Malcolm accepted an invitation of the Student Nonviolent Coordinating Committee (SNCC) in Selma, Alabama, in an effort to connect his work with their work in the rural South. Yet he was cognizant that his presence could make the nonviolent efforts of Dr. King and others within the region difficult, as evidenced when he stated, "I want Dr. King to know that I didn't come to Selma to make his job difficult." Malcolm placed his work with black Americans within the larger context of the black nationalist effort. While traveling to Ghana, he consulted with Prime Minister Kwame Nkrumah, representatives of the African National Congress (ANC) of South Africa, and the South African Pan-Africanist Congress of Azania Africa (PAC). In addition, he reached out to other world black nationalists throughout his work, as "he deepened that link with the forces of liberation in Africa on his second trip to Africa, especially at the OAU Summit Conference of Heads of State in Cairo, representing American blacks and was housed while there on a boat with other representatives."[4] He said of the experience, "I was blessed with the opportunity to live on that boat with the leaders of the liberation movements, because I represented an Afro American liberation movement."[5] Stokely Carmichael, another black nationalist with ties to the Black Belt, also linked his work to a larger African peoples movement. William W. Sales found not only a connection of American black struggles but also connections between the ideology of Carmichael and Malcolm in their black liberation approach: "Stokely Carmichael's All African Peoples Revolutionary Party (AAPRP) believed as did Malcolm X, that the basis for Black Revolution

---

[4] William W. Sales, *From Civil Rights to Black Nationalism: Malcolm X and the Organization of Afro-American Unity* (Cambridge MA: South End Press, 1994) 104.
[5] Ibid.

could not be located solely with the United States." Stokely saw his work in the Black Belt as part of a larger struggle of the world's black people.[6]

As with the early twentieth century, midcentury efforts for change were accompanied by a cultural awakening. The Black Arts Movement of the 1960s and 1970s married political activism with artistic expression, producing such arts activists as Maya Angelou, Nikki Giovanni, and Haki R. Madhubuti, whose experiences in the South helped develop their artistic craft and their civil rights work.

Although the battle for civil rights was eventually won and blacks within the Black Belt received their social and political rights, their economic rights went largely unfulfilled. Historically, it had been proven that political rights did not result in economic freedom for blacks in the region, and the economic circumstance of blacks within the Black Belt lagged behind both whites and blacks elsewhere. Slavery and its legacy of segregation continued to have a negative impact on the lives of black people in the Black Belt region decades after the civil rights movement, as the lack of generational wealth and economic opportunity were highlighted there. By the 1980s, the region could be summed up by horrifying social and economic statistics, always assembled well below the national average in all quality-of-life indicators. Plagued by generations of persistent poverty, consistently low educational attainment, continued substandard housing, and inadequate healthcare, the Black Belt region of the late twentieth and early twenty-first century emphasizes the lack of a comprehensive Southern rural development policy and the failure of the "one size fits all" approach to solving regional economic problems. In addition, it shows the price paid for the South's reliance on cheap low-skilled labor and the recruitment of low-rung manufacturing.

This book tells the story of rural black people within the Black Belt and their unique American experience. It describes the lack of comprehensive federal and state plans to incorporate them into the

---

[6] Malcolm X speech, "The House Negro and the Field Negro," to SNCC in Selma, Alabama, 4 February 1965. www.pbs.org/wgbh/amex/malcolmx/peopleevents/e_civilrights.html, accessed 12 December 2012. Sales, *From Civil Rights to Black Nationalism*, 104 and 177.

economic system on an equal basis. It also highlights the inability of the region to adapt to the new knowledge-based, high-skilled economy due to a lack of investment in rural education and physical infrastructure. In addition, it sheds light on the current circumstances of rural blacks of the region and the need for a greater emphasis on developing regional solutions to address regional problems.

*Why Focus on the Black Belt Region?*

Some may ask why study the Black Belt region. Or wonder what could be so different about this area in comparison to the entire Southern region. Wouldn't it be more beneficial to study the South in its entirety? Wouldn't it be better for the country to forget the ugly past of the Black Belt and move on? Well, besides the fact that the region is a rewarding exercise in research, this area reveals invaluable information about American political history. The Black Belt exposes significant information about the development of political ideology of rural African Americans, the development of American political parties, the class and racial divisions within our society, and how legal and extralegal mechanisms were used to create a split-race society that in many substantive areas continues into the twenty-first century. In addition, a unique culture, developed out of the distinct societal structures developed so long ago, is revealed. The Black Belt region and its difficult past have significant bearing on the present day Black Belt society and warrants exploration.

*Why Is This Research Unique?*

The Black Belt region and its people have been studied historically by focusing on the glorious pre-Civil War past of the South, with its wealthy landed Black Belt aristocracy. Or the region has been studied by focusing on the poverty and despair of rural African Americans that led to the modern civil rights movement. However, there are few present-day examinations of the Black Belt region, and those that do exist often have conflicting definitions. This book defines the Black Belt region presently, encompassing not only socioeconomic data but also a comprehensive history and review of the political economy of the region and how these factors shape the Black Belt in the twenty-first century. Addressing a rarely studied group, rural African Americans, the work explores the history and experiences of this group within the region and the factors that have shaped and continue to shape their lives. African American rural poverty in the twenty-first century continues a legacy for many that began with the importation of enslaved Africans to the New World. Most current research on black poverty focuses on those African Americans living in urban areas, and the lives of impoverished rural African Americans is often overlooked in a nationalistic perspective of poverty. Even when studying urban poverty, very few works relate the conditions of the Black Belt South and African American migratory patterns to urban poverty, which should be an important component of any explanation of black urban poverty. These populations and associating factors are strongly connected. There are even fewer works that focus on African American Southern rural poverty and the effects of the global economy and transnational policy on this population. Most works focusing on African Americans in the rural South look only at issues of culture or history and do not address the interdependence of history, culture, public policy, and present-day social, political, and economic conditions that influence and encompass the Black Belt experience for this group.

The preface begins the Black Belt regional journey by defining the area and its culture. Chapter 1 continues the definition of the region and the history of the black population within. Chapter 2 focuses on slavery and the history of the Black Belt South. Specifically, by examining the people, the culture, and the socioeconomic and political factors that created this unique locale, a place of interesting contradictions is revealed. Chapter 3 looks at the fascinating political history of the region and the factors that shaped the political environment and political culture. The rise of African American elected officials, paralleled with the rise of political conservatism and the Republican Party in the region, will be covered. Chapter 4 focuses on racialized politics in the region and its influence on political participation and policy. In addition, the political reality of nonelected, appointed boards in the region is also addressed, along with how this negatively affected democracy and the people of the Black Belt region. Chapter 5 provides a twenty-first-century exploration of the Black Belt region composed of current demographic factors associated with the residents of the Black Belt region. Factors such as racial composition, unemployment percentages, and educational attainment levels are all important points of comparison in defining the twenty-first century Black Belt region. Chapter 6 focuses on the development of the political economy of the region, specifically on the history of development policy as a remedy for economic and social ills. The absence of a comprehensive national rural development policy and its effect on this region, in particular, will be discussed. Additionally, the power of the transition to the global economy on the quality of life in the rural South will be assessed. Chapter 7 focuses on recent proposed national initiatives for the Black Belt that are patterned after initiatives in the Appalachian region and reveals how they are ill-equipped to handle the unique conditions of the Black Belt region. Chapter 8 concludes the book with final discussions on the issues addressed in the text and present prescriptions for change that are rational within the unique context of the socioeconomic political environment of the Black Belt region.

Therefore, although this book will define the Black Belt region in the twenty-first century through a comprehensive theoretical approach, it will also explore how governmental responses, culture and tradition, and civil society have played and continue to play a significant role in the sociopolitical and economic development of the region. This narrative will chronicle how the systemic inadequacy or lack of governmental responses, discriminatory and racist components of the Black Belt culture, and traditions of the region and civil society unfairly target rural African Americans, impeding the group's ability to take advantage of socioeconomic progresses occurring in the region. These actions have resulted in an underdeveloped region that is ill-equipped for twenty-first-century challenges.

# THE BLACK BELT REGION DEFINED

The Black Belt region is grounded in the Old South and was key in shaping and developing it. The Old South has been described in various ways within academia and throughout popular culture, often illustrated as a legendary place, based on a Southern mythology. This mythology was essential in the creation of the region's unique culture, particularly the strong racial divisions, as well as the promotion of regionalism and Southern white nationalism that permeates within the traditions of the Old South. Yet the race mythology within the South, particularly in the Black Belt, was far more complex than just white over black. In fact, it also included elements of intrawhite superiority, as the Southern antebellum race mythology even included intraracial theories that assisted in creating a chasm between Northern and Southern whites as it presented a clear reason for differences in regional culture. These perceived differences, along with conflicting theories of federalism and politics, would eventually result in armed combat between the two regions and centuries of political and social ideological differences. Often highlighted are the political and economic differences of the North and South, yet many Southerners viewed themselves culturally superior to the North as a separate race of people. This difference has been described as a "deep cultural and racial division that had originated over two hundred years ago in England in the antagonism between Puritan and Cavalier."[1] Accordingly, Southerners viewed themselves as descendants of the Cavaliers, whom they felt represented the descendants

---

[1] I use the terms "black" and "African American" interchangeably throughout this book. Ritchie Watson, "'The Difference of Race': Antebellum Race Mythology and the Development of Southern Nationalism," *Southern Literary Journal* (2002)1. A. Clarkson, *The Basis of Northern Hostility to the South*, 7–16 in J. D. B. DeBow 28/1 (July 1860). http://quod.lib.umich.edu/m/moajrnl/acg1336.1-28.001/11:5?rgn=full+text;view=image, accessed 12 December 2012.

of a more enlightened English society. Clarkson published in 1860 that the Northerners were descended from the English puritans, "who were among the very worst developments of human nature." While Southerners were descended from the "more enlightened classes of Great Britain and France.... In our descent, we, of the South, have advanced rapidly on the intellectual, moral, and social development of our ancestors; perfecting the great work they began in 1688 establishing a free, representative, and constitutional republic, with an open Bible, and with the noblest, most cultivated and enlightened, and most Christian social system that has ever existed."[2] With this understanding, Southerners theorized that they were culturally superior and more representative of a pure Anglo-Saxon bloodline than their Northern counterparts and viewed their way of life superior to that of the North. Yet this division in "whiteness" between North and South did not theoretically play out within Southern society itself, as whiteness proved important, regardless of ethnicity or class. Within the Black Belt region of the South, whiteness became an important factor of solidarity, as described in an 1864 publication: "There the white man wears an eternal badge of honor in his white skin, which, however, poor he may be, if he is an honest, upright, and intelligent citizen, is always acknowledged at all times, and in all places.... There the social ban is on the black race...."[3] Applying this race mythology to the history of the Black Belt allows for a basis for historical racism against blacks and provides explanation for the racial cohesiveness of Southern whites while serving as a possible explanation of how racism influenced the policy and socioeconomic decisions of the region, including the development of social and political institutions.

Therefore, the Southern race mythology directed the development of "blackness" and the placement of blacks outside of Black Belt society, which was not just a gradual process but developed simultaneously with

---

[2] A. Clarkson, *Northern Hostility*, http://quod.lib.umich.edu/m/moajrnl/acg1336.1-28.001/20:5?page=root;size=100;view=pdf, accessed 12 December 2012.

[3] C. C. Burr, *The Old Guard* (New York: 1864) 102. http://quod.lib.umich.edu/m/moajrnl/aag2687.0002.005/113:1?rgn=full+text;view=image, accessed 12 December 2012.

the region itself and became an integral part of the traditions and norms there. The first census in 1790 found that blacks in the South were numbered at 689,784. By 1910, 89 percent of blacks lived in the South, while 25 percent of whites resided there. According to John Cummings, "Throughout the period from 1790 to 1860, Virginia maintained her preeminence as regards Negro population over all other states. At the census of 1860, 5 Southern states reported Negro populations in excess of 400,000—Virginia 548,907; Georgia, 465,698; Alabama, 437,770; Mississippi, 437,404; South Carolina, 412, 320, and 7 other Southern states reported Negro populations in excess of 100,000." In 1910, the black population was 1,176,987, in Georgia, the largest in the country, and all of the 13 states that had black populations over 200,000 were located in the South. There were very few foreign-born whites in the South in 1910, as this population was 726,171, or 5.4 percent of the total foreign white population in the country.[4] Table 1.0 shows the small percentage of white foreign population in each region during 1910, revealing the low percentage within the Southern region and highlighting the fact that there was no need for white, cheap, immigrant labor in the South, since black labor was dominant.

Table 1.0 Percentage of Race in Region, 1910

| Geographic Region | Black | White Native | White Foreign Born |
|---|---|---|---|
| The South | 29.8 | 67.4 | 2.5 |
| The North | 1.8 | 77.7 | 20.3 |
| The West | 0.7 | 76.9 | 19.0 |
| U.S. | 10.7 | 74.4 | 14.5 |

John Cummings, "Negro Population: 1790–1915," Department of Commerce, Bureau of Census (Washington DC: Government Printing Office, 1918): 46.

*The Development of Blackness*

Although black indentured servants were residents of the original colony in Jamestown, Virginia, the collective group transformation from

---

[4] John Cummings, "Negro Population: 1790–1915," Department of Commerce, Bureau of Census (Washington DC: Government Printing Office, 1918) 35 and 39.

indentured servant to the enslaved began soon after. By 1640, Africans within colonial America, those already stateside and new arrivals, would eventually be snared in the nightmare of involuntary servitude.

Extended terms of indentured servitude demonstrated the deteriorating status of blacks after 1619, often the result of concocted violations of contracts that would extend the term of the contract for the black servant, thereby developing the distinctiveness of blackness. The *John Punch Case* (1640) is illustrative of this phenomenon. John Punch, of African descent, James Gregory, a white man, and another white man named Victor were all indentured servants contracted to Virginia planter Hugh Gwyn. All three men ran away, hoping to obtain their freedom. They were apprehended and Gwyn took them to court. The two white indentured servants were sentenced to four additional years of labor beyond their initial seven-year contract, but John Punch was sentenced to "serve his master or his assigns for the time of his natural life," becoming the first enslaved black American.[5] Remarkably, as early as 1640 in this country, law was used to distinguish blackness and the consequence of its membership upon newly arriving individuals and those who were already living there. This resulted in the development of an agriculturally built slave empire that fueled the socioeconomic and political development of the country, particularly within the Black Belt region. The Southern race mythology and its promotion of blackness as negative and separate created and sustained a dual society membership within the region, one black and one white.[6] Table 1.1 below shows the significant black population during colonial and antebellum America.

---

[5] John Punch, *Slavery and the Making of America*, http://www.pbs.org/wnet/slavery/experience/responses/spotlight.html, accessed 12 December 2012. For additional information on the case, see H. R. Mcilwaine's "Minutes of the Council and General Court of Colonial Virginia, 1622–1632, 1670–1676," 2nd ed. (Richmond: Library of Virginia, 1979).

[6] Don Jordan and Michael Walsh White, *Cargo: The Forgotten History of Britain's White Slaves in America* (New York: NY Press, 2008) 174. Theodore Wilson, *The Black Codes of the South* (Tuscaloosa: University of Alabama Press, 1965) 18.

Table 1.1 Population 1790–1910

| Date | Black Population | Black Percentage | White Population |
|---|---|---|---|
| 1910 | 9,827,763 | 10.7 | 81,731,957 |
| 1900 | 8,833,994 | 11.6 | 66,809,196 |
| 1890 | 7,4888,676 | 11.9 | 55,101,258 |
| 1880 | 6,580,793 | 13.1 | 43,402,970 |
| 1870 | 4,880,009 | 12.7 | 33,589,377 |
| 1860 | 4,441,830 | 14.1 | 26,922,537 |
| 1850 | 3,638,808 | 15.7 | 19,553,068 |
| 1840 | 2,873,648 | 16.8 | 14,195,805 |
| 1830 | 2,328,642 | 18.1 | 10,537,378 |
| 1820 | 1,771,656 | 18.4 | 7,866,797 |
| 1810 | 1,377,808 | 19.0 | 5,862,073 |
| 1800 | 1,002,037 | 18.9 | 4,306,446 |
| 1790 | 757,208 | 19.3 | 3,172,006 |

Source: John Cummings, "Negro Population: 1790–1915," Department of Commerce, Bureau of Census (Washington DC: Government Printing Office, 1918): 29.

Within this Old South mythology emerged not only theories and the practice of racial superiority (both inter- and intra-), but also the linking of sociopolitical theories of development and advancement to Christianity and religion. The Christianity practiced within the South also supported the Southern race mythology and upheld theories of racial superiority that were used in sanctioning and justifying black slavery and racial and gender discrimination. After all, the enslavement of the Africans was well within the doctrine of fundamentalist regional Christianity, as blacks were thought to be descendants of Ham, who had been cursed and, through their ancestry and blackness were chained to Genesis 9:25. Englishman William Archer wrote about the complex relationship between segregation and Christianity as he traveled through the Black Belt in the early twentieth century:

> The Southern goes to the Gospels for his rule of life, and has never heard of Nietzsche; yet I am wholly unable to discover how the system of race

> discriminations is reconcilable with the fundamental precepts of Christianity. It is far easier to find in the Old Testament the justification of the Jim Crow car, the white and black school, and the white and black church. This is not necessarily a condemnation of the Southerner's attitude: I do not think that the color problem was foreseen in the New Testament. Christianity's one thing, sociology another, and the Southerner's logical error perhaps lies in not keeping the distinction clear. But I am sure there are many sincere an earnest Christians in the South who will scarce be at ease in Heaven unless they enter it, like a Southern railway station, through a gateway marked "For Whites."

Archer illustrates how segregation may have found justification by whites in the Old Testament and the integral part it played in the lives of people of the region.[7]

So this Southern mythology served as the basis for not only white supremacy, but also white Southern nationalism, which became an important factor in developing the character of the South and bred a Southern white resistance philosophy that disconnected the region from other parts of the country on many issues, particularly those of slavery and civil rights. The South, however, is not homogenous and is composed of many subregions. According to renowned sociologist Howard Odum,

> Within the South, there are not only the old cultural subregions, such as Charleston, New Orleans, but more than a score of demographic subregions including the Black Belt, the Cotton Piedmont, Tobacco Piedmont, Northern Cotton-Tobacco, Blue Ridge, Atlantic Tidewater, Semi-Tropical, Citrus Vegetable, Vegetable Citrus, Southern Cotton-Tobacco, Northern Piedmont, Coast, Tennessee Valley, Cumberland, Blue Grass, Tobacco Cattle, Muscle Shoals-Nashville Basin, Mining, Black Belt, Gulf Coast Plain, Gulf Tidewater, Rice-Cane, Bluffs, Interior Ridge, Delta, Interior Plain, Ozark, Red River Bottoms, Shenandoah Valley.[8]

---

[7] William Archer, "An Englishman's Study of Black and White: Use of the 'Jim Crow Car' in the Black Belt: Some Racial Prejudices," *The New York Times,* 7 March 1909. http://query.nytimes.com/mem/archive-free/pdf?res=F70615FA3E5D12738DDD AE0894DB405B898CF1D3, accessed 12 December 2012.

[8] Howard W. Odum, "Regionalism vs. Sectionalism in the South's Place in the National Economy," *Social Forces* 12/3 (March 1934): 348.

Yet although all of these subcultures were unique, distinct, and Southern, the Old South's mythical model was perfected in the Black Belt region, and the South as a whole took on the sociopolitical character of the Black Belt region. Therefore, it is important to understand the region in order to understand its underdevelopment, particularly the unique experiences of the rural blacks within.

*The Black Belt Region*

The Black Belt is a crescent-shaped region that extends from eastern Texas to the eastern shore of Virginia and encompasses the bulk of the old plantation South. Booker T. Washington designated it as a part of the country that had rich, black soil, a history of enslaved Africans, counties with majority African American populations, and the execution of extreme racial politics, often promoted through violent attacks on blacks. In this eminent work *Up from Slavery*, the inimitable connection between black people and the land, the primary source of economic security in the Black Belt South, was discussed. This economic dependence between the two was established as the first enslaved Africans appeared on the Carolina and Georgia coasts. Although the Black Belt region thrived economically through the promotion of an agrarian economy, it developed more slowly socially as its peculiar racial and social relationships created a "closed society," isolated from many of the socioeconomic and political developments taking form in other regions of the country.[9]

This closed society was eloquently illustrated by W. E. B. Du Bois in his famous work *The Souls of Black Folk* (1903), which described the Black Belt as "a strange land of shadows at which even slaves paled in the past, and whence come now only faint and half-intelligible murmurs to the world beyond."[10] This portrayal of the Black Belt as an eccentric, mysterious, irrational, and shadowy place, closed from the society beyond, is often discarded in recent literature, which describes the region based solely on cold, socioeconomic factors that lack the totality of the

---

[9] Booker T. Washington, *Up from Slavery* (Garden City NY: Doubleday, 1901).
[10] W. E. B. Du Bois, *The Souls of Black Folks* (Chicago: A. C. McClurg, 1903).

circumstances that give explanation to the region.[11] Table 1.2 below highlights the large percentages of blacks within the Southern states at the turn of the twentieth century.

Table 1.2 Black Population Percentages within Southern States, 1910

| State | Black Population Percentage |
|---|---|
| Mississippi | 56.2 |
| South Carolina | 55.2 |
| Georgia | 45.1 |
| Louisiana | 43.1 |
| Alabama | 42.5 |
| Florida | 41.0 |
| Virginia | 32.6 |
| North Carolina | 31.6 |
| Arkansas | 28.1 |
| Tennessee | 21.7 |
| Maryland | 17.9 |
| Texas | 17.7 |
| Delaware | 15.4 |
| Kentucky | 11.4 |
| Oklahoma | 8.3 |
| West Virginia | 5.3 |

John Cummings, "Negro Population: 1790–1915," Department of Commerce, Bureau of Census (Washington DC: Government Printing Office, 1918): 49.

The interconnectedness of race, class, and gender was clearly evident in the antebellum Black Belt South, historically playing an extremely important role in the lives of people within the region. Yet for blacks in the rural South, blackness underscored the power or privilege of maleness, the alleviations of class, and the protections and praise of

---

[11] Ibid.

womanhood more formally than anywhere else, since blackness revoked the social graces and charms promoted within the Black Belt region. The intrinsic nature of racism and the societal structure of the region successfully perfected racial and gender discrimination as they were used to perpetuate the mythology of the region. This mythology kept blacks within the region out of all aspects of power and helped shape blackness as a major factor of inequality within the region. So although initially Africans came to America in a similar fashion as white indentured servants, their transformation to involuntary servitude was complete by the late seventeenth to early eighteenth centuries. This transformation was most significant in the Black Belt since it developed its economy exclusively on black enslaved labor. The Black Belt region and its development proved central to the development of the South:

> In such states as Alabama and Georgia, for example, a compelling case can be made that the Black belt served as their cultural hearths, the progenitors of their Antebellum cultures. Likewise, in the twentieth century, many of the South's preeminent battles during the civil rights movement were fought in the Black Belt. Thus, the Black Belt region played a prominent if not dominant role in the two most important events in the South's history, the Civil War and the Civil Rights Movement.[12]

The legacy of racial discrimination and violence within the region has negatively influenced the lives of blacks there as the legacy has been "shaped by slavery, sharecropping, segregation, marginal employment opportunities and limited educational choices."[13] According to Wimberley and Morris, the Black Belt region is a product of the 1700s and 1800s and consists of 11 states and 623 counties in the Old South with higher than the national percentage of black population. These counties have historically been linked to low quality-of-life conditions,

---

[12] Margaret L. Andersen and Patricia Hill Collins, *Race, Class, and Gender: An Anthology* (Belmont CA: Wadsworth, 2001). Gerald R. Webster and Jerrod Bowman, "Quantitatively Delineating the Black Belt Geographic Region," *Southeastern Geographer* 48 (May 2008): 3.

[13] Louis E. Swanson, Rosalind P. Harris, Jerry R. Skees, and Lionel Williamson, "African Americans in the Southern Rural Regions: The Importance of Legacy," *The Review of Black Political Economy* 22 (1994) 110.

such as persistent poverty, low education levels, poor quality of health, and high economic dependence.[14]

The region has also been politically described: "The Black Belt sketches the section of the nation where the smallest proportion of adults exercise the franchise and it defines the most solid part of the Solid South,"[15] as historically the region has been dominated by a solidly Democratic party. Internationally, the Communists believed "the Southern Black Belt constituted a colonized 'nation' in need of liberation." Harry Haywood, an internationally known black Communist, defined the region as "the area in which the plantation economy is most firmly rooted; the peon farms today correspond to the slave plantations of yesterday."[16] Haywood's understanding of the Black Belt highlights the connection between the lack of development within the region and its unusual past and explains how many of the ills of the region can be linked to the history of the place.

The Black Belt region has also been described as a foreign place and linked to the African continent by way of its large black population, even being referenced as the "Africa of America." Geographically it has been depicted as "centring at Alabama, borders along the Atlantic and the great Gulf, reaching along the Mississippi valley to upper Missouri, and along the Ohio Valley as far east as Pittsburg. All of these vast tracts of land are included within the Black Belt."[17]

Although numerous and diverse, each definition of the Black Belt region includes the exceptional size and position of the blacks within the

---

[14] Ibid. Joyce E. Allen-Smith, Ronald C. Wimberley, and Libby V. Morris, "America's Forgotten People and Places: Ending the Legacy of Poverty in the Rural South," *Journal of Agricultural and Applied Economics* 32/2 (2000): 319–29.

[15] Arthur Raper, *Preface to Peasantry: A Tale of Two Black Belt Counties*, (Chapel Hill: University of North Carolina, 1936) 4–5.

[16] *Modern Black Nationalism: From Marcus Garvey to Louis Farrakhan*, ed. William L. Van Deburg (New York: New York University Press, 1997) 59. Raper, *Preface to Peasantry*, 4–5. Harry Haywood, *Negro Liberation* (New York: International Publishers Inc., 1948) 11.

[17] Reverend E. L. Quade, "Our Africa," *Catholic World* 62 (1896): 830–35. http://quod.lib.umich.edu/m/moajrnl/bac8387.0062.372/868:16?rgn=full+text;view=image, accessed 12 December 2012.

region. The difficulty of their existence was recognized in an 1896 article.

> It is difficult to fancy a people in a worse plight than the Negroes of the South. Living amid our civilization, vast numbers of them are yet not of it; men by civil law. Yet in very great part children; citizens by constitutional amendment, yet babes in the exercise of their rights, apparently Christians, they are really of no religion; free men in the eyes of world, yet really shackled with the fetters of superstition; strong in the exercise of imaginative power, yet weak in their ability to comprehend real ideas; in the sight of the law they are everything, in its hands they are nothing..[18] This is, in fine, their present moral, social, and political standing.

These trials would define the Black Belt existence for blacks for generations to come, as they were seen not as men and women but children who must be "protected" and "disciplined."

Geographically, the Black Belt is located within a traditionalistic political culture, which political scientist Daniel Elazar has described as a hierarchically structured society established by elites who dominate politics and governmental activities while discouraging any participation by the masses that may result in change within the society. According to Elazar, these elites use government to their advantage and make policy that benefit them in an effort to maintain the status quo and discourage innovation and impede inclusion. This exclusive political culture of the Black Belt had significant implications on African American social and political inclusion and economic progress within the region and serves as a backdrop for a long history of social and political resistance by blacks as well as a strong movement of white resistance and backlash politics.[19]

This political exclusion was used to shape a unique economic system that was historically driven by an agricultural economy. The founding of this agricultural economy and its connection to black people has historical and present-day importance, since there has been a lasting linkage between blacks and the land of the South because the land served as the basis for the agricultural economy that developed the Black Belt

---

[18] Quade, "Our Africa," 830–35.
[19] Daniel J. Elazar, *American Federalism: A View from the States* (New York: HarperCollins, 1984).

society in which they lived. The oppressive and hierarchically structured society it produced firmly planted African Americans at the bottom, first as enslaved people and next as free, often landless people with few opportunities for advancement. Whether by economic, social, or political effort, the rural African American population was positioned outside of the mainstream of Black Belt society, yet was an integral part of the success and development of the region, primarily through their working of the land, their free labor, and their population size.

*The Unique Cultural-Institutional Arrangement of the Black Belt Region*

So what is this unique cultural-institutional arrangement of Southern society—in particular rural Black Belt society—that has had a negative generational influence on African American residents of the region? Scholars have analyzed inequalities in society based on social-cultural and structural-institutional factors. The social-cultural factors suggest family structure, social norms, and socialization processes result in differences of socioeconomic experiences among people. Structural-institutional theorists suggest societal institutions such as labor markets, political structure, and educational systems play significant roles in the socioeconomic experiences of people.

    This work theorizes that inequality in the Black Belt region is a result of a unique cultural-institutional arrangement. Other theorists have defined this arrangement as legacy. Swanson, Harris, Skees, and Williamson suggest legacies are "the social values, cultural framing assumptions, hopes, and fears passed from one generation to the next."[20] The conditions of the rural South have resulted in the continued marginalization of African Americans in the Black Belt region because of their legacy of slavery, segregation, and inequality of economic and social opportunity. Additionally, the exclusion of political participation or the reliance on simplistic, descriptive representation at the expense of true participatory power in the political arena in Black Belt communities

---

[20] Louis Swanson, Rosalind Harris, Jerry Skees, and Lionel Williamson, "African Americans in Southern Rural Regions: The Importance of Legacy," *The Review of Black Political Economy* 22/4 (Spring 1994): 109–10.

is common. The exceptionalism of the cultural arrangement in the Black Belt region has been, and in some areas, still is, the exclusive nature of socioeconomic and political institutions and the omission of blacks, and to a lesser extent, poor whites, from key decision-making roles. This exclusion of African Americans, who make-up such a large population within the Black Belt region, created a tradition in which this group was viewed, and is still sometimes perceived, as occupying a position outside of "true citizen" and therefore unworthy of the benefits thereof. Add to this quandary a very traditional hierarchical social structure that is not conducive to the needs of the less fortunate, especially those with a darker hue, and what emerges is an inaccessible local, political, and social system with few chances for any hope of progress. Link this with a politically conservative political culture and a restrictively controlled local government that is limited in scope and for the most part inactive, but which has played a significant role in the subjugation of those out of power, and the result is generational poverty and hopelessness for many rural African Americans or, more succinctly, generational disparity.

This unique cultural arrangement created a very uncomfortable position in the Black Belt for poor Southern whites, in that although economically they had more in common with African Americans of the region than the financially successful white land and business owners, they were required to go against their own economic interests in many cases to adhere to the social structures and norms of the Black Belt South. This irrational social arrangement began during the antebellum South, as defined in this quote by Lewis: "Even as the racial basis of American slavery hardened over the decades, masters and slaves endured in a codependency based on coercion, manipulation, antagonism, and consanguinity that required of the millions of excluded poor whites little more than political passivity and police work."[21] This unusual cultural arrangement made it impossible for poor and working-class whites and blacks to create a lasting socioeconomic and political alliance that could benefit them both and develop the region on their behalf.

---

[21] David Levering Lewis, *W. E. B. Du Bois: The Fight for Equality and the American Century, 1919–1963* (New York: Henry Holt & Company, 2002) 370.

Racism ensured that the Black Belt region would make important decisions about development, education, business, and policy creation and implementation along racial lines, which crippled the region and many of its people. Unfortunately, the region has yet to recover from this very successful strategy, and in some areas of the Black Belt, the strategy continues to be implemented.

Historically, the small, local white elite class was very politically active and ideologically conservative, not requiring or needing an active government with a significant public service provision. In fact, the development or establishment of a local government with significant social welfare provision would be counter to their need for economic dependence from the majority black population or poor white population within the county. This ruling group particularly was opposed to a government, whether local, state, or national, that was inclusive in composition, innovative and supportive in service provision, or could result in the economic independence of the blacks whom they depended upon for financial survival. Therefore, regional leaders established a Black Belt society that produced a government with limited social responsibility and strength, which then served as an accomplice to the discrimination of blacks in the region. This government was established by, composed of, and ruled by white Southern elites for many generations. Williams argued that the early Alabama Black Belt aristocracy was not always politically successful, but the power of this elite group was recognized as early as the 1830s.

> By nature, through environment, and because of training, a majority of these black-belt slaveholding cotton producers felt themselves well qualified to pass judgment upon the administrative policies of governors and of presidents.... They were quite willing to criticize their own institutions, but they felt that they best understood their own problems and that whatever changes were to be made would be made cautiously and then not by means of outside interference.... They respected the constitutions under which their security had grown and they intended to protect their position.[22]

---

[22] Clanton W. Williams, "Early Ante-Bellum Montgomery: A Black-Belt Constituency," *The Journal of Southern History* 7/4 (November 1941): 517–18.

These feelings of privilege remained long after the antebellum Black Belt disappeared. Gibson found that Southern aristocracy, although a "vanishing cultural element has lingered long in the Black Belt," and that the region represented the sharpest color line in the South with a significant dependence on blacks by whites.[23] This observation was made long after Emancipation and well into the twentieth century.

A Black Belt regional dialectic emerged, with blacks opposing their subservient role within the region and a majority of the white population, regardless of class, primarily resisting efforts for change. Decades after Emancipation, blacks were still looked upon as vital to the economic success of the region, as illustrated in this *New York Times* article in which a former plantation owner stated of blacks, "They are industrious for awhile, but they lack persistence and intelligent methods. I don't see what the country is to do; they will never restore it, I fear.... They are the only people that will endure the labor here. A white man can't stand it. They are just what is needed here. But they have no ambition or pride in the country."[24] The article displayed the bewilderment and disappointment of this and many former masters in the newfound social structure of the Black Belt, who were anxious and often opposed to the readjustments to the social order of the region and what it meant for their relationship with blacks.

These difficult social dynamics notwithstanding, after the Civil War, one thing linked most peoples of the Black Belt South, regardless of race: poverty. As the Black Belt society transformed, economic opportunities existed for only a privileged few. And so the Black Belt and the Southern region as a whole continued to be intrinsically linked to high levels of poverty that were often cyclical and generational. Many of those who were of means before the war fell on hard times. Systemic poverty within the region had been well above the national average

---

[23] J. Sullivan Gibson, "The Alabama Black Belt: Its Geographic Status" *Economic Geography* 17/1 (January 1941): 22–23.
[24] "The Planter and the Poor White: The Black Belt As It Was, and As It Is—the Contrasts Which Twenty Years Present," 23 February 1877. http://query.nytimes.com/mem/archive-free/pdf?res=F50E12FA3F55107A93C1AB1789-D85F438784F9, accessed 12 December 2012.

before the Civil War and did not remain in the past, in the Old Black Belt South. On the contrary, poverty persisted well into the twenty-first century and continues to play a significant role in the present modern Black Belt South. According to a report by the Population Reference Bureau, the Southern region has higher poverty rates than other regions around the country, and the Black Belt South within the Southern region maintains the highest rate. The report acknowledged that while the region is narrowing the gap, the gap is changing slowest within the Black Belt among black people.[25] Social scientists Webster and Bowman found the extreme level of poverty currently defines the region as "the preeminent characteristic of the Black Belt today. One must ask how a region of substantive importance to the history of the South as a whole has continued to be characterized by its levels of poverty and not by successful efforts to improve the socioeconomic conditions of its people."[26] This severe concentration of poverty is most prominent among the black population of the Black Belt, yet all of the population of the region is influenced by its unusual economic condition.

W. E. B. Du Bois wrote, "Once accustomed to poverty, to the sight of toil and degradation, it easily seems normal and natural; once it is hidden beneath a different color of skin, a different stature or a different habit of action and speech, and all consciousness of inflicting ill disappears."[27] To see current Black Belt rural poverty strictly as a contemporary black crisis disregards the acknowledgement of systemic inequality and its influence on the present Black Belt and its link to the past. This distinctive regional poverty tends to be depicted for the most part as a black rural dilemma that results in the nation and the region's inability to look at rural Black Belt poverty through nondiscriminatory lens. Yet the region's stagnant sociopolitical culture has resulted in its

---

[25] Mark Mather, "U.S. Racial/Ethnic and Regional Poverty Rates Converge, but Kids are Still Left Behind," Population Reference Bureau (August 2007) http://www.prb.org/Articles/2007/USRacialEthnicAndRegionalPoverty.aspx, accessed 12 December 2012.
[26] Gerald R. Webster and Jerrod Bowman, "Quantitatively Delineating the Black Belt Geographic Region," *Southeastern Geographer* 48/ (May 2008): 15.
[27] David Levering Lewis, *W. E. B. Du Bois: The Fight for Equality and the American Century, 1919–1963* (New York: Henry Holt & Company, 2002) 588.

inability to keep up with the larger South and other regions in terms of socioeconomic development, trapping many Black Belt dwellers, particularly blacks, in generational cycles of poverty which stifle the development of the region and the future of the people who live there.

# 2

## HOW SLAVERY SHAPED THE HISTORY OF THE BLACK BELT

> Here, then is the dilemma,... What, after all, am I? Am I an American or a Negro? Can I be both? Or is it my duty to cease to be Negro, as soon as possible and be an American?[1] —W. E. B. Du Bois, 1897

Framers of the Constitution theorized that the protection of the basic rights of life, liberty, and the pursuit of happiness are interwoven into the basic role and responsibility of government and that their protection is indeed government's major purpose. Yet early on, the Constitution set in motion a federal system that allowed issues of state sovereignty and regionalism to deny blacks basic rights provided by the Constitution. In fact, three passages of the Constitution commenced centuries of legalized discrimination against blacks, serving as the basis for their disparate treatment. Article I Section 2 established the inferiority of African people within colonial America by classifying them as three-fifths human. Next, in Article I Section 9, the sanctioning of the continued importation of Africans for forced servitude in this country, until 1808, demonstrates a lack of civil rights support for Africans within America and highlights the verification of the duality of American society's membership based on race, characterizing their relationship in both national and state governments as a unique one. Finally, in Article IV Section 2, in an attempt to regulate relations between participating governments within this federal system, the Constitution allowed for the return of escaped Africans and, unfortunately, sometimes freedmen to the ruthless subsistence of slavery, forfeiting any responsibility by the national government to uphold the liberties discussed in the Constitution.

---

[1] *The Conservation of Races*, Vol. 2 of The American Negro Academy Occasional Papers (Washington DC: American Negro Academy, 1987).

Historically, the Constitution created a separate grouping for blacks outside of the status of citizen, thereby not including them as part of the American social contract. This extraordinary categorization legally sanctioned centuries of discrimination against black Americans based on the Constitution and the federal make-up of the political system.[2]

*Federalism Becomes an Enabler of Oppression*

The federal system and its division of power between national and state governments has proven to be a conflicting factor in the determination of which level of government is responsible for the civil rights and liberties of black people. Although the Constitution was created to ensure that basic human rights and protections be granted to the American people, it did not begin as a grantor of these rights to blacks. In fact, the relationship of black people with this document began as a very negative one. In addition, the Constitution created a system of dual federalism that served as the basis for the constitutionality of slavery, segregation, and racial discrimination. States' rights advocates believed and advocated that the Constitution allowed for the sovereignty of state power that gave states the power to participate in the discrimination of blacks within their borders as part of this federal system. However, the supremacy of the national government in Article VI lays the foundation for national supremacy within our federal system affirming, *"the Authority of the United States, shall be the supreme Law of the Land."* This supremacy clause gives the national government the authority to take precedence over conflicting state laws and actions.[3]

However, initially, the civil rights and liberties of blacks were not included in national government law, and, in fact, the national government used its supremacy to discriminate against blacks. So although the national government eventually became the protector of the rights of blacks, it did not play this role early in American history. In addition to the Constitution, early Supreme Court rulings also created an unequal place in the American system for blacks, such as the *Dred Scott* (1857) decision, which promoted the limitation of national governmental

---

[2] US Const. art. 1 sec. 2 cl. 3. US Const. art. 1 sec. 9 cl.1. US Const. art. 4 sec. 2 cl. 3.
[3] US Const. art. 6. Sec. 2.

power and the sovereignty of state power in racial discrimination and defining the status of blacks within the United States on an inferior basis. The court ruled against Dred Scott, a slave who believed that a federal law, the Missouri Compromise of 1820, which made slavery illegal in free states or territories, could free him because he resided in a free state for four years. The court ruled that blacks were not citizens of this country and were instead property and therefore could not sue for their own freedom. In addition, the court ruled that the Missouri Compromise was unconstitutional because Congress had no authority to outlaw slavery. This precedent allowed for decades of legally sanctioned inequality and brutality of blacks based heavily on the doctrine of states' rights and ordained by the high court. The states' rights doctrine was an important tool used before and after the Civil War and reigned for decades as a counter tool to the principles of liberty and equality for blacks. This foundation of inequality, based on the Constitution and early Supreme Court rulings, reveals the exceptional experience of blacks, particularly within the Black Belt, and their relationship with the founding doctrines of the society. With limited constitutional coverage, blacks existed outside of full American citizenship well into the twentieth century. In addition, Black Belt society used this limitation to perpetuate inequality and racial discrimination and a slave system that eventually exclusively used blacks.[4]

Slavery was the primary way of life for blacks in the Black Belt region until the Civil War, and this institution was built on both the Southern race mythology, which established blacks as an inferior race, and the complicity of an inactive national government as it related to the protections of black people. The severity of the slave experience within the Black Belt was unique to blacks, although slavery was not initially. As stated by Theodore Wilson in *The Black Codes of the South,* slavery did not begin as exclusively black. Native Americans were enslaved as infidels, and their treatment was justified by their masters through the Old Testament, similar to the early justification of black slavery. Yet the Native American experiment was short-lived and, for the most part, replicated by black slavery. Black slavery also rested in the philosophy

---

[4] *Dred Scott v. Sandford*, 60 U.S. 393 (1857).

of biblical sanctions, but soon a more successful doctrine was established, the doctrine of black inferiority: "The theory which gradually developed…was that the Negro race was far inferior to other races and was unfitted by nature for any condition except slavery. Being manifestly convenient, the theory received ready acceptance. Thus, during the last half of the seventeenth century the philosophical and legal justification for slavery in America was changed from captivity and heathenism to racial inferiority alone."[5] The motivation for establishing the institution of slavery in relation to race has initiated the research of many scholars. Because slavery was a great wealth-producing system, many scholars have argued that the basis of slavery was not merely racial but economic. Nantambu (1998) found that slavery was created for the generation and accumulation of profit, with financial success being the primary motive for slavery. Williams (1961) found, "Both Indian slavery and white servitude were to go down before the black man's superior endurance, docility and labor capacity. The features of the man, his hair, color dentifrice, his 'subhuman' characteristics so widely pleaded, were only the later rationalizations to justify a simple economic fact: that the colonies needed labor and resorted to Negro labor because it was the cheapest and best."[6]

Although this book is focused on the Black Belt South, it is important to note that slavery as an institution was not exclusively Southern. "Thirteen years after the debarkation at Jamestown—the first Negroes were brought into James River in a Dutch vessel; and forthwith they were put to their appropriate use, others followed in their train; it rapidly became recognized, active and lucrative branch of trade, and at length we find slaves in all the colonies from New Hampshire to Georgia." In fact, the institution was critical to the development of the country, as shown in an article from 1855 in the *Southern Literary Messenger*. The piece published a discussion regarding the importance of

---

[5] Theodore Wilson, *The Black Codes of the South* (Tuscaloosa: University of Alabama Press, 1965) 18.
[6] Kwame Nantambu, "Pan-Africanism Versus Pan-African Nationalism: An Afrocentric Analysis," Journal of Black Studies 28/5 (May 1998): 561–74. Eric Williams, *Capitalism and Slavery* (New York: Russel & Russel, 1961) 5–21.

slavery and the black race in the country's growth: "We maintain that THE SLAVERY OF THE BLACK RACE ON THIS CONTINENT IS THE PRICE AMERICA HAS PAID FOR HER LIBERTY, CIVIL AND RELIGIOUS, AND HUMANLY SPEAKING, THESE BLESSINGS WOULD HAVE BEEN UNATTAINABLE WITHOUT THEIR AID."[7] Yet it was the colonies of the South that built their economy on free black labor forced from enslaved black people. This system was perpetuated by the significance of the white race mythology promoted in the South, which allowed the region to institute the practice of white racial superiority in its institutions and law.

The institution of slavery within the Black Belt region was the driving force of the economy and the structure that held the social fabric of the society together as an institution. It held the future and past for the community, it played an integral part in dowries and inheritance, fortune or ruin, class standing and family name, and all of this was connected to black slavery. This institution clearly cannot be separated from the American experience or Southern experience because it played such an important role in the foundation of the country and particularly the Black Belt region. It even colored the region in which it dominated.

Du Bois (1903) described the Black Belt of Georgia, specifically Dougherty County, often calling it the Egypt of the Confederacy.

> Then came the black slaves. Day after day the clank of chained feet marching from Virginia and Carolina to Georgia was heard in these rich swamp lands. Day after day the songs of the callous, the wail of the motherless, and the muttered curses of the wretched echoed from the Flint to the Chickasawhatchee, until by 1860 there had risen in West Dougherty perhaps the richest slave kingdom the modern world ever knew. A hundred and fifty barons commanded the labor of nearly six thousand Negroes, held sway over farms with ninety thousand acres of tilled land, valued even in times of cheap soil at three millions of dollars...and men that came there bankrupt made money and grew rich.

---

[7] R. Thompson, ed., "The Black Race in North America: Why Was Their Introduction Permitted?" *Southern Literary Messenger* 21 (November 1855): 656 and 647.

In a single decade[8] the cotton output increased four-fold and the value of lands was tripled.

Slavery was integral to the development of the Black Belt region and its significant wealth-building properties, as well as the conspicuousness of the black population. The Black Belt as a region was built out of slavery and this institution was built for the most part on the misery of enslaved black people. Acknowledging this experience helps us to better understand the region.

Georgia had a large enslaved population that grew each year until the Civil War, and the state and its people prospered as a result. It was also an original colony and a prominent state member of the Black Belt region. Hancock County, located within the Georgia Black Belt, created very wealthy land barons, with their wealth grounded largely in black people and the labor they produced. Table 2.0 below shows the population increase of Africans in the county over four decades. Interestingly, it also shows how the institution of slavery became increasingly centralized by a few owners with larger enslaved forces over time. However, the state of Georgia was not the only state, or the South the only region, that utilized enslaved labor. Table 2.1 shows how quickly the number of enslaved Africans rose in forty years within the nation, particularly in the lower South, which illustrates the significant rise in the black population and the obvious importance of the institution within the Southern region, particularly the Black Belt region.

---

[8] W. E. B. Du Bois, *The Souls of Black Folk Essays and Sketches* (Chicago: A. C. McClurg, 1903) 123.

## Table 2.0 Slave and Slave Owner Population in Hancock County, Georgia

| Year | No. of Slave Owners with less than 10 slaves | No. of Slave Owners with 20-59 Slaves | No. of Slave Owners with 100 slaves | Total No. of Slave Owners | Total No. of Slaves |
|---|---|---|---|---|---|
| 1802 | 656 | 26 | 0 | 819 | 4,823 |
| 1821 | 437 | 88 | 0 | 678 | 6,331 |
| 1835 | 277 | 77 | 2 | 480 | 5,680 |
| 1844 | 256 | 53 | 2 | 445 | 5,787 |
| 1856 | 256 | 95 | 3 | 487 | 7,516 |

Source: From Growth of Slaveholding in Selected Counties of the Georgia Cotton Belt table in "The Origins and Growth of the Southern Black Belts" by Ulrich B. Phillips, *The American Historical Review* 11/4 (July 1906): 811.

## Table 2.1 US Slave Population, 1820 and 1860

|  | 1820 | 1860 |
|---|---|---|
| United States | 1,538,125 | 3,953,760 |
| North | 19,108 | 64 |
| South | 1,519,017 | 3,953,696 |
| Upper South | 965,514 | 1,530,229 |
| Delaware | 4,509 | 1,798 |
| Kentucky | 127,732 | 225,483 |
| Maryland | 107,397 | 87,189 |
| Missouri | 10,222 | 114,931 |
| North Carolina | 205,017 | 331,059 |
| Tennessee | 80,107 | 275,719 |
| Virginia | 425,153 | 490,865 |
| Washington DC | 6,377 | 3,185 |
| Lower South | 553,503 | 2,423,467 |
| Alabama | 41,879 | 435,080 |
| Arkansas | 1,617 | 111,115 |
| Florida | * | 61,745 |
| Georgia | 149,654 | 462,198 |

| | | |
|---|---|---|
| Louisiana | 69,064 | 331,726 |
| Mississippi | 32,814 | 436,631 |
| South Carolina | 258,475 | 402,406 |
| Texas | * | 182,566 |

Source: Ira Berlin, *Slaves Without Masters: The Free Negro in the Antebellum South* (New York: New Press, 1974): 396–97.

Yet the influence of the brutality of slavery on the psyche of both master and the enslaved—the effect on the human spirit—is something that can never be fully quantified. Slavery, according to Hahn, "was a system of extreme personal domination in which a slave had no relationship that achieved legal sanction or recognition other than with the master, or with someone specially designated by the master." This system had very little appreciation for standard family and kinship. Hahn also found, "on farms and small plantations, fewer than half of the slaves at any one time lived in 'standard nuclear families' (both parents and children), and even on larger plantations, the developmental cycle of birth, aging, and death made for periods of social and familial imbalance, at times casting slaves into a succession of different family settings." This inhumane and brutal system was supported by laws used to maintain the system by force, such as the infamous slave codes. For example, the state of South Carolina used sadistic means to perpetuate slavery and to discourage runaways: "The black code of South Carolina in which a man was authorized to kill a runaway negro, whether he resisted or not—he was authorized to bring him in dead or alive. If he was brought in alive he had his nose slit and his ears cut off. If he ran away a second or third time he either had one of his legs sawed off, or suffered the penalty of death." To try to psychologically understand the effects of one human being having total control over another human being and the toll that position plays in the judicious processes of that individual or the immeasurable influence of total powerlessness without remedy and what effect this has on the mentality of a people over time is critical to the discussion of the Black Belt region's legacy on the people within.[9]

The support of the institution by both private and public sectors reveals how vital the institution of slavery was to the development of the country and its essential function in the development of Southern society, particularly the Black Belt. This institution not only supported the agricultural economy of the South, it was also important in the industries of the South, as "Southern industry's most distinctive aspect was its wide and in-tensive use of slave labor. In the 1850's, for example, 160,000 to 200,000—about 5 per cent of the total slave population—worked in industry. About four-fifths of these industrial slaves were directly owned by industrial entrepreneurs; the rest were rented by employers from their masters by the month or year. Most were men, but many were women and children." Industries utilizing enslaved labor included Southern textile mills, iron manufacture, Southern tobacco factories, manufacturing, and most secondary manufacturing—shoe factories, tanneries, bakeries, paper-makers, printing establishments, and brick makers. Additional industries that used slaves included those associated with sugar refining, rice milling, and grist-milling, the production of salt, the building of railroads as well as most Southern roads, bridges and other transportation facilities.[10] The institution of slavery and the use of black labor was a primary force behind the Southern economy, particularly the Black Belt, and the white power structure used every means available to maintain dominance in the region, working inside and outside of the political system. Blacks also used every means available to them to escape or at least lessen the shackles of slavery. These historical struggles have shaped the sociopolitical fortunes of the Black Belt region in the past and protest against oppression continues to influence its present and future.

---

[9] Steven Hahn, *A Nation under Our Feet: Black Political Struggles in the Rural South from Slavery to the Great Migration* (Cambridge: Harvard University Press, 2003) 16–18. "The *Recent Southern Convention at Vicksburg," Debow's Review, Agricultural, Commercial, Industrial Progress and Resources* 27/3 (September 1859): 361 http://name.umdl.umich.edu/acg1336.1-27.003, accessed 15 December 2012.
[10] Robert S. Starobin, "Economics of Industrial Slavery in the Old South," *The Business History Review* 44/2 (Summer 1970): 131–33.

*Protest and Rebellion*

Protest against oppression has been a principal factor of the American political culture from the beginning, and the rural black experience within the Black Belt region has been no exception. Africans developed maroon communities within the Black Belt as a way to escape slavery early on. Africans escaping the British colonies often settled in Florida or the coastal areas of South Carolina and Georgia. Many joined the Seminole Indian nation, and the Seminole War of 1835–1842 was partly fought for this reason. During slavery, blacks protested and resisted in many ways, including participating in work stoppages, feigning illness, refusing to procreate, killing crops, and poisoning or making ill their masters and farm animals, but the violent slave revolt was the protest tool most feared by slave owners and the community at-large. Many laws were passed to combat this form of protest. Four revolts in particular have been repeatedly recorded in the annals of American history. All of these revolts occurred in the Southern region, including the Stono Rebellion in Stono, South Carolina, in 1739, which resulted in enactment of oppressive slave codes that existed until Emancipation and may help to explain the harshness of the South Carolina codes. The next attempt at revolt was Gabriel's Revolt, in 1800, in Richmond, Virginia, in which more than a thousand enslaved Africans reportedly participated. The Denmark Vesey Plot in Charleston, South Carolina, in 1822, proved the dreaded connection between free and enslaved blacks and their collaborative efforts to end slavery. Finally, Nat Turner's Insurrection, in 1831, near Southampton, Virginia, presented the possibility of widespread chaos and danger at the hands of the large populations of enslaved people in the Black Belt region. This was particularly frightening as word of the Haitian revolution and the success of the enslaved blacks put fear in the minds of whites, particularly in the places with the largest black population, the Black Belt region.

These acts of protest continued until Emancipation and additionally, blacks also sought to participate in the ultimate American hailed act of protest: fighting for freedom through military service. Blacks have a strong history of military service in this country, and although generally not widely discussed, blacks in significant numbers even fought in the Civil War, continuing the American tradition of actively fighting for liberty. After much debate regarding their participation and finally being given the opportunity in an act in July 1862 to enlist in the military, black men responded to the call of service, resulting in some being recognized for valor. For example, fourteen black soldiers were awarded the country's medal of honor on 29 September 1864 as they helped Union troops drive the Confederates back into Virginia. By 1865, roughly 180,000 blacks had served in the Union Army, over one-fifth of the adult male black population under forty-five years of age.[11]

Yet their service was not just on land, as they also participated in the Navy. As a correspondence of the Superintendent of the Naval War Records Office found, "During the Civil War the Negro was enlisted in the squadrons for one year. In the absence of specific data it is suggested that as several vessels report during the Civil War having a crew of one-fourth negroes that the actual number of enlistments must have been about one-fourth of the total number given above, or 29,511."[12]

As with all other Americans, and drawing from a history of rebellion and revolution, blacks actively participated militarily in the pursuit of their own freedom. The road to freedom began on 1 January 1863, with Lincoln's Emancipation Proclamation. Although the proclamation was limited in scope, since it only applied to enslaved blacks in rebellious states and depended on a Union victory, Lincoln stated, "And by virtue of the power, and for the purpose aforesaid, I do order and declare that all persons held as slaves within said designated States, and parts of States, are, and henceforward shall be free; and that the Executive government of the United States, including the military and naval authorities thereof, will recognize and maintain the freedom of said persons."[13]

---

[11] "American Experience: Reconstruction: The Second Civil War," http://www.pbs.org/wgbh/amex/reconstruction/states/sf_timeline.html, accessed 12 December 2012.

[12] Robert E. Johnson, ed., "Battlefield in Virginia Finally Will Honor Heroics of Black Civil War Soldiers," *Jet* 6/22 (November 2000): 20. Herbert Aptheker, "The Negro in the Union Navy," *The Journal of Negro History* 32 (April 1947): 179.

[13] "Slavery and the Making of America: The Emancipation Proclamation 1863," National Archives, Old Military and Civil Records (LICON) http://www.pbs.org/wnet/slavery/experience/freedom/docs4.html, accessed 12 December 2012.

*Black Codes of the South*

Even with the promise of freedom in 1865, Southern states began to enact "black codes" that stripped blacks of any illusions of social inclusion. These codes were oppressive because of their restrictive provisions to the civil rights and liberties of blacks, including the exclusion of their free movement after slavery. These black codes restricted all aspects of black life in the Black Belt, including occupation, marriage, educational opportunities or lack thereof, and social norms, particularly in relation to whites. By developing a sociopolitical caste system, these black codes limited the lives of blacks within the Black Belt society and were instrumental in putting into place previous antebellum social codes, the remnants of slavery. In addition, it also promoted racial violence and exploitation by placing blacks near the status of involuntary servitude without the protections of citizenship and law.

For example, in Mississippi, the codes included restrictions on all aspects of life, including travel, work, and marriage. Section 9 focused on the enticement of black labor, which stated,

> *Provided,* if any person shall, or shall attempt to, persuade, entice, or cause any freedman, free negro, or mulatto to desert from any legal employment of any person, with the view to employ said freedman, free negro, or mulatto without the limits of this State, such person, on conviction, shall be fined not less than fifty dollars, and not more than five hundred dollars and costs; and if said fine and costs shall not be immediately paid, the court shall sentence said convict to not exceeding six months imprisonment in the county jail.

This denied blacks the opportunity to negotiate labor contracts for their best interest or have the opportunity to leave employment if they desired, and particularly when coupled with vagrancy laws, these codes were very damaging to the freedmen. For example, Section 2 stated,

> All freedmen, free negroes and mulattoes in this State, over the age of eighteen years, found on the second Monday in January, 1866, or thereafter, with no lawful employment or business, or found unlawfully assembling themselves together, either in the day or night time, and all white persons so assembling themselves with freedmen, free negroes or mulattoes, or usually associating with freedmen, free negroes or mulattoes, on terms of equality, or living in adultery or fornication with a

freed woman, free negro or mulatto, shall be deemed vagrants, and on conviction thereof shall be fined in a sum not exceeding, in the case of a freedman, free negro or mulatto, fifty dollars, and a white man two hundred dollars, and imprisoned at the discretion of the court, the free negro not exceeding ten days, and the white man not exceeding six months.

These laws trapped blacks in a vicious circle of poverty and hopelessness as their opportunities for employment and negotiation were restrained and the needs of the planters were put ahead of their own. These acts also included the usage of the criminal justice system to maintain or reestablish the social norms of the prewar Black Belt, and it began decades of utilizing the political institutions of the state and localities to discriminate against blacks. More importantly, these codes were instrumental in reestablishing the social order of the Old South and were reflective of the fact that the Southern states were confident that the national government would not be proactive in protecting the freedmen.[14]

Left victim to state laws and injustice, blacks found themselves under enormous brutality, as described by Du Bois.

> Some planters held back their former slaves on their plantations by brute force. Armed bands of white men patrolled the country roads to drive back the negroes wandering about. Dead bodies of murdered negroes were found on and near the highways and by-paths. Gruesome reports came from the hospitals—reports of colored men and women whose ears had been cut off, whose skulls had been broken by blows, whose bodies had been slashed by knives or lacerated with scourges. A number of such cases I had occasion to examine myself. A veritable reign of terror prevailed in many parts of the South. The negro found scant justice in the local courts against the white man. He could look for protection only to the military forces of the United States still garrisoning the "States lately in rebellion" and to the Freedmen's Bureau.[15]

---

[14] "The Mississippi Black Codes (1865)," http://wps.ablongman.com/long_longman_lahdemo_1/0,8259,1546454-,00.html, accessed 12 December 2012.

[15] W. E. Burghardt Du Bois, "Reconstruction and Its Benefits," *The American Historical Review* 15/4 (July 1910): 785.

These reports highlighted just how far the Southern region was willing to go to reestablish the old social order and to limit black progress. Responding to the codes and other issues, blacks began to meet in black conventions throughout the country to protest their treatment and to organize for their rights. They were particularly upset about the reinstatement of former Confederates to positions of power. For example, in South Carolina under President Johnson's Reconstruction, former Confederates were placed in several state leadership positions, such as appointed Governor Benjamin Perry, who was a proslavery former Confederate state legislator, who, along with many other former Confederates, began to reestablish the old sociopolitical order in South Carolina.

In response, in November 1865, blacks met in South Carolina at a well-attended convention to discuss their grievances with Reconstruction efforts. They assembled a petition and presented it to the state legislature to publicize their needs: "We ask that those laws that have been enacted that apply to us on account of Color, be repealed. We do not presume to dictate, but we appeal to your own Sense of justice and generosity, Why should we suffer this, is it because of the color an All Wise Creator has given us? Is it possible that the only reason for enacting such stringent laws for us is because our color is of a darker hue?"[16]

These appeals were presented throughout the South as the freedmen protested their position in the establishment of the postwar South. They had supporters such as Republicans Charles Sumner of Massachusetts, Lyman Trumball of Connecticut, and Thaddeus Stevens of Pennsylvania, who were dedicated to furthering the progress of blacks in the South. Thaddeus Stevens sponsored legislation in 1865 to provide acreage to the freedmen, and Sen. Lyman Trumball sponsored legislation to protect blacks from violence, which would become the Civil Rights Act of 1866. In a speech on 6 September 1865, Thaddeus Stevens proposed the confiscation of rebel estates worth $10,000 or over 200 acres. He also insisted that the poor and those who were coerced into the conflict be spared because they had been led by the elites of their community, and

---

[16] Herbert Aptheker, "South Carolina Negro Conventions, 1865," *The Journal of Negro History* 31/1 (January 1946): 96.

he was confident that they would not have seceded without the leadership of the elites. Focusing on the freedmen, Stevens discussed their need for land.

> There are about six millions of freedmen in the South. The number of acres of land is 465,000,000. Of this, those who own above two hundred acres each number about 70,000 persons, holding, in the aggregate, (together with the States,) about 394,000,000 acres, leaving for all the others below 200 each about 71,000,000 of acres. By thus forfeiting the estates of the leading rebels, the government would have 394,000,000 of acres, beside their town property, and yet nine tenths of the people would remain untouched. Divide this land into convenient farms. Give, if you please, forty acres to each adult male freedman.[17]

This idea of providing to the freedmen forty acres was widely supported by the freedmen and their supporters. Yet there was significant opposition. These discussions often reflected the sentiments of many whites, who felt the freedmen were undeserving of the land, as highlighted in this *New York Times* response in 1867:

> Emancipation from bondage is not enough now. Absolute equality before the law falls short of what is required. There must be "dominance instead of equality," and ready-made farms of forty acres besides! That is the latest version of the platform on which the noisy friends of the freedmen profess to stand and the knowledge of it will assuredly not tend to make the negroes more orderly in their demeanor or more moderate in their requirements. There can be no hope of peace for the country until the negro be banished, as a distinct and separate element, from its politics.[18]

Interestingly, the separate treatment of blacks legally was often used as an argument to deny blacks any special remedy despite centuries of disparate treatment and living, "as distinct and separate elements under the law" as enslaved people. Yet the issue of land provision went unfulfilled during Reconstruction, a time, according to Du Bois, that was

---

[17] Beverly Wilson Palmer and Holly Byers Ochoa, "Reconstruction, September 6, 1865," *Pennsylvania History* 60/2 Thaddeus Stevens and American Democracy" (April 1993); 204.

[18] "The Freedmen and Their Friends," *The New York Times*, 13 May 1867 http://select.nytimes.com/gst/abstract.html?res=f70d15fc3c5a1a7493c1a8178ed85f438684f9, accessed 15 December 2012.

the best opportunity to initiate and settle the matter: "The vision of landowning, however, the righteous and reasonable ambition for forty acres and a mule which filled the freedmen's dreams, was doomed in most cases to disappointment. And those men of marvelous hind-sight, who today are seeking to preach the Negro back to the soil, know well, or ought to know, that it was here, in 1865, that the finest opportunity of binding the black peasant to the soil was lost."[19]

The governmental entity that became responsible for the freedmen and confiscated land was established in an act in 1865, which created the Bureau of Refugees, Freedmen, and Abandoned Lands within the War Department. This effort was vehemently opposed by President Johnson, who vetoed the legislation. However, an 1866 act finally organized the Freedmen's Bureau, as it was called. The Bureau focused on assigning black labor to plantations instead of land provision for blacks and black self-sufficiency, as land was imperative for economic sufficiency within the Black Belt as an agricultural economy. This decision resulted in blacks being forced to work in peasantry on Black Belt plantations for the most part for another century.

An excerpt from a speech on the work of the Freedmen's Bureau, given by Major General Howard, who led the agency, states,

> The first business was to regulate labor.... The plan adopted was to have former owners, as far as practicable, who had work to do, employ each the men who had been his slaves. I mean where they had not left their own homes, or voluntarily returned. I knew that they had been able to support their slaves on their plantations, or rather that the masters had been supported, by the labor of their slaves, and that very large fortunes had been made, so that it is wonderful how many people there are at the South who are worth more than twenty thousand dollars. The system of contracts was chosen.[20]

---

[19] W. E. Burghardt Du Bois, "The Freedmen's Bureau" *Atlantic Monthly* 87/519 (March 1901): 354–65. http://history.eserver.org/freedmens-bureau.txt, accessed 15 December 2012.

[20] "The Freedmen: Organization of the Freedmen's Bureau Its Objects, and What It Has Accomplished," 20 August 1865 http://www.nytimes.com/1865/08/20/news/

This speech highlights the necessity of blacks being given an opportunity for self-sufficiency by finding work, but it also becomes obvious that land provision was not in thoughtful consideration. Finally, it reveals the missed opportunity for the needs of the freedmen to be given priority by the federal government instead of the former landowners, many who had participated in treason years before.

There were many discussions about what to do with blacks after the war. Besides providing land, there were also discussions about colonizing them in other locations. During a board meeting of the board of directors of the American Colonization Society, whose membership included very prominent men, including senators and those in leadership at the Freedmen's Bureau, the idea of removing the freedmen from America was widely discussed. Gen. Howard supported the mission of the American Colonization Society and expressed his "willingness to aid them in their work of colonizing the negroes." There were also discussions of possible black violence and the need for Southern states to organize militias against the possibility, which was opposed by Republicans such as Sumners, who "presented a remonstrance against the arming of a militia in Alabama, which is stated to have been done for the purpose of repressing disorders among the colored people. The remonstrance alleges that there is no danger of such disorders."[21]

All of these efforts highlight the uncertainty of the lives of the freedmen. It became obvious in the political environment that they would only be provided their rights through national legislation, as the states were incapable of seeing them as citizens.

*Southern Backlash*

---

freedmen-organization-freedmen-s-bureau-its-objects-whatit-has.html?pagewanted=print, accessed 12 December 2012.

[21] "Washington News: The Reconstruction Question in the Senate. Special Dispatches to the New-York Times," 18 January 1866 http://query.nytimes.com/mem/archivefree/pdf?res=FB0911FC3E59137A93CAA8178AD85F428684F9, accessed 12 December 2012.

After the Civil War and Lincoln's assassination, and with hope provided by President Johnson, most Southern white leaders moved quickly to restore the oppressive nature of the Black Belt region and were very successful with the help of a complacent national government and with presidential approval. On 29 May 1865, Johnson issued a proclamation of a blanket amnesty, citing Lincoln's original attempts at reconstruction as a subtext. Johnson provided exceptions only to those who had held prior positions in the Confederate government, however assuring that those persons would be dealt with by "special application" of the president to ensure "the peace and dignity of the United States." Over the next couple of months, Johnson provided pardons abundantly to many former high-ranking Confederates and took great pleasure in ruling over the former Southern elites, many of whom had held him in great disdain. The following excerpt from the proclamation highlights the requirement of ending slavery or ownership of enslaved people as part of the terms for amnesty.

> To the end, therefore, that doubts may be removed, that the authority of the government of the United States may be restored, and that peace, order, and freedom may be established, I, Andrew Johnson, President of the United States, do proclaim and declare that I hereby grant and assure to all persons of color who have, directly or by implication, participated in the existing rebellion, a free pardon; and that I hereby grant and assure to all white persons who have, directly or indirectly, participated in the existing rebellion, except as hereinafter excepted, a full pardon, but upon the condition, nevertheless, that every such person will, in aid of the emancipation proclamation, the legal validity of which is hereby affirmed, freely and forever disclaim, and will never assert, right or title to slaves, and that every such person will never thereafter own a slave or any interest therein.[22]

Although recognizing blacks as free people, Andrew Johnson set the stage for over a century of racial discrimination and violence against blacks in the South when he failed to utilize the federal government to

---

[22] "Slavery and the Making of America: A Proclamation of Amnesty and Reconstruction," 29 May 1865, Library of Congress, Rare Book and Special Collections Division, Ephemera Collection http://www.pbs.org/wnet/slavery/experience/freedom/docs7.html.

protect them or provide any economic recourse beyond returning them to the fields as contract labor in positions only slightly better than enslavement. In his first address to Congress, President Johnson revealed the prominent role of the state in the treatment of blacks, while at the same time allowing former Confederates the opportunity to retake power within the South, personally appointing many himself. In an 1865 address, Johnson stated, "The public interest will be best promoted if the several States will provide adequate protection and remedies for the freedmen. Until this is in some way accomplished, there is no chance for the advantageous use of their labor; and the blame of ill-success will not rest on them."[23]

President Johnson also saw the New South not as a place for the equal treatment of blacks, but as a place where whites and white immigrants from Europe could now thrive and participate as the Civil War had opened up the "closed society's" economy to external factors. According to Johnson,

> Slavery was essentially a monopoly of labor, and as such locked the States where it prevailed against the incoming of free industry. Where labor was the property of the capitalist, the white man was excluded from employment, or had but the second best chance of finding it; and the foreign emigrant turned away from the region where his condition would be so precarious. With the destruction of the monopoly, free labor will hasten from all parts of the civilized world to assist in developing various and immeasurable resources which have hitherto lain dormant. The eight or nine States nearest the Gulf of Mexico have a soil of exuberant fertility, a climate friendly to long life, and can sustain a denser population than is found as yet in any part of our country. And the future influx of population to them will be mainly from the North, or from the most cultivated nations in Europe.[24]

The lack of leadership by Johnson to assist in the development of economic opportunities for the freedmen set the stage for Southern

---

[23] Andrew Johnson, "Our Official History: The First Message of President Johnson," *The New York Times,* 6 December 1865. http://www.nytimes.com/1865/12/06/news/our-official-history-first-message-president-johnsonhis-views-relations-duties.html, accessed 12 December 2012.

[24] Ibid.

states, and Black Belt leaders reinstated many of the principles of the previously important white race mythology and set socioeconomic and political limitations on blacks within the region. Just as their economic rights had been thwarted by the president's inaction, so too did their political rights slip away as he saw little usefulness in blacks being afforded full citizenship or political participation, stating to Congress in December 1867, "Negroes have shown less capacity for government than any other race of people. No independent government of any form has ever been successful in their hands. On the contrary, wherever they have been left to their own devices, they have shown a constant tendency to relapse into barbarism."[25]

With the Chief Executive unwilling to view blacks as human beings and citizens who deserved a role in the government or protection from the Southerners who sought revenge for their economic and social troubles after the Civil War, blacks within the Black Belt found themselves in an awful dilemma where they existed outside of Black Belt society again, yet were instrumental in its rebirth and future development. Those in charge in the Black Belt were unwilling to accept them in their new role as free people, and most whites were not willing to see them on equal terms. However, there were whites in the Republican Party from northern states who fought for the civil rights of blacks in the Black Belt and used the national government to achieve these goals.

*The Constitution, Civil Rights Laws, and Blacks*

The national government outlawed slavery with the Thirteenth Amendment to the Constitution, which states: *Neither slavery nor involuntary servitude, except as a punishment for crime whereof the party shall have been duly convicted, shall exist within the United States, or any place subject to their jurisdiction.* This amendment ended generations-old states' rights beliefs in the supremacy of state sovereignty within the federal system and provided the national

---

[25] James Richardson, *A Compilation of Messages and Papers of the Presidents 1789–1897,* vol. 6 (Washington DC: Government Printing Office, 1897) 565.

government with the authority to ensure freedom to blacks, regardless of state of residence.[26]

Other national actions included the Civil Rights Act of 1866, sponsored by Lyman Trumbull, and the Reconstruction Act of 1867, which provided African Americans with rights as citizens and the ability to participate in the development of new constitutions in the Southern states. These rights were given permanence with the passage of the fourteenth and fifteenth amendments to the Constitution. The Fourteenth Amendment, Section One, was ratified in 1868, and states: *All persons born or naturalized in the United States, and subject to the jurisdiction thereof, are citizens of the United States and of the State wherein they reside. No State shall abridge the privileges or immunities of citizens of the United States; nor shall any State deprive any person of life, liberty, or property, without due process of law; nor deny to any person within its jurisdiction the equal protection of laws.* This section of the Fourteenth Amendment asserts the concept of dual citizenship and declares the limitations of states' rights in the inequitable treatment of state residents, specifically blacks. As a result of this amendment, blacks became citizens of this country with all of the rights and privileges thereof. Yet upholding this assurance to African Americans in the Black Belt region proved a daunting feat.[27]

The Fifteenth Amendment's sections one and two provide political life for African Americans for the first time. Section one: *The right of citizens of the United States to vote shall not be denied or abridged by the United States or by any State on account of race, color, or previous condition of servitude.* Section two: *The Congress shall have power to enforce this article by appropriate legislation.* Through these amendments, blacks were given the opportunity to participate in the governance of their communities and expected the national government to uphold and protect their ability to do so. This provided great optimism for the future for blacks throughout the country, but especially in the Black Belt. Yet most whites in the region felt it was inconceivable that former enslaved men would be able to take part in the political system

---

[26] US Const. 13th amend.
[27] US Const. 14th amend. Sec.1.

that governed them, and they went to great lengths to keep them from participating. Additionally, other laws, such as the Civil Rights Act of 1875, prohibited discrimination in public accommodations, but like other efforts to promote equality, were short-lived.[28]

Support for the freedmen was not universal and attacks against their success were not just locally or state-based. Unfortunately, President Johnson vetoed the Reconstruction acts, believing them to be disadvantageous to white Southerners. Republicans in Congress, who, by 1866, had two-thirds majority, succeeded in passing the measures without Democratic support and overrode Johnson's vetoes, and Reconstruction was implemented under the Republican Congress. It sectioned the Southern region into five military districts under the command of a military officer and elected delegates from the states to create a new state constitution for voter approval. Once the states wrote a new constitution and accepted the Fourteenth Amendment, they were readmitted back into the United States and could participate in the national legislative body. With new suffrage rights, African American males could participate in elective office for the first time.[29]

*Supreme Court Attacks African American Citizenship*

However, the rights provided by the legislation to African Americans were quickly under assault by the Supreme Court through several important decisions such as the Slaughter House cases, *U.S. v. Reese*, and *U.S. v. Cruikshank*. Although the Slaughter House cases were not brought by African Americans, they found that "state and federal citizenships are separate and distinct" and weakened the usage of the Fourteenth Amendment. The Supreme Court voided many of the civil rights progresses of Reconstruction, and two opinions in 1876, *U.S. v. Reese* and *U.S. v. Cruikshank*, "ruled unconstitutional or largely unenforceable those sections of the 1870–72 Enforcement Acts that

---

[28] US Const. 15th amend. Sec. 1 and sec. 2.
[29] Eric Foner, *Reconstruction: America's Unfinished Revolution, 1863–1877* (New York: HarperCollins, 1988).

attempted to protect all citizens against violence or fraud, state-sponsored or private, in connection with state or local elections."[30]

The Supreme Court decision in *U.S. v. Reese* declared "the 15th amendment extends no positive guarantees of the franchise and does not 'confer the right of suffrage upon anyone.' The *U.S. v. Cruikshank* ruled that the 'Fourteenth amendment prohibits a state from depriving any person of life, liberty or property'…but…as long as the 'state' was not a party to a deprivation of the right to vote, there was no infringement of the Fourteenth Amendment."[31]

In another assault on civil rights, the Civil Rights Act of 1875, which prohibited discrimination in public accommodations, was declared unconstitutional by the civil rights cases of 1883. Upholding the ideas of states' rights and establishing a Jim Crow system in the South in the *Plessy* decision (1896), the Supreme Court ruled, "In the nature of things it could not have been intended to abolish distinctions based upon color, or to enforce social, as distinguished from political equality, or a commingling of the two races unsatisfactory to either." In short, segregation does not in itself constitute unlawful discrimination.[32]

By the time *Plessy v. Ferguson* (1896) was decided, African Americans had been relegated to citizenship abyss. All of these decisions were made using legal mechanisms within our political system and proved the national government ineffective in securing civil rights for blacks. In addition to legal means of intimidation and deprivation, extralegal means were also employed to limit the constitutional rights of African Americans during the time and highlighted the lack of action by the national government to adequately support and protect blacks against those who attacked them legally and extralegally.

Violence was used frequently during the period after the Civil War and during Reconstruction, creating a legacy that continued well into the

---

[30] *United States v. Reese*, 92 U.S. 214 (1876), *United States v. Cruikshank*, 92 U.S. 542 (1876). The Slaugherhouse cases 83 U.S. 36 (1873). J. Morgan Kousser, *Colorblind Injustice: Minority Voting Rights and the Undoing of the Second Reconstruction* (Chapel Hill: University of North Carolina Press, 1999) 49.

[31] Lawrence Hanks, *The Struggle for Black Political Empowerment in Three Georgia Counties* (Knoxville: University of Tennessee Press, 1987) 17.

[32] *Plessy v. Ferguson*, 163 U.S. 537 (1896).

twentieth century. During electoral processes such as the 1868 elections, for example, in Louisiana, 1,081 mostly black individuals were killed trying to participate in the political process. Scholars have suggested that the violence that occurred after the Civil War against African Americans has been unparalleled in this country's history. Kousser found that "this extensive, systematic political terrorism has no parallel in the modern civil rights movement, and in sheer extent it far surpassed the lynching spree of the last decade of the nineteenth century and the first two decades of the twentieth."[33]

Although these hardships placed extraordinary burdens on the freedmen, they were eager to begin their lives as citizens and attempted to use their rights to further themselves. Astonishingly, "from Virginia to Georgia, from the Carolinas to the Mississippi Valley and Texas, the free people showed 'a remarkable interest in all political information,' were 'fast becoming thoroughly informed upon their civil and political rights,' and most consequentially, were avidly 'organizing clubs and leagues throughout the counties'"[34] The Reconstruction period allowed blacks the opportunity to shape American democracy by their own design.

This division was widened by the Southern political culture that traditionally excluded blacks and proved a challenge to the inclusion of blacks. Chapter 3 will focus on the unique political culture of the region and how it shaped politics and policy implementation within.

---

[33] Kousser, *Colorblind Injustice*, 23.
[34] Hahn, *A Nation under Our Feet*, 177.

# THE UNIQUE POLITICAL CULTURE OF THE REGION

"Seek ye first the political kingdom and all else shall be added onto you" —Kwame Nkrumah, 1960

Creating the environment to include blacks as citizens proved a difficult challenge as Southerners, although defeated in war remained diligently opposed to black citizenship and political inclusion. In addition to state governments opposing black rights, localities of the South also proved they would work to continue discrimination against black residents. The local governing structures were quickly returned to the leadership of whites who had their political rights restored after the Civil War. Local authorities immediately utilized their positions to return African Americans to a status slightly above involuntary servitude and a role outside of traditional citizen. These local authorities refused to prosecute acts of personal violence against African Americans and supported plantation and other unscrupulous employers in contract disputes with black workers. Local governments also unarmed African Americans by confiscating their firearms and leaving them virtually defenseless against violence in the region. In addition, blacks could not testify against white people in legal proceedings and often were fined excessively. Sentences resulting in imprisonment for minor infractions were common for African Americans who refused to work for white people or who tried to increase their economic or political success. This new social order quickly reestablished blacks at the lowest level of the social and political order in the Black Belt region.

In addition, the social order was reestablished and controlled by the unique political system that was shaped by the historical control of a one-party structure. This was the environment in which blacks entered politics for the first time as freedmen.

Although slavery was no longer legal after the Civil War, the financial make-up of the Black Belt region economically enslaved many African Americans long after the Emancipation Proclamation and the

Reconstruction Era's civil rights amendments to the Constitution. The institutional legacy of slavery had far-reaching implications for African Americans in the Black Belt region, because they continued to be tied to the plantation financially. As a result, this economic dependence was used to manipulate them politically, as shown in this 1868 newspaper article.

> It is unfortunately true that the colored vote is very seriously jeopardized by the disgraceful action of the rebel planters. The fiat has gone forth in South Carolina, Georgia, Alabama and elsewhere, that employment shall not be given to the freedmen who dare to vote for GRANT. They are not simply to forfeit favor. They are to be deprived of bread, so far as it is at the disposal of those who furnish employment. A system of terrorism is being inaugurated as supplementary to fraud; and by the two agencies combined the rebels expect to either to keep freedmen from the polls or to compel them to aid the Democracy.[1]

The system of terrorism promoted during the Reconstruction Era proved historically violent as Shapiro found, "The 1871 Southern States Convention declared that from the start of Reconstruction some 1500 to 1600 murders had been committed in Georgia alone, and that in the entire South there had been about 20,000 such murders during that period."[2] This violence further alienated blacks from the traditional political system.

Due to a lack of a national comprehensive plan to determine the future of the freedmen and protect their political participation, many freedmen began to create their own institutions of change. Several organizations were developed around the Southern region to improve the situation of African Americans. One such organization was established by William Edwards, an educator within the Alabama Black Belt, who organized the Black Belt Improvement Society in Wilcox County, Alabama. This society was affiliated with the Snow Hill Institute and focused on making improvements within the Black Belt. Its constitution

---

[1] Anonymous, "The Electoral Votes," *The New York Times* 12 August 1868, accessed 12 December 2012. http://query.nytimes.com/mem/archive-free/pdf?res=F00E11FC38541B7493C0A81783D85F4C8684F9.

[2] Herbert Shapiro, "Afro-American Responses to Race Violence during Reconstruction," Science & Society 36/2 (Summer 1972): 158.

identified several objectives such as (1) uplifting people in the Black Belt, (2) supporting farmers and agriculture, (3) developing a system of farm co-ops for the people, (4) discussing topics of interest to the Black Belt community, particularly related to the general welfare of the people, especially farmers, (5) teaching people to be thrifty economically, and (6) helping each other in sickness and death.[3]

Each of these objectives was selected to focus on the needs of the people of the Black Belt region and provide solutions to problems that affected them. What is most impressive about many of these organizations, such as the BBIS, is that they were grounded in self-help philosophy. Organizations like this assisted the community in times of need and were supported and operated, for the most part, by the people of the Black Belt. The BBIS is just one of many groups created to address the problems of the region by the people. Elective power and addressing the challenges of African Americans within the political arena, however, proved more difficult.

## *Non-Elective Leadership in the Black Belt*

African American theorists and ideologues developed varying opinions about the direction toward success for African Americans and the role of Southern whites in this success. The direction of African American equality perplexed black leadership, which often had differing opinions. One example occurred between the opposing opinions of W. E. B. Du Bois and Booker T. Washington. A Du Bois quote from "Of Mr. Booker T. Washington and Others" illustrates the Du Bois conflict with Washington:

> In his failure to realize and impress this last...Mr. Washington is especially to be criticized. His doctrine has tended to make the White, North and South, shift the burden of the Negro problem to the Negro's shoulders and stand aside as critical and rather pessimistic spectators; when in fact the burden belongs to the nation, and the hands of more of us are clean if we bend not our energies to right the great wrongs The South ought to be led, by candid and honest criticism, and assert her

---

[3] William James Edwards, *Twenty Five Years in the Black Belt* (Boston: Cornhill Company, 1918).

better self and do her full duty to the race she has cruelly wronged and is still wronging.[4]

Booker T. Washington did not express this view of white Southerners, and in an essay entitled *The Educational Outlook in the South,* Washington wrote,

> Any movement for the elevation of the Southern Negro in order to be successful, must have to a certain extent the cooperation of the southern whites. They control government and own the property—whatever benefits the black man benefits the white man.... My faith is that reforms in the South are to come from within. Southern people have a good deal of human nature. They like to receive the praise of doing good deeds, and they don't like to obey orders that come from Washington telling them that they must lay aside at once customs that they have followed for centuries.[5]

These differing ideas about race relations prevailed for many years and would define African American political participation for decades. The role of Southern whites in the success of African Americans proved to be and continues to be a part of the Black Belt development discussion. Yet the lack of significant white, Black Belt progressive voices fighting against racism and inequality resulted in a strong chasm between the races.

Yet the dilemma for southern blacks was complicated, as the rancid political environment in which their futures were being decided grew more and more tense. As shown in an Atlantic Monthly article in 1901,

> Then, amid all this crouched the freed slave, bewildered between friend and foe. He had emerged from slavery: not the worst slavery in the world, not a slavery that made all life unbearable—rather, a slavery that had here and there much of kindliness, fidelity, and happiness—but withal slavery, which, so far as human aspiration and desert were concerned, classed the black man and the ox together. And the Negro knew full well that, whatever their deeper convictions may have been, Southern men had fought with desperate energy to perpetuate this

---

[4] W. E. B. Du Bois, "Of Mr. Booker T. Washington and Others," (1903) http://www.bartleby.com/114/3.html, accessed 12 December 2012.

[5] *Booker T. Washington and His Critics: Black Leadership in Crisis*, 2nd ed., edited by Hugh Hawkins (Lexington MA: D. C. Heath and Co., 1974) 12–14.

slavery, under which the black masses, with half-articulate thought, had writhed and shivered. They welcomed freedom with a cry. They fled to the friends that had freed them. They shrank from the master who still strove for their chains. So the cleft between the white and black South grew.[6]

Due to the lack of federal government success in including blacks in the economy as independent participants, their economic needs served as a vehicle for the former Confederates to continue to determine their future. Because the Freedmen's Bureau resorted to forcing blacks back onto the plantation instead of allowing them the opportunity to become small-land owners, they sealed their fate as a dependent class of people for many decades. Very few African Americans owned land or were economically independent after slavery and Reconstruction. "As Henry Grady remarked in 1881, "the planters were still lords of acres, though not of slaves."[7] Even an effort to promote savings by the freedmen was ill-conceived. As part of an effort to teach the freedmen thrift and savings and to promote the reconstruction effort, the Freedman's Savings and Trust Company, popularly known as the Freedman's Bank, was incorporated by Congress on 3 March 1865 and included thirty-seven offices in seventeen states and the District of Columbia. Due to mismanagement, fraud, and other economic factors such as a national economic downturn, the Freedman's Bank failed in 1874, leaving tens of thousands of its depositors in economic ruin.[8] Depositors received only a small portion of their savings back, if any, which resulted in many blacks distrusting the American banking system for generations. It also signaled to the freedmen that the national government was not particularly interested in their economic well-being.

Therefore, the only true opportunity for economic progress for black individuals was in the land they worked. After the Civil War, the

---

[6] W. E. Burghardt Du Bois, "The Freedmen's Bureau," *Atlantic Monthly* 87 (1901): 354–65. http://history.eserver.org/freedmens-bureau.

[7] Douglas R. Hurt, *American Agriculture: A Brief History*, rev. ed. (West Lafayette IN: Purdue University Press, 2002) 166.

[8] Reginald Washington, "The Freedman's Savings and Trust Company," http://www.archives.gov/research/african-americans/freedmans-bank.html, accessed 12 December 2012.

relationship between people and the land in general resulted in many forms.

> By 1880 the organizational variety that would persist for more than a half century could be clearly discerned: some farms were cultivated by their owners, often with the assistance of wives and children; others by hired workers receiving a fixed wage; some by tenants paying a stipulated amount of products (standing rent) or money (cash rent) for the use of the land; still others by tenants paying a definite share of the crops as rent. The "mix" of these arrangements varied widely from place to place, even within a given state, and changes occurred over time.

These varied relationships to the land provided sustenance but limited many economic and social mobility opportunities for blacks within the region. Despite these challenges, the concentration of blacks within this agriculturally based society provided the base for the promotion of political power if allowed to be practiced without interference; however this did not occur.[9]

Because most blacks in the Black Belt before the Civil War were connected to agricultural work after the war they used this agricultural work and their population size for political progress. Thus, the work and land became more than just survival; they linked blacks to political and economic mobilization. Black political participation during this first era developed through organizing and mobilizing newly freed black men and women and was often initially promoted through the activities of the Republican Party. The large number of newly freed people provided a formidable power base. Due to the brutality being imposed on them as Black Belt society was being reconstructed, they quickly linked their work in agriculture with mobilization activities, issues of self-defense and protection, and labor negotiations. During this time, their power base and exercise of power, as it was connected to farming, proved to be an effective strategy. In addition, they also utilized their power through the Republican Party, which provided them entry into mainstream political activity. These Republican activities created organizations around farming and agriculture allowing African Americans to assemble and

---

[9] Robert Higgs, "Patterns of Farm Rental in the Georgia Cotton Belt, 1880–1900," *The Journal of Economic History* 34/2 (June 1974): 468.

facilitate political discourse in conjunction with self-defense and economic self-sufficiency efforts. These activities also supported mobilization efforts resulting in black leadership and elective-office holding within the Black Belt region.

Although different types of political groups for black advancement were organized after the Civil War, ranging from militia groups to more traditional Republican organizations, the Loyal Leagues proved to be an important tool in the transition to citizenship for many Black Belt African American men: "Agents of the Freedmen's Bureau were quick to inform the freedmen of their new political rights; and within a few months it was claimed that 58,000 blacks were members of the Union Leagues."[10]

Mysterious, ceremonial, and accustomed to spreading Republican politics throughout the South, the league's political rhetoric often revolved around agriculture and the need for political participation by the freedmen. Focusing on issues such as land redistribution, voter registration, and agriculture practices such as gang labor, these organizations proved to be instrumental in promoting the reconstruction of Southern society. The leagues were cloaked in secrecy and ceremony, as shown in a description of its meetings in Georgia.

> Meetings of the League were held at night in old school houses or churches, or even in barns or deserted houses. Radical Republicans made fiery speeches. Initiation ceremonies were frequent both for the benefit of new members and to keep the old members fully impressed with the organization. The emblems were the altar, the Holy Bible, the Declaration of Independence, the United States Constitution, the flag of the Union, a censer of incense, the sword, the gavel, the ballot box, the sickle, the shuttle, the anvil, and other emblems of industry. In a room lighted perhaps by the flare of pine knots or perhaps by one or two smoky kerosene lamps or lanterns, the members of the League would gather.[11]

---

[10] John M. Matthews, "Negro Republicans in the Reconstruction of Georgia," *The Georgia Historical Quarterly* 60/2 (Summer 1976): 147.

[11] Roberta F. Cason, "The Loyal League in Georgia," *The Georgia Historical Quarterly* 20/2 (June 1936): 132.

These leagues were actively involved in transforming agricultural practices from gang labor to tenant farming, thus allowing greater autonomy for the freedmen. Therefore, some of their first issues revolved around labor, and "though the leagues and similar bodies were not labor unions, the politicization of the freedmen after military Reconstruction had a pronounced agrarian character.... Radicals openly promised major changes in plantation life that would secure freedmen greater autonomy in their day-to-day lives."[12]

But more importantly, the leagues tended to utilize existing African American social and cultural organizations, thereby recognizing black culture and shaping the league to fit these racially structured groups. In addition, the league was instrumental in the development of the Republican Party within the Black Belt. Michael Fitzgerald discusses its role in the Alabama Black Belt: "League membership rose from a reported three thousand whites in December 1865 to several times that number a few months later.... Local league councils maintained considerable autonomy, but they were brought into a working relationship with the Republican leadership in Washington. The Union League thus paved the way for the emergence of the Republican party in Alabama."[13]

These organizations were financially sponsored by congressional Republicans and tended to be well organized, becoming extremely powerful by 1867. Impending violence in the Black Belt by angry whites assisted in the recruitment of the Union League in the Black Belt and resulted in significant Union activity. As a result of violence in Alabama, for example, several Union League chapters took on a military character, and the chapter in Greensboro, in the heart of the Alabama Black Belt,

---

[12] Michael W. Fitzgerald, *The Union League Movement in the Deep South: Politics and Agricultural Change during Reconstruction* (Baton Rouge: Louisiana State University Press, 2000). Michael Fitzgerald, "'To Give Our Votes to the Party': Black Political Agitation and Agricultural Change in Alabama, 1865–1870," *The Journal of American History* 76/2 (September 1989): 503.

[13] Michael W. Fitzgerald "Radical Republicanism and the White Yeomanry during Alabama Reconstruction, 1865–1868," *The Journal of Southern History* 54/4 (November 1988).

numbered around 500 men.[14] Because of the history of the agricultural base of the Southern economy, the creation of organizations around farming allowed African Americans to assemble and attempt to move toward economic and social independence within the region. Eager for economic independence, blacks quickly tried to make the agricultural activities work for them economically as Fitzgerald wrote, "In May 1868 one overseer complained that hands were scarce because of 'so many freedmen working on their own hook,' with some so eager for independence that they were trying to farm 'without horse or plow.'" Politics and agriculture were intrinsically linked during this time, with Republican leaders and the freedmen consistently connecting the two.[15]

Political scientist and father of Southern politics V. O. Key theorized that the threat of black domination created distinctly violent politics in the Black Belt that was perpetuated by a one-party region. He found that the Democratic Party had a monopoly on politics in the South and used it as a mechanism to ensure a locally subordinate black population and to block external forces that could threaten these local arrangements. The white exclusivity of Democratic membership limited African American participation and the ability of blacks to shape policy agenda for many generations.

*The Power of Partisanship and the Black Belt*

Political parties are deeply connected with the African American experience in this country, and partisanship became a major factor in politics of the South and was used in determining support for civil rights legislation during Reconstruction. The region supported the Democratic Party and opposed the Republican Party, since it was usually seen as the party of the North and civil rights for blacks. Table 3.0 shows the trend of Republican support for the Civil Rights bills and Democratic opposition to them in Congress.

---

[14] Fitzgerald, "To Give Our Votes," 493.
[15] Ibid., 497.

Table 3.0 Partisan Lineups in House and Senate Votes
on Civil Rights Laws, 1866–1890

| Year | Law | House Vote Republicans | House Vote Democrats | Senate Vote Republicans | Senate Vote Democrats |
|---|---|---|---|---|---|
| 1866 | Civil Rights Bill | 111-5 | 0-33 | 33-2 | 0-10 |
| 1866 | Fourteenth Amendment | 138-0 | 0-36 | 33-4 | 0-7 |
| 1869 | Fifteenth Amendment | 144-3 | 0-41 | 39-2 | 0-11 |
| 1870 | Enforcement Act | 133-0 | 0-58 | 48-1 | 0-10 |
| 1871 | Ku Klux Klan Act | 93-0 | 0-74 | 36-2 | 0-11 |
| 1872 | Enforcement Act | 102-0 | 0-79 | 36-2 | 0-11 |
| 1875 | Civil Rights Bill | 147-14 | 0-79 | 38-7 | 0-19 |
| 1875 | Enforcement Act | 135-51 | 0-78 | No vote | No vote |
| 1890 | Lodge Bill | 155-2 | 0-147 | 34-8 | 0-27 |

Source: J. Morgan Kousser, *Colorblind Injustice Minority Voting Rights and the Undoing of the Second Reconstruction* (Chapel Hill: University of North Carolina Press, 1999): 39.

This partisan approach to civil rights served as a missed opportunity for our country and the Southern region to unite behind the promotion of the principles of democracy, liberty, and equality. It created a political environment within the Southern region that tolerated discrimination and in essence required it from Democratic politicians. But more importantly, it created a political environment in which the two major parties of our society were defined by race. At this time in the Black Belt region, the Republican Party was seen as the party of the black man and the Democratic Party was seen as the party of the white man. The role of race in political parties continues to be an issue in modern politics, yet the political party affiliation has reversed. However, political power in the Black Belt region historically came from the strict control of the region by a small group of white elites who controlled the Democratic Party. During Reconstruction, the Republican Party, particularly because of the freedmen, briefly became a player in Black Belt politics. With the help of the national Republican Party, the politics of the region changed, civil rights legislation was passed, African Americans were elected to office, and the political system was briefly opened to more than the elites of the Black Belt.

*Early National African American Leadership in the Black Belt*

During Reconstruction, which began in 1867 and ended by 1877, African Americans in the Black Belt received descriptive representation for the first time by sending black men to state constitutional conventions as delegates. Hines, Hines, and Harrold found, "Of the 1,000 men elected as delegates to the ten state conventions, 265 were black. Black delegates were a majority only in the South Carolina and Louisiana conventions. In most states, including Alabama, Georgia, Mississippi, Virginia, North Carolina, Arkansas and Texas, black men made up 10 percent to 20 percent of the delegates. At least 107 of the 265 had been born slaves; about 40 had served in the Union Army." Although Reconstruction is characterized by black political participation, whites played a major role in politics of the time as well.[16]

Although African Americans were often portrayed as childlike, sometimes irrational, and unfit to serve in government, these conventions proved that they were fully capable of leadership. Soon, African Americans held office in state legislatures in both chambers and were elected to state offices throughout the South. They also took local offices such as mayor, sheriff, and police chief. This temporarily inclusive politics made tremendous change in the political landscape of the Black Belt community and the power structure there. According to Hahn (2003),

> During Reconstruction, black men held political office in every state of the former Confederacy. More than one hundred won election or appointment to posts having jurisdiction over entire states, ranging from superintendent of education, assistant commissioner of agriculture, superintendent of the deaf and dumb asylum, and member of the state land commission to treasurer, secretary of state, state supreme court

---

[16] Darlene Clark Hines, William Hines, and Stanley Harrold, *The African American Odyssey,* 4th ed. (New York: Pearson/Prentice Hall, 2008) 324.

justice and lieutenant governor. One African American even sat briefly as the governor of Louisiana. A great many more—almost eight hundred—served in the state legislatures. But by far the largest number of black officeholders was to be found at the local level: in counties, cities, smaller municipalities, and militia districts.... [B]lacks clearly filled over 1,100 elective or appointive local offices, and they may well have fill as a many as 1,400 or 1,500, about 80 percent of which were in rural and small-town settings.[17]

These black lawmakers took part in drafting new constitutions and legislation that transformed the Southern region. For example, in Alabama, "the 1868 document, crafted by a biracial convention dedicated to new ways of commerce, education, state government, and race relations, was a constitution devoted to raising additional revenue, providing universal education and expanded state services, enlarging the size and scope of state government, and encouraging business and industry."[18] These efforts resulted in significant changes in governmental responsiveness and scope.

However, racial discrimination was not unique to the South, and there was great conflict between white Republican leaders and black Republicans on many issues, including the role of federal protection in the South. Although, the African Americans were members of the Republican Party, these lawmakers had very little in common politically with white Northern Republicans who ran the party. Many Northern Republicans did not support governmental activism within the South as it related to civil rights and liberties, nor financial remedies for the financial situations of the freedmen. Blacks as a minority within a majoritarian system found it difficult to address the specific needs of the freedmen within the existing system, so they participated in colored men conventions to address their unique concerns.

These "colored men" conventions allowed for the full participation of African American men and were used as vehicles to address the

---

[17] Steven Hahn, *A Nation under Our Feet: Black Political Struggles in the Rural South from Slavery to the Great Migration* (Cambridge MA: Harvard University Press, 2003) 219.

[18] Wayne Flynt, "Alabama's Shame: The Historical Origins of the 1901 Constitution," *Alabama Law Review* 53/1 **[issue?]** (2001): 67.

grievances of the race and served as centers for strategic planning and decision-making. Some of these conventions focused on African Americans leaving the rural South for western areas, where they could be safe and prosper.

Therefore, these colored conventions began a history of Black Power strategy through the development of all-black organizations. One example occurred in the Black Belt of Georgia after two major events that shook the faith of blacks in the political process and the federal government's willingness to protect them. It also resulted in them questioning whether the Republican Party had the ability to truly assist them. The first event was a riot in Camilla, Georgia, as blacks tried to organize a political rally, and the second event was the expulsion of elected black legislators from the state legislature in September 1868. As a result black individuals took action:

> The expelled representatives decided to organize a "purely colored" Civil and Political Rights Association to seek redress for the freedmen's grievances. Henry M. Turner, president of the all-black organization, called for a Colored State Convention to meet in Macon in early October…the 136-delegate meeting where "issues ranging from finances, to murders and outrages, to whether freedmen might vote unmolested in November" were discussed. When the convention adjourned, delegates returned home to establish black Civil and Political Rights Associations throughout the state. Although the associations comprised "Georgia's first broadly based 'black power' organization," they never developed into a separate political party.... [B]lack leaders apparently recognized that any achievements for blacks could only be made through the national Republican party and its state level organization.

These efforts were just some of the Black Power efforts that would emerge from within the Black Belt region to address the issues influencing the lives of black people. Although blacks sought alternative approaches to political participation, they still worked with traditional institutions for change, as reconstruction efforts allowed for African American descriptive representation in all levels of government. Yet

---

[19] Lee W. Formwalt, Robert Crumley, and Philip Joiner, "Petitioning Congress for Protection: A Black View of Reconstruction at the Local Level," *Georgia Historical Quarterly* 73/2 (Summer 1989): 308.

impoverished African Americans of the Black Belt were caught in a political predicament because although they had elected representation, this representation was a minority in a majoritarian system and was not able to address their unique economic and political circumstances through minority elective-office holding. Table 3.1 shows the names of early African American congressional representatives and the years they served. All of these were residents of the South, which also reveals the fact that white Northerners, like white Southerners, did not elect Africans Americans as representatives at the time, and like today, very few white Americans are represented by African American congressional representatives.

Soon, the political tides were changing, and black tenure in Congress was short-lived. The interest in the freedmen by the North and the Republican Party began to weaken. As a result of the disputed presidential election of 1876 between Republican Rutherford Hayes and Democrat Samuel Tilden, the national Republican Party negotiated with Southern Democrats for the election of Hayes. In return for Southern conservative support, the Republican Party agreed to withdraw all federal troops from the South, officially ending Reconstruction in 1877.[20]

Table 3.1 African Americans in Congress During Reconstruction

| NAME | STATE | YEARS IN OFFICE | |
|---|---|---|---|
| Hiram Revels | Mississippi | 1870-1871 | Senate |
| Blanche Bruce | Mississippi | 1875-1881 | Senate |

---

[20] Rutherford B. Hayes, a Republican, and Samuel J. Tilden, a Democrat. The first returns indicated a victory for Tilden, who had won the popular vote with 4,284,020 votes to Hayes's 4,036,572. But Tilden's 184 electoral votes—the votes that would decide the presidency—were still one short of a majority, while Hayes's 165 electoral votes left him 20 ballots away. The votes of three Southern states and one western state still had not been counted. The 20 electoral votes remaining in dispute were one from Oregon and 19 from the three Southern states that still retained Republican-controlled electoral boards—Florida (4), Louisiana (8), and South Carolina (7). After a heated debated, the stalemate ended with the Democrats agreeing to support Hayes if Reconstruction efforts were ended.

| Joseph Rainey | South Carolina | 1869-1879 | House |
| Jefferson Long | Georgia | 1871 | House |
| Benjamin Turner | Alabama | 1871-1873 | House |
| Robert DeLarge | South Carolina | 1871-1873 | House |
| Robert Elliot | South Carolina | 1871-1875 | House |
| Josiah Walls | Florida | 1871-1875 | House |
| Richard Cain | South Carolina | 1873-1875 1877-1879 | House |
| Alonzo Ransier | South Carolina | 1873-1875 | House |
| James T. Rapier | Alabama | 1873-1875 | House |
| John Lynch | Mississippi | 1873-1877 1882-1883 | House |
| Jeremiah Haralson | Alabama | 1875-1877 | House |
| John Hyman | North Carolina | 1875-1877 | House |
| Charles Nash | Louisiana | 1875-1877 | House |
| Robert Smalls | South Carolina | 1875-1879 1881-1887 | House |
| James O'Hara | North Carolina | 1883-1887 | House |
| Henry Cheatham | North Carolina | 1889-1893 | House |
| Thomas Miller | South Carolina | 1889-1891 | House |
| John Langston | Virginia | 1889-1891 | House |
| George Murray | South Carolina | 1893-1897 | House |
| George White | North Carolina | 1897-1901 | House |

Source: Clay, William. *Just Permanent Interests Black Americans in Congress 1870–1992*. (Amistad. New York, 1993)

By the late 1800s, the Republican Party had abandoned African Americans in the South and redefined itself as the party of limited government and economic and business issues. The South was left to the Democratic Party, which had always fought Reconstruction, passage of the early civil rights legislation, and fought African American progress, and which now was the party in charge of the South. This Democratic Party was a party traditionally dedicated to limited government, agrarianism, states' rights, and slavery, and it sought to reestablish the Old Order in the South, using the one-party system to recreate the closed political system of the Black Belt. C. Vann Woodard examined the control of this party in Virginia and illustrated the power of local organizations and moneyed elites and their control of an entire county.

> Through "these election officials and the use of money and local pressure," the county chairman "was able to see that only his men were chosen as treasurer, sheriff, clerk of court, commissioner of revenue, member of the legislature and supervisors." Since the General Assembly by custom appointed the county judge recommended by the member from the county, it could be accurately said "that the county chairman and his immediate assistants determined who would be chosen to every office in the county." This tiny group was the "courthouse clique" and "In them lay the real power of the only organization that could control Virginia."[21]

This image of Virginia provides a tiny glimpse of the strict political power structure in most of the Black Belt counties. Political power was restricted to those of a particular race and class, and for the most part gender. The policy preferences and use for government of the ruling class was unique to their status, and they utilized government to their advantage. There can be no underestimation of the power of the locals and the promotion of racial discrimination as the power at the local level allowed control of politics by a few people in the Black Belt region. In many places, an elitist tradition continues. African Americans within the Black Belt region were left out of the political process, often victims of the policies it produced, and were without remedy by state and national governmental forces.

In addition to the total domination of local, state, and national affairs by the Southern Democratic party, African American political participation was also being attacked. Even the small representation in Congress during Reconstruction would soon be abandoned as between 1901 and 1928 there were no African Americans serving in Congress at all. Politically, African Americans were considered mute and their issues were null by the turn of the twentieth century. They had been completely forced out of elective political life in the South. In his farewell address, Congressman George H. White of North Carolina, the last African

---

[21] C. Vann. Woodard, *Origins of the New South, 1877–1913* (Baton Rouge: Louisiana State University Press, 1995) 52.

American in Congress for twenty-eight years stated, "This, Mr. Chairman, is perhaps the Negroes' temporary farewell to the American Congress. But let me say, phoenix-like, he will rise up someday and come again. These parting words are in behalf of an outraged, heartbroken, bruised and bleeding people, but God-fearing people, faithful, industrious, loyal people…rising people, full of potential."[22]

After Reconstruction, the use of terrorism by the political and economic establishment resulted in an almost century-long hiatus of African American elective political leadership in the Black Belt region. This did not, however, result in a lack of leaders within the community. On the contrary, many African Americans took up leadership positions within other segments of the African American community, such as in the black church, schools, and charitable organizations. These organizations allowed for the social progress and development of an African American cohort of leaders. When focusing on the history of the Black Belt and changes within the region, one constant factor that was never fully addressed by national, state, nor local leaders was the lack of economic opportunity for African American residents. Even when the region was being politically refurbished to include African Americans during Reconstruction, Republicans failed to overhaul the economic inequality in the region. To this date, this issue has yet to be addressed comprehensively by the national government.

*Post-Reconstruction Politics in the Black Belt*

After Reconstruction, forms of Jim Crow laws quickly swept the Black Belt region, and within a couple of years they were passed throughout, beginning in 1881 in Tennessee, 1887 in Florida, 1888 in Mississippi, 1889 in Texas, 1890 in Louisiana, and 1891 in Alabama, Arkansas, Kentucky, and Georgia. Soon, many of these laws would be tested by the Supreme Court in the *Plessy* decision, which resulted in almost a hundred years of *separate-but-unequal* public accommodations. However, disastrous the former *Dred Scott* decision was to African

---

[22] George White Farewell Address to Congress, 29 January 1901, Washington, DC, http://www.edchange.org/multicultural/speeches/george_white_farewell.html, accessed 12 December 2012.

Americans in this country, and particularly those who resided within the Black Belt region, the *Plessy* decision established segregation throughout the South and lent a legal guideline for Southern inequality for decades. In *Plessy v. Ferguson* (1896), the courts established a separate-but-equal doctrine that ruled for a significant part of the twentieth century and hindered educational, economic, and political opportunities for Southern blacks, particularly Black Belt residents. This decision impeded progress of the Fourteenth Amendment to allow full citizenship for African Americans and constructed a society that, although founded on a constitution that eventually outlawed slavery and ultimately denounced African American subordination, also created a system where denying African Americans the right to be treated as full citizens was tolerated. This separate-but-equal doctrine ruled the Black Belt society legally until the Brown (1954) decision overturned it.[23]

After Reconstruction, Southern states rewrote their constitutions to ensure the new Black Belt society (or the New South), like the former Old South, would be structured around their own social norms and traditions. The redevelopment of the old discriminatory social contract for the region was first on the agenda, as this redesigned social contract would preserve preordained social norms and institutions of the Old South. These efforts included the exclusion of African Americans from the electoral processes and stripped them of all of the civil rights and liberties provided by the Constitution. In 1890, Mississippi became the first Southern state to disenfranchise African Americans by constitutional convention, beginning a trend of political exclusion in the South that lasted well into the twentieth century. For example, John B. Knox, the president of Alabama's 1901 constitutional convention stated, "Why it is within the limits imposed by the Federal Constitution to, establish white supremacy in this state. This is our problem, and we should be permitted to deal with it unobstructed by outside influences…but if we would have white supremacy," he rationalized, "we must establish it by law—not by force or fraud…. To discriminate against the Negro," Knox concluded, "was not based on race, but on the Negro's inferior intellectual and moral

---

[23] *Dred Scott v. Sandford*, 60 U.S. 393 (1857), *Plessy v. Ferguson* (1896) 163 U.S. 537. *Brown v. Board of Education* (1954) 347 U.S. 483.

condition."[24] As a result of the hostile environment, many blacks left the region as discussed in this newspaper article addressing the Alabama Black Belt.

> The Census returns will show that in Alabama the race problem is rapidly approaching a peaceful and satisfactory solution. The immigration of white laborers from the North and from Europe and the exodus of negroes to the Mississippi Valley is settling this vexed question better than legislation could. In nearly all the counties in the "black belt" of Alabama there has been a falling off in population, and the decrease is among the negroes. In Hale, one of the largest black counties, a decrease of 3,500 in population since 1880 is shown.[25]

Many black migrants left for various reasons, such as economic opportunity, political disenfranchisement, or other issues, but one of the most important factors was the continued brutality faced by these individuals and the lack of civil rights protection. In both the Black Belt of Alabama and Georgia after the Civil War and Emancipation, blacks were targeted for ill treatment and abuse, both legal and extralegal in nature. For example, in Alabama, cases of peonage were brought in Tallapoosa, Coosa, and Lowndes counties. According to accounts, political and law enforcement leaders were complicit in the atrocities, including Sheriff Dixon and his five brothers, who dominated Lowndes County by violence. Lowndes County had a black population that was ten times the size of whites and historically had been characterized as tremendously brutal in its treatment of its black residents. The Dixon clan used their positions to victimize black residents and limit their basic rights. In another example, John Pace, who was the former sheriff of Tallapoosa County, forced blacks into a contract that "empowered Pace to treat the laborer as a convict. Pace reserved the right to lock him up, deprive him of clothing and to bring him back with bloodhounds if he undertook to escape." Beatings and violence were major components of the peonage exhibited in the Black Belt at this time. The state of Georgia

---

[24] Flynt "Alabama's Shame," 71.
[25] Anonymous, "The Alabama Race Problem," *The New York Times*, 31 August 1890 http://query.nytimes.com/mem/archive-free/pdf?res=f5061ff93a5d15738ddda80b94d0405b8085f0d3, accessed 15 December 2012.

was no better, as it hosted convict camps where "Negroes [were] housed in stockades and camps, whipped for trivial offenses and compelled to marry against their will and without legal ceremony." One woman, Lula Frazier, was enslaved for fourteen months to work off a $50 debt.[26] The outrageous treatment of blacks was also coupled with significant political abuse. Fraud was everywhere in the Black Belt. In one observation of the political process, it was stated, "The entire negro vote is Republican...and that the enormous Democratic majorities returned from the Black Belt counties are entirely fictitious.... [I]n these counties the trouble is not that the negroes are not allowed to vote, or that their votes are thrown out, but that their votes are counted, whether cast or not, for men whom they did not vote."[27] All of these situations were after the thirteenth, fourteenth, and fifteenth civil rights amendments to the constitution and provide glaring proof of the flaws in the federal system for protecting the rights of blacks after the Reconstruction period.

As a result, blacks began to utilize the only leverage they had to economically progress themselves: their agricultural labor. As with the Union League and Republican activity, politics was linked to agriculture. Because of the inability of the national government to protect them, black individuals began to develop self-reliant political ideologies to address problems within their own communities. The Colored Farmers' Alliance represented one such endeavor of this self-reliant ideology, and this organization was crucial in the continued development of an organic Black Belt Black Power ideology. As one of the largest black organizations in American history, it hailed from Houston County, Texas, in 1886 and spread to every state in the South. By 1891, the organization boasted a membership of an estimated one million members, yet most scholars suggested the number was smaller. As part of its self-reliant strategy,

---

[26] J. L. Brady, ed., "How Slaves Are Made," *Lawrence* (KS) *Daily World*, 22 June 1903 http://news.google.com/newspapers?id=AuFWAAAAIBAJ&sjid=PEINAAA-AIBAJ&pg=2863,5677358&dq=black+belt+region&hl=en, accessed 15 December 2012.

[27] Felix Agnus, "Their Votes Are Stolen. Alabama Negroes Counted for Democrats," *Baltimore* (MD) *American*, 18 October 1892 "http://news.google.com/newspapers?id=8jxCAAAAIBAJ&sjid=RLkMAAAAIBAJ&pg=3555,1789540&dq=black+belt+region&hl=en, accessed 20 December 2012.

The Colored Alliance urged its members to learn new farming techniques, acquire ownership of their homes, and improve their level of education. It sponsored cooperative stores and in the ports of Norfolk, Charleston, Mobile, New Orleans, and Houston established exchange through which members bought goods at reduced prices and obtained loans to pay off mortgages. It published newspapers and in some cases raised money to provide longer public school terms.[28]

Like the Loyal Leagues, the Alliance promoted a Black Belt black political power ideology that was based on the agricultural connection between African Americans and the land. Initially, the alliance was successful in its pursuit of economic self-sufficiency, particularly through its farm techniques and cooperative efforts. These efforts also focused on political inclusion, such as the St. Landry Parish, Louisiana, chapter, which described its purpose as being "for the purpose of trying to elevate our race, to make us better citizens, better husbands, better fathers and sons, to educate ourselves so that we may be able to vote more intelligently on questions that are of vital importance to our people."[29] The organization of a cooperative was instrumental in developing black self-sufficiency and would be key to other black efforts in the region in the future.

However, one chapter in Leflore County, Mississippi, drew the wrath of local whites, who viewed the group as economic competitors and a political threat. Community leaders asked the leaders of the group to leave, but they refused and racial tensions became heated. Things were so tense that the sheriff called the governor for troops, fearing a race riot. As a result, roughly 200 white men formed a posse and hunted down the Colored Alliance group members. Eyewitness reports stated that African

---

[28] William F. Holmes, "The Leflore County Massacre and the Demise of the Colored Farmer's Alliance," *Phylon* 34/3 (May 1973): 267–74. William F. Holmes, "The Demise of the Colored Farmer's Alliance," *The Journal of Southern History* 41/2 (May 1975): 187.

[29] Darlene Clark Hines, William Hines, and Stanley Harrold, *The African American Odyssey: The Combined Volume* ((Upper Saddle River NJ: Pearson Prentice Hall, 2008): 355.

Americans were "shot down like dogs"[30] and *The Detroit Plains Dealer* reported "that a brave colored man risked his life to investigate the extent of the massacre. He too claimed the whites killed many blacks, but he was sure the whole truth would never be obtained because the Negroes in Leflore County were so terrified that they dare not speak of the matter, even to each other." After the massacre, the white planters ordered "the Durant Commercial Company, the Alliance store with which many blacks had been doing business, to desist from selling goods or loaning money to Colored Alliance or to any of its members."[31]

This effort, like many others, was viewed by the majority community as a threat, and the Old South social order of black economic dependence and social control was maintained. Just as the Colored Alliance sought to make African Americans economically self-sufficient in the Black Belt region, one majority white farmer organization sought to disenfranchise blacks and keep them economically dependent on the white power elite. The Southern Alliance, a very powerful white farmer organization, fought against measures such as the Lodge Election bill, which promised federal protection for black voting rights, and other efforts to give civil rights and freedom to blacks. In addition, the organization also fought measures that could potentially provide land ownership and local power to African Americans. For example, "In Screven County, Georgia, the Southern Alliance, issued orders in 1889 that no land could be leased to blacks; instead, negroes should work for white farmers," again ensuring black economic dependence.[32]

This dominant organization influenced agriculture and national policy, and many Southern state legislatures were controlled by the Southern Alliance. It has been credited with the motivation for many anti-black pieces of legislation, including Jim Crow laws and poll taxes as well as literacy tests. The necessity of keeping African Americans under total economic, political, and social control was a constant goal for

---

[30] William F. Holmes, "The Leflore County Massacre and the Demise of the Colored Farmer's Alliance," Phylon 34/3 (May 1973): 272.
[31] Holmes, "Demise," *Journal of Southern History*, 187. Holmes, "Leflore County Massacre," 274.
[32] Holmes, "Demise," *Journal of Southern History*, 194.

those who controlled the Black Belt, and the Southern Alliance was used as a tool to accomplish this goal. The region was delicately built on a tower of racially colored cards, and if one card was removed from their control, the tower would collapse. This carefully built race tower required its residents to remain in prescribed roles without opportunities for change and individualism. Yet blacks were developing political ideologies that fit their unique circumstances and challenging the very structure of the race tower by focusing on self-help and independence.

The discrimination and violence against blacks in the region increased, as whites quickly moved to restore the "old order." To find solutions to their problems, in 1879, African American delegates representing fourteen states participated in a convention in Nashville to discuss emigration efforts to western territories. Issues addressed at the convention included transportation to the territories and the consequences of leaving the Black Belt region in addition to the violence facing African Americans in the Black Belt. Tens of thousands of African American "Exodusters," as they were called, moved to Kansas by 1880. Yet Kansas was not the only attractive western site for fleeing blacks, they settled in other areas such as California, New Mexico, and Oklahoma, to name a few.[33]

Many black individuals decided that relocating was their best option, as Damani Davis describes:

> Thus the Kansas Exodus was an inconvenient blow to both whites, who expected the masses of black workers in the South to quietly conform to their new role as a cheap, compliant labor force, and to African American elites, who expected them to blindly follow the dictates of the official "black leadership" as well as the Republican Party. It also challenged the idea that freed blacks were incapable of intelligently assessing their own predicament, drawing their own conclusions, and taking action to improve their situation. No member of the educated elite segment of the black community directly organized or led the Exoduster movement. This grassroots movement, generated by indigenous leaders among the

---

[33] Billy D. Higgins, "Negro Thought and the Exodus of 1879," *Phylon* 32/1 (1960) (1st quarter 1971): 39–52.

masses of black sharecroppers and tenant farmers, sought the full benefits of freedom.[34]

The movement was seen as a problem of national proportion because it could potentially change the labor demographics of the South, so the US Senate held hearings to address the issue.

Although the exodus looked promising, many others remained in the Black Belt and continued to struggle under great odds with little internal or external support in their efforts. However, this large power base of black rural laborers who remained on Southern lands would become a stable political and social power source well into the twentieth century. Unfortunately, their large numbers did not translate into significant economic power because of the economic structure of the region, and most remained economically stagnant.

By 1900, 75 percent of Southern black farmers were sharecroppers or tenants. This economic dependence resulted in many generations of black residents of the Black Belt South without generational wealth, framing the economic circumstances for future generations of blacks in the region. It also shaped their ability to politically shape their communities, since economic powerlessness means political powerless in the Black Belt at the end of the twentieth century. Indeed, the stagnant economic circumstance of blacks at the time was an institutional legacy of slavery and socioeconomic and political oppression. Yet these large numbers of blacks allowed for a ready power base for future Black Belt political activity.[35] Table 3.2 below shows the large number of farm operators in the South in 1910. Table 3.3 also reveals that most blacks were workers of the land and not owners, so their ability to become economically self-sufficient was quite limited.

---

[34] *Damani Davis,* "Exodus to Kansas: The 1880 Senate Investigation of the Beginnings of the African American Migration from the South." http://www.archives.gov/publications/prologue/2008/summer/exodus.html, accessed 17 December 2012.

[35] C. Vann Woodard, *Origins of the New South, 1877–1913* (Baton Rouge: Louisiana State University Press, 1995).

## Abandonment in Dixie

Table 3.2 Farm Operators in the South in 1910

| Race | Total number | Owners free of mortgage | Owners with Mortgage | Part owners | Cash tenants | Share tenants | Managers |
|---|---|---|---|---|---|---|---|
| Black | 890,141 | 128,557 | 46,733 | 42,177 | 285,950 | 384,524 | 1,200 |
| White | 2,207,406 | 908,211 | 245,889 | 171,944 | 229,461 | 636,877 | 15,084 |

Source: 1910 Agriculture Census: Chapter XX-Agriculture: Acreage of Farmers, Value of Farm Property; Livestock; Crops; Term of Occupancy; Mortgage Indebtedness, and Tenure Classes (Washington DC: Government Printing Office, 1910): 585.

Table 3.3 Black Farm Owners in 1910

| State | Total farm population | Owners free of mortgage | Percentage | Owners with mortgage | Percentage |
|---|---|---|---|---|---|
| Delaware | 406 | 231 | 56.9 | 171 | 42.1 |
| Maryland | 3,950 | 2,582 | 65.4 | 1,334 | 33.8 |
| Virginia | 32,228 | 26,209 | 81.3 | 5,609 | 17.4 |
| West Virginia | 558 | 478 | 85.8 | 78 | 14.0 |
| North Carolina | 21,443 | 15,433 | 72.0 | 5,609 | 26.1 |
| South Carolina | 20,372 | 15,208 | 75.0 | 4,336 | 21.5 |
| Georgia | 15,698 | 5,842 | 80.0 | 1,284 | 17.6 |
| Kentucky | 5,929 | 4,488 | 75.7 | 1,319 | 22.2 |
| Tennessee | 10,700 | 7,781 | 72.7 | 2,687 | 25.1 |
| Alabama | 17,082 | 9,951 | 58.3 | 6,551 | 38.3 |
| Mississippi | 25,026 | 12,803 | 51.2 | 11,385 | 45.5 |
| Arkansas | 14,662 | 9,111 | 62.1 | 4,913 | 33.5 |
| Louisiana | 10,725 | 7,736 | 72.1 | 2,637 | 24.6 |
| Oklahoma | 11,150 | 7,806 | 70.0 | 2,633 | 23.6 |
| Texas | 21,232 | 15,686 | 73.9 | 5,004 | 23.6 |

Source: 1910 Agriculture Census: Chapter XX-Agriculture: Acreage of Farmers, Value of Farm Property; Livestock; Crops; Term of Occupancy; Mortgage Indebtedness, and Tenure Classes (Washington DC: Government Printing Office, 1910): 587.

Land was the key to economic success in the South, and blacks were eager to obtain it. "By 1900 more than 100,000 black families owned their own land in the eight states of the deep South.... Black land ownership increased more than 500 percent between 1870 and 1900." African American land ownership peaked in 1910 with 15 million acres: 175, 000 farms were fully owned while 43,000 were partially owned and 670,000 were sharecropped. Sadly, these ownership numbers would not last, and efforts to keep land and farms would result in a unique definition of political ideological exploration in Black Power.[36]

*Agriculture and Socialism in the Black Belt*

Democratic Party dominance in the Black Belt set up a regional political system where political freedom and exploration of political ideology could be difficult. The lack of political ideological examination had a major influence on policy and governmental operations, such as providing exclusionary political party membership in the Black Belt region and impeding political competition. Resulting consequences included the dominant economic class of the Black Belt controlling the Democratic Party and an economically biased policy agenda. Therefore, lower class citizens found little remedy in political activism through the one active political party in the region. As a result, planters and businessmen, whom lower class agricultural workers worked for, had control of the only party that mattered in the region. This resulted in the brief formation of an agricultural group sponsored by the Socialist movement in the South that addressed the needs of lower class agricultural workers and began to examine alternative political and economic theories. According to Foner, the Socialist Party dismissed racism in the South early in the twentieth century and promoted interracial endeavors. As a result, the Socialist Party included blacks

---

[36] Darlene Clark Hine, William C. Hine, and Stanley Harrold, *The African-American Odyssey* (Upper Saddle River NJ: Prentice Hall, 2008) 369–70. Manning Marble, "The Land Question in Historical Perspective: The Economics of Poverty in the Blackbelt South, 1865–1920," in *The Black Rural Landowner-Endangered Species: Social, Political and Economic Implications*, edited by Leo McGee and Robert Boone (Westport CT: Greenwood Press, 1979).

from throughout the South: "In the states from Maryland to Texas, there were about 900 members in 1933, or 5 percent of the national total, and about 700 in 1935, or about 4 percent of the national total. In the six states of the Deep South—North and South Carolina, Georgia, Alabama, Mississippi, and Louisiana—where the largest number of Negroes lived, there were 270 party members in 1933 and about 80 in 1935."[37]

Although the numbers suggest that the Socialist Party had little appeal to African Americans and didn't address issues that concerned them, their membership proved their openness to alternative approaches to change. Even with these small numbers, the Socialist Party helped to sponsor a venture in union organizing in the Deep South: the Southern Tenant Farmers' Union (STFU), which at one time boasted membership of over 25,000 members. The union organized strikes to demand fair payment for crops and protested the horrible social and economic conditions in the agricultural industry. The union had a largely African American membership, and by 1937, this population was over 80 percent of the group's total membership. However, as with other integrated political organizations during the time, the leadership of the organization was not diverse, and this fact and external pressures eventually resulted in African American laymen and the small number of African American leaders losing confidence in the union, eventually abandoning the effort. Power brokers within the community were threatened by the union, as "the union aroused the enmity of planters and businessmen. Local officials harassed organizers, and when this tactic failed, a campaign of violence followed."[38]

As with reconstruction activities and the Colored Farmers Alliance, violence was used to end political activities that did not fall within the

---

[37] Philip Foner, *American Socialism and Black Americans From the Age of Jackson to World War II* (Westport CT: Greenwood Press, 1977) 348.

[38] Jerold S. Auerbach, "Southern Tenant Farmers: Socialist Critics of the New Deal," The Arkansas Historical Quarterly 27/2 (Summer, 1968): 113–31. Alexander Yard, "'They Don't Regard My Rights at All': Arkansas Farm Workers, Economic Modernization, and the Southern Tenant Farmers Union," The Arkansas Historical Quarterly 47/3 (Autumn 1988): 201–29. Foner, *American Socialism*. Lowell Dyson, "The Southern Tenant Farmers Union and Depression Politics," *Political Science Quarterly* 88/2 (June 1973): 230.

traditional routes of political progress, and these were closed to blacks within the Black Belt. Yet by joining and participating in STFU activities, black members exhibited many concepts of Black Belt Black Power ideology. More importantly, their abandonment of the effort when it was clear that they could not play a leadership role demonstrated that Black Belt Black Power activities would be defined by black people on their own terms.[39]

The mostly black membership proved that they were willing to seek alternative solutions beyond traditional political parties due to their exclusion from the Democratic Party. However, the true exercise of Black Belt Black Power resulted in the black membership's rejection of the Socialist union's inability to provide true autonomous black leadership and decision-making opportunities. Rural black people would not merely accept a subservient role in their progress—they demanded to lead it. This desire for black leadership in the alternate pursuits of advancement was briefly realized in Communist-driven efforts in Alabama with the Sharecroppers Union (SCU) or the Alabama Sharecroppers Union, which was founded in 1931. It was the largest Communist-led, black-led mass organization in the Deep South during the 1930s. Black sharecroppers, tenant farmers, and agricultural wage laborers were all represented in the group's membership. This effort was a part of a larger Communist effort to organize blacks around a separatist agenda, with the espoused ultimate goal of assisting a separate Black Belt nation. The life circumstances of rural blacks in the South was a topic of the Communist Party at the highest levels in the 1920s: "During the Second Congress of the Comintern (1920) John Reed passed a note to the rostrum asking, 'Should I say something about Negroes in America?' Lenin scribbled back, '*Yes*' absolutely necessary."[40] In 1928, the Sixth World Congress of the Communist International recognized the Black Belt region as an independent nation within the American South. This

---

[39] V. O. Key, *Southern Politics in State and Nation* (New York: Knopf, 1949). *Encyclopedia of the American Left* edited by Mary Jo Buhle, Paul Buhle, and Dan Geogakas (New York: Garland Publishing, 1990).

[40] Woodford McClellan, "Africans and Black Americans in the Comintern Schools, 1925–1934," *The International Journal of African Historical Studies* 26/2 (1993): 371.

recognition was prominent, as "the central hypothesis upon which the Communist position rested was that a Negro nation, conforming to Stalin's definition of a nation as 'an historically developed lasting identity of language, territory, economic life and psychology,' existed in the heart of the American South." So "'self-determination of the Black Belt' was affirmed to be a major objective of the party."[41] The Communist Party found in the Black Belt willing participants in carving out their own place in Black Belt society.[42]

The Sharecroppers Union (SCU) in Dallas and Lowndes counties, in the heart of the Alabama Black Belt, promoted and negotiated or renegotiated contracts with landowners and supported cooperatives to market their own crops. The group's power base rested on the large black population of sharecroppers and tenants who exercised their power through their numbers. Due to the limitation of political and economic opportunities, this group used its members' work in agriculture to negotiate contracts and develop cooperatives for economic improvement. This group illustrates Black Belt Black Power through agriculture and economic innovations and continued a very successful strategy of linking agriculture, political activism, and attempts at economic self-sufficiency. They were strong promoters of self-defense, as "in the early 1930s, rural blacks in Alabama armed themselves to organize the Share Croppers' Union. Their own experience had taught them, one recalled, that 'the only thing going to stop them from killing you, you got to go shooting.'"[43]

Although the focus on self-defense and protection is noteworthy, the cooperative would prove to be a long-lasting solution for change in the Black Belt region. Black Communists during the 1930s in Alabama

---

[41] John Beecher, "The Share Croppers' Union in Alabama," *Social Forces* 13/1 (1934): 124.
[42] Beecher, "The Share Croppers' Union in Alabama," 124.
[43] D. G. Robin Kelley, *Hammer and Hoe: Communists in Alabama during the Great Depression* (Chapel Hill: University of North Carolina Press, 1990) 45. Theodore Rosengarten, *All God's Dangers: The Life of Nate Shaw* (New York: Vintage Books, 1984). Timothy Tyson, "Robert F. Williams, 'Black Power,' and the Roots of the African American Freedom Struggle," *The Journal of American History* 85/2 (September 1998): 545–46.

appealed to black sharecroppers and tenants because of their stance on economic sufficiency. So although the Communist Party did not promote Black Nationalism, they did provide blacks with economic possibilities for economic independence, which was more than the traditional American political system allowed.

Agricultural unions linked the civil rights efforts of blacks and their agricultural work, thereby developing a grassroots community organizing approach that was then supplanted in urban areas around the country. Those efforts proved to illustrate Black Belt Black Power theory in its most complete form, as the efforts promoted organic black participation and were flexible enough to adapt to varied circumstances. These groups also involved interracial efforts in a desire to promote the agenda of the people and served as a warning to the power elites that if successful, they could prove potentially detrimental to the existing political and economic structure. The planters were well aware of the changes to come if these unions became a stronghold in the Black Belt, and they used legal and extralegal means to squelch them. The closed political culture of the region thrived on the one-party arrangement it had with the Democratic Party, and those in power within the region were determined to keep the relationship strong and exclusive. These, like most efforts to organize for political and economic advancement, were hindered in the Black Belt South, and so the economic dependence there continued, influencing the economic well-being of many generations of blacks in the Black Belt as well as their ability to socio-politically shape their communities.

In order to thrive within our system, there is required participation in the key systems of our society, democracy and capitalism. Yet these systems were not allowed to take root and grow in the Black Belt initially, being a region that was culturally built on racism, elitism, patronage, and terrorism. The forbiddance of this Black Belt society to allow inclusive politics and economics resulted in the exclusion of blacks in key societal institutions and policy agenda-setting roles.

*Pan Africanism in the Black Belt*

As a result of their exclusion from traditional political processes, blacks began to focus on blackness and Pan Africanism and helped to formulate political theories that were exclusive to their own experiences in the

Black Belt. These ideologies included W. E. B. Du Bois's well-known integrationist theories and Booker T. Washington's accommodationist theories as major blue prints for the direction for black success. Both Du Bois and Washington, in addition to the aforementioned theories, participated in Pan Africanist approaches to progress, although Du Bois's efforts are far more well known than Washington's. Du Bois attended the first Pan African Congress in London in 1900 and subsequently was instrumental in four additional Pan African congresses that were held between 1919 and 1927 in several international cities, such as Paris, Lisbon, and New York. Du Bois also utilized his editorship at *The Crisis* to advocate for black economic self-sufficiency through the development of black enterprise and became a major voice in linking black peoples of the world and their experiences of oppression.[44]

Booker T. Washington, working in the Black Belt region, utilized his position at Tuskegee Institute to also promote Pan Africanism. His influence on African educational policy proved strong, as his efforts on behalf of "Tuskegee-in-Africa" linked the Black Belt region to the African continent. Washington also hosted the International Conference on the Negro at Tuskegee Institute, in 1912. The conference focused on ways that black education efforts in the Black Belt could be applied on the continent, and twenty-one countries and colonies were represented.[45] An announcement of the conference a year before the actual date stated that "the object of calling this Conference at Tuskegee Institute is to afford an opportunity for studying the methods employed in helping the Negro people of the United States, with a view of deciding to what extent Tuskegee and Hampton methods may be applied to conditions in these

---

[44] J. R. Hooker, "The Pan-African Conference 1900 Transition" 46 (1974): 20–24. Clarence G. Contee, "Du Bois, the NAACP, and the Pan-African Congress of 1919," The Journal of Negro History 57/1 (January 1972): 13–28. Du Bois's definition of Pan-Africanism states, "An effort to bring together leaders of various groups of Negroes in African and in America for consolidation and planning for the future." From W. E. B. Du Bois, "Pan-Africanism: A Mission in My Life," *United Asia* (April 1955): 23.

[45] Tuskegee-in-Africa was an effort to start a school in Liberia based on the Tuskegee model of self-help and industrial education. Edward H. Berman, "Tuskegee-in-Africa," *The Journal of Negro Education* 41/2 (Spring 1972): 99–112.

countries, as well as to condition in Africa."[46] The conference was developed to answer the call for inquiries on black educational efforts worldwide.

> For a number of years, we have received here at Tuskegee letters from various parts of the world, from missionaries in foreign fields, from governmental officials, especially in Europe, asking for some education employed at Tuskegee. It occurred to us, after receiving a number of these communications, that it would be perhaps a wise thing and a natural development for us to ask these persons representing missionary organizations, representing government that have to do with the darker races of the world, to come here and spend a few days in observing the methods that we are trying to employ at Tuskegee.[47]

This pan-African effort resulted in an international central committee organizing future efforts with representatives from Jamaica, the United States, England, Sierra Leone, Liberia, Barbados, and the Congo. Washington and Du Bois worked diligently on behalf of American blacks but also expanded their efforts to the African diaspora, which would continue through the 1960s modern civil rights movement.[48]

Other theories of Pan Africanism supported within the region were not totally separate from Washington and the Du Bois theories, but focused significantly on a black pride edict. Black Belt black nationalism in its purest form early on was revealed in Bishop Henry Turner of the Georgia Black Belt, who became the premier regional black nationalist of his time.[49]

---

[46] Louis R. Harlan and Raymond W. Smock, eds., "An Announcement of a Conference at Tuskegee Institute, Tuskegee AL, March 1911," Vol. 11 of Booker T. Washington Papers (Champaign: University of Illinois Press, 1981): 72.

[47] *Opening Address: The International Conference of the Negro*, http://www.btwsociety.org/library/speeches/07.php?PRINT=True, accessed 17 December 2012.

[48] "An Announcement of a Conference at Tuskegee Institute," The Booker T. Washington Papers Tuskegee, Alabama, March 1911. Maurice S. Evans, "Declarations of the First International Conference on the Negro," *Journal of the Royal African Society* 11/44 (1912): 426.

[49] Edwin S. Redkey, "Bishop Turner's African Dream," The Journal of American History 54/2 (September 1967): 271–90. Melbourne S. Cummings, "The Rhetoric of

However, Turner's nationalism was distinctive to the region and often misunderstood as shown in Redkey's discussion: "Bishop Turner, who built his nationalist appeal not on the culture of black people but on an Africanized American dream, thereby lost one of the basic appeals that has strengthened other nationalisms, the call for a people with a distinct culture to establish a state in which that culture could flourish." Instead of calling for a separate black state, Turner called for African Americans to demand equality within the United States while also connecting with the African continent and their roots.[50]

Turner used the black Church, the African Methodist Episcopal Church in particular, to promote racial pride and duty. He coupled Black Nationalism with the necessity of political participation as the only true way black people could survive and thrive as a race. Bishop stated, "I don't believe any race will ever be respected, or ought to be respected, who do not show themselves capable of founding and manning a government of their own creation." In addition, he was a strong proponent of uplifting the continent of Africa and African Americans simultaneously. He felt this could be achieved through reparations and was a great voice in the reparations movement: Turner assessed, "that the American government should appropriate money to assist blacks who volunteered to settle in Africa. For services rendered during slavery, the nation owed the ex-slaves some 40 billion dollars. Turner calculated, "one hundred dollars a year for two million of us for two hundred years."[51] His call for reparations also became an added discussion among black nationalists in the future.

Turner's belief that African Americans had a duty to aid Africans against European colonization resulted in this warning: "Wait till the whites go over and civilize Africa, and homestead all the land and take us along to black their boots and groom their horses. Wait till the French

---

Bishop Henry McNeal Turner," Journal of Black Studies 12/2 (June 1982): 457–67. E. Merton Coulter, "Henry M. Turner: Georgia Negro Preacher-Politician during the Reconstruction Era," The Georgia Historical Quarterly 48/4 (December 1964): 371–410.
[50] Edwin S. Redkey, *Black Exodus: Black Nationalist and Back-to-Africa Movements, 1890–1910* (New Haven CT: Yale University Press, 1969): 301.
[51] Ibid., 39.

or English find some great mines of gold, diamonds or some other precious metal or treasures, so we can raise a howl over it and charge the whites with endeavoring to take away our fathers' inheritance, and lift a wail for sympathy of the world."[52] Turner sought to forge a strong connection between African Americans and Africans that could be beneficial to both groups against segregation and colonization.[53] However, Turner was not above having colonial viewpoints about the work of American blacks in Africa, as he viewed them as a vital part of *civilizing* Africa. Turner's nationalism proved an important political continuum of developing black political ideologies. Yet he was not the only black leader to bring Black Nationalism to the Black Belt, as Marcus Garvey was also active within the region and set Black Nationalism on America's center stage.

## *Garveyism and the Black Belt*

Most have described Marcus Garvey's Universal Negro Improvement Association (UNIA) as an urban movement, but there is strong evidence that Garvey's organization was also prevalent within the Black Belt region. According to Rolinson,

> Not just in Georgia, but all over the South, ministers and their churches formed a crucial part of the UNIA infrastructure. Although they were not exclusively in charge of organizing and leading local UNIA divisions, at least thirty-two ministers, extent record fragments show, headed southern divisions, while eight served as local secretaries in 1926 through 1927. Many more provided access to their congregations, use of their facilities, and support to local lay organizers. The *Negro World* also provides evidence of abundant ministerial support for Garveyism in the Southland.[54]

Many worked diligently within the region to promote membership, such as Hon. S. V. Robertson, who boasted of organizing sixteen divisions of

---

[52] Ibid., 36.
[53] Ibid., 36.
[54] Mary Rolinson, *Grassroots Garveyism: The Universal Negro Improvement Association in the Rural South, 1920–1927* (Chapel Hill: University of North Carolina Press, 2007) 93.

the UNIA as commissioner of Louisiana and Mississippi during a convention meeting in 1924.[55]

During the period after World War I, lynchings increased significantly in the region, and Mary Turner's lynching in 1918 highlighted its horrors on a national level, becoming a battle cry for Garvey and others as it resulted in a call to participate in change and/or emigration. Mary Turner was an eight-month pregnant black woman who had protested the lynching of her husband, for which she was hung upside down and bisected. Her fetus, cut from her womb, was stomped to death by the mob, igniting the black community. When addressing a packed audience at Carnegie Hall in 1919, Garvey attacked her lynching: "In America, below the Mason and Dixon Line, what did they do to Mary Turner? Oh I will not repeat because it is common knowledge to the world."[56] His ability to fill Carnegie Hall revealed the support of his message and the growing support of a black nationalist agenda.

Garvey had mass appeal in the South. Rolinson found 423 UNIA divisions in the 11 former Confederate states. Unfortunately, Garvey's organization faltered as he was sentenced to five years in prison for mail fraud. Yet there were mass meetings held for Garvey's release from prison between 1923 and 1927 in Alabama, Arkansas, Florida, Georgia, Louisiana, Mississippi, South Carolina, Tennessee, Texas, and Virginia. During the decades of 1910 and 1920, most blacks lived in extreme conditions in southwest Georgia and the Arkansas Delta, and Garvey's message of hope was of interest to many downtrodden blacks. Although not long-lived, the Garvey movement continued the ideology of Black Nationalism within itself. UNIA members also were connected to other important political activities in the region such as the Southern Tenant Farmers Union, as the union's vice-president E. B. ("Britt") McKinney was a tenant farmer and preacher and a former Garveyite.[57]

---

[55] Robert Hill, "The Marcus Garvey and the Universal Negro Improvement Association Papers, June 1921–December 1922," vol. 5 (Berkley: University of California Press, 1987): 663. Rolinson, *Grassroots Garveyism*, 94.

[56] Rolinson, *Grassroots Garveyism*, 127.

[57] Hill, "Marcus Garvey Papers," 658. Rolinson, *Grassroots Garveyism*, 127.

## Migration as Remedy

The horrors of the Southern rural black experience continued to motivate blacks to leave the region, as many reasoned that circumstances would not change and opted for migration during the early twentieth century. Although Black Nationalists' ideologies were overshadowed by accommodationist and integrationist efforts by the mainstream press and academicians, they proved to be an important part of the political history and culture of the region. The region's overall traditionally conservative political culture would not and could not tolerate the perceived extreme ideologies espoused by black nationalists Turner and Garvey that supported black pride and black self- sufficiency, particularly in a region in which those in power were economically and politically dependent on African Americans remaining out of power.

So many African Americans left the Southern states, particularly the Black Belt, and moved to urban areas in both the South and the North. From 1900 to 1920, one-fourth of the African American population in the Black Belt of Alabama left. According to Gibson (1941), "industrial development particularly in Birmingham and to a less degree in the North and Middle West provided thousands of jobs for unskilled workmen, and many of the more industrious and ambitious negroes left the Black Belt and other parts of the South in response to this newly-opened opportunity for employment." However, many stayed behind in these rural places, and the lack of opportunity in the Black Belt resulted in a majority of remaining African Americans being locked in an intergenerational cycle of poverty.[58]

## History of Black Belt Political Culture

The continued control of the region by the Democratic Party proved beneficial to White Southerners as most within the party saw it as "the White Man's party in a section where the White Man is a minority of the population." Kennedy describes a political system during the 1930s in the region in which men of means ruled and used the Democratic Party

---

[58] Gibson, J. Sullivan, "The Alabama Black Belt: Its Geographic Status," *Economic Geography* 17/1 (January 1941): 15.

as their own tool to control the state and the country: "The Belt has always been politically powerful in the State.... [M]ost of its counties, some of them with a total qualified vote of less than 2,000, have one senator and two representatives in the State legislature, while in other sections of the state two or more counties are grouped to form a district with the same representation."[59] This political rule of the state by the Black Belt region in state legislatures resulted in rural communities and rural interests, more precisely, the interests of those in power in the Black Belt, successfully ruling the Democratic Party and the agenda of state politics and the actions of state lawmakers.

"The post-Reconstruction Democratic Party together was a commitment to maintaining white supremacy.... The success of the Democrats' efforts to convince whites that they alone could be trusted blacks might hold the balance of power in close elections—resulted in saddling the South of the first half of the twentieth century with a one-party system that helped retard the region's economic and social development."[60]

The Democratic Party's rule in the South lasted until 1948, when the national Democratic Party began to split because of growing support for civil rights legislation. This unique one-party arrangement had been significant, allowing the Black Belt areas of Southern states to control politics in the South for centuries, establishing and maintaining a unique political culture that was based on inequality, contrary to the espoused principles of American democracy. Discriminatory laws were established and utilized in the region for centuries to subjugate blacks politically and economically and were sanctioned not just by the Democratic Party, since the Republican Party also played a dubious role. The Democratic Party created and implemented discriminatory policies while the Republican party sanctioned the system by refusing to provide an alternative.

---

[59] Renwick Kennedy, "Black Belt Aristocrats: The Old South Lives on in Alabama's Black Belt," *Social Forces* 13/1 (October 1935): 80–85.
[60] George Fredrickson, *White Supremacy: A Comparative Study in American & South African History* (Oxford: Oxford University Press, 1981): 278.

These arrangements allowed for the dominance of white rural issues and the maintenance of the plantation economy that benefitted those in power. Because of their control of the Democratic Party within their states, the Black Belt elites controlled their states' congressional delegates from the late nineteenth century until the mid-twentieth century, which also allowed them the opportunity to wield power beyond the Black Belt and their state capitols. The traditions of the South and the power of Southern Democrats received national prominence as they dictated key national legislation. During the era of the New Deal, they shaped some of the most important national legislation in American history to fit the plantation economy of the Black Belt and continued Black Belt social norms such as segregation through "progressive" legislation.

Roosevelt's New Deal policies and programs were based on the acknowledgement that the Southern region and its traditions and culture would not be interrupted by New Deal programs. These programs would be administered according to local customs of racial discrimination. Therefore, "in the early Roosevelt years, Southern political power was enhanced by a tacit deal between Roosevelt and the Southern contingent: Support for the New Deal was exchanged for a relatively free hand in writing and rewriting legislation to fit the peculiarities of the South."[61] As during Reconstruction, it was soon evident that the national government under Roosevelt would not challenge the inequalities of the rural South. Allowing local customs of segregation and discrimination to be applied to national programs demonstrates the vulnerability of African American citizenry at the time and the lack of national enforcement of national laws, in relation to blacks. It also revealed the fundamental flaws of the federal system in supporting the rights of blacks.[62]

The national government continued to serve as accomplice to the mistreatment of African Americans well into the twentieth century through legislation such as the Tydings Amendment, in 1942, and the

---

[61] Frederickson, *White Supremacy*, 44.
[62] Alston Lee and Joseph Ferrie, *Southern Paternalism and the American Welfare State Economics, Politics, and Institutions in the South, 1865–1965* (Cambridge University Press, 1999): 39 and 44.

Selective Service Act of 1940, which provided deferments to agricultural workers so that blacks could stay in the fields of the Black Belt. Also important were the Pace amendments to the Farm Labor Act of 1943, which prevented the expenditure of federal funds for the transportation of agricultural workers out of a county without the permission of the county farm agent, thus limiting the opportunities of black labor in the South. These are just a few examples of amendments that allowed for the continued availability of rural African American labor for the Black Belt elites, and they demonstrate the significant power of this group to shape and move national legislation that supported their agenda. These examples highlight the continued subordination of blacks as economic pawns within the plantation economy and the lack of governmental support to assist them in issues of importance.[63]

The need for labor was a top legislative priority for those controlling the region, and through the national government, and with the assistance of state and local implementation, they were able to maintain control over the local economy and black workers. They opposed any interference by the national government in Southern farm labor, as King Agriculture required a large, cheap, and dependable labor force, and so they did not want or need any governmental programs that would compete for the small wages offered within the region. Powerful Southern congressional Democrats managed to insulate the Black Belt region from social development for many decades, and as a result, managed to pigeonhole rural blacks from any economic progress from New Deal policies, including participation in Social Security by domestics and agricultural workers. This was detrimental to the black economic future, as during the 1930s 65 percent of blacks worked as domestics and in agriculture.[64]

---

[63] Lee and Ferrie, *Southern Paternalism*, 10. John Brueggeman, "Racial Considerations and Social Policy in the 1930s: Economic Change and Political Opportunities," *Social Science History* 26/1 (Spring 2002): 139–77.
[64] Larry Dewitt, "The Decision to Exclude Agricultural and Domestic Workers from the 1935 Social Security Act." http://www.ssa.gov/policy/docs/ssb/v70n4/v70n4p49.html, accessed 17 December 2012.

## Court Cases Change Political History

Yet two important cases helped change the Southern political party landscape. *Smith v. Allwright* (1944) was the case in which the court acknowledged the Democratic Party as the dominant party in the South and the primacy of their primary. By the Democratic Party declaring itself "a voluntary association," it violated the civil rights of African Americans since it allowed only whites to participate. The second landmark case was *Gomillion v. Lightfoot* (1960), which focused on a 28-sided political gerrymander drawn by the white elite power structure in Macon County, Alabama, to keep African Americans from gaining control of local politics. The court in this case found that the electoral structure in Macon County was a denial of equal protection, revealing that racially discriminatory intent could be proven based solely on its effect, not just intent. These two decisions allowed for the beginning of African American political inclusion in electoral politics in the Black Belt region for the first time since Reconstruction, and they ushered in a national focus on civil liberties in the region and reinforced the need for the national government to promote change.[65]

## Civil Rights Becomes Key Focus of National Government

The protection of civil rights and liberties of blacks became a focus of the national government mid-twentieth century. The Supreme Court ruled favorably on African American civil rights in the *Brown v. Board of Education* (1954) decision, finding that the separate-but-equal system created in the South was unconstitutional, which proved to be the catalyst for dismantling the separate-and-unequal legal system of the South.[66]

How different the developments might have been if there had been a demand by the majority residents of the Southern region for their leaders to adhere to the amendments of the constitution (thirteenth, fourteenth, and fifteenth) that supported the citizenship of African Americans. How different it might have been if Southern leaders had acknowledged their

---

[65] *Smith v. Allwright*, 321 U.S. 649 (1944), *Gomillion v. Lightfoot*, 364 U.S. 339 (1960).
[66] Ibid. *Brown v. Board* (1954) 347 U.S. 483.

roles as representatives within a representative democracy and carried out the responsibility of representing the black population within their respective districts and states, and not just the whites. Yet there was very little white Southern support for civil rights legislation initially within the South, and the precarious socioeconomic and political situation of poor whites within the Black Belt allowed for consolidation of power based on the promotion of white supremacy, connecting all aspects of the white community and revealing the irrationality of its use in the Black Belt. Most poor whites were excluded from full participation: "Though some poor whites prospered as a result of the South's system of social control, many did not because some of the mechanisms for social control, such as poll taxes, were based on class rather than race. Through their promotion of a racist ideology, Southern politicians were able to maintain the support of poor Southern whites who were hurt by these mechanisms."[67]

Southern politicians, either themselves a part of the aristocracy or tools of the aristocracy, victimized poor whites under the system, because their denial of support for progressive policy efforts denied them to all who resided there, poor white included. This absence of support for progressive policies resulted in Southern politicians using a states' rights policy agenda at the expense of promoting economic and social developmental strategies that would move the entire region forward, regardless of race. There was little effort made to draw the connection between a lack of development in the region and racism, and the ability of many Southern politicians to rally the white community to support measures that inevitably negatively influenced them was a tragedy for all. Not only did a lack of development hurt African Americans, it also negatively influenced whites who were not members of the elite class. Yet because of the widespread support for white supremacy and the protection of the "Southern way of life," change was seen as negative and something to be blocked. Organizations such as the White Citizens Council and the Ku Klux Klan grew and were instrumental in the promotion of fear, as "the Klan attracted small businessmen, shop keepers, clerks, Protestant clergymen, farmers, and professional

---

[67] Lee and Ferrie, *Southern Paternalism*, 39.

people,"[68] which illustrates that all aspects of white society fought black political participation throughout the region.

Many whites within the region did not support social changes and developed reactionary activities to the civil rights changes sweeping the region. As a reaction to integration efforts, many Southern leaders took action, developing and supporting efforts such as the Southern Manifesto of 1956, which promoted Southern white supremacy and states' rights, signed by roughly 100 nationally elected officials from the South, aggressively opposing national governmental intervention in civil rights issues in the region. Remarkably, these senators and House members represented most African Americans in the South. Yet the perilous political opportunities for African Americans within the region through these leaders were well apparent in the numbers of Southern leaders who supported the manifesto. The apparent inequalities in the federal system, which allowed the Southern region with its significant African American population the opportunity to victimize its own citizens for centuries, should not be overlooked when discussing the uniqueness of the rural black experience within our representative democracy. However, there were a few Southern white leaders who did not sign the manifesto, proving that there were some white Southerners who were willing to accept the imminent changes coming or did not support oppression. Southerners Albert Gore, Sr., of Tennessee, Senate Majority Leader Lyndon Johnson of Texas, and Estes Kefauver of Tennessee did not sign the manifesto. However, some of these lawmakers cannot be considered true progressives, as they opposed other key civil rights legislation. For example, Senator Gore voted against the Civil Rights Act of 1964. The lack of white progressive voices in the South, and the Black Belt region in particular, circumvented many attempts to implement civil rights for

---

[68] Darlene Clark Hine, William C. Hine, and Stanley Harrold, *The African American Odyssey* (Upper River Saddle NJ: Prentice Hall Publisher, 2005) 404.

blacks and resulted in an "us" versus "them" approach to civil rights within the South against the activities of the national government.

# 4

# MODERN RACIALIZED POLITICS IN THE BLACK BELT

The Black Belt political culture historically facilitated the extreme racialization of politics within the region, with the ultimate goal of rendering blacks politically neutral. And efforts to design political mechanisms to defeat African American political power often were based on the size of the population and the immediate threat of the political success of the group. Historically, several legal arrangements were employed to ensure African Americans would not participate politically in the South, or if they did participate, they would have little political power. These efforts continued well into the twentieth century, and some would argue that some tactics are currently employed. According to Kousser (1999), tools such as gerrymandering, at-large elections, the white primary, annexation and de-annexation were all used to fight African American political power. These tools focused specifically on manipulating the system using the size of the African American population as a directive for tool selection.

> If majorities were too large to be overcome, bonds for officeholders could be set so high as to deter from running any but the extremely affluent or those with rich and brave friends, or the authorities might arbitrarily refuse to accept the bonds as valid, or election officials might consolidate polling places to such an extent as to make the trip to the polls or the line at the polls intolerably long, or they might just fail to open the polls altogether. In extremes, the legislatures could impeach or otherwise displace elected officials or do away with local elections altogether and vest the power to choose local officials in the legislature or governor or their appointees.[1]

---

[1] J. Morgan Kousser, *Colorblind Injustice: Minority Voting Rights and the Undoing of the Second Reconstruction* (Chapel Hill: University of North Carolina Press, 1999) 26.

Historically, these devices allowed for continued white domination and control in the Black Belt, resulting in roughly eighty years of mostly exclusive white power there.

## Fighting Back

As shown in this work, the Black Belt region has a history of African American resistance against oppression. Yet most of the popular and scholarly attention on the South has been focused on nonviolent strategy and the use of the judicial system during the modern civil rights movement. Groups such as the National Association for the Advancement of Colored People (NAACP) and the Montgomery Improvement Association (MIA) both played important roles in civil rights legal efforts and the desegregation of buses in Montgomery, Alabama. The Southern Christian Leadership Conference (SCLC), a group of civil rights organizations and ministers dedicated to working in local communities to fight injustice and discrimination, and the Student Nonviolent Coordinating Committee (SNCC), which was composed of young activists of the movement, and consisted of both high school and college students, were also active in the Black Belt.

The campaigns of Dr. Martin Luther King, Jr., the legal work of the NAACP, as well as the mobilization of the SCLC for the Montgomery bus boycott, and the SNCC and the Albany movement employed nonviolent approaches. Finally, the *Brown* case during the 1950s in Arkansas, all support this thesis of a strong nonviolent Black Belt strategy. The Birmingham and Selma, Alabama, and Nashville, Tennessee, campaigns, which resulted in the national civil rights and voting rights legislation of the mid-1960s, were also viewed as part of this larger nonviolent strategy. This strategy was deeply connected with the black church, "as the most resource-rich institution in the African-American community and the one most closely associated with civil society, the church had much to contribute. The resource mobilization literature notes that the black church could offer social communication networks, facilities, audience, leadership, and money to the movement."[2]

---

[2] Allison Calhoun-Brown, "Upon This Rock: The Black Church, Nonviolence, and the Civil Rights Movement," *PS: Political Science and Politics* 33/2 (June 2000): 170.

The resources of the black church provided the movement with its leaders and participants, as the members of the black church served as the driving forces behind the strategy of passive resistance. It was a moral directive of efforts within the movement and served as a just power in its peaceful demonstrations and sit-ins and song, in contrast to the violence and murder by its opponents.

Yet there were other groups and other strategies employed in the Black Belt that proved influential in the movement and built upon a history of self-defense laid there long ago by the enslaved. These strategies were developed to combat the violent Black Belt society and defend African Americans against terrorist attacks as they worked within the modern civil rights movement. Groups such as the Deacons for Defense and Justice, organized in Louisiana, Alabama, and Mississippi; the Student National Coordinating Committee (formerly the Student Nonviolent Coordinating Committee); and the Lowndes County Freedom Organization or the Black Panther Party, in Lowndes County, Alabama, were African American groups working within the Black Belt who followed a self-defense philosophy and/or took up arms during the modern civil rights movement, countering or supporting the nonviolent strategy so often publicized. These groups organized and operated on ideologies of proactive protectionism. They did not participate in preemptive violence but felt it was imperative that African Americans fight back against terrorism and focus on self-protection as they struggled for civil rights. Again, as in the Old South immediately after the Civil War, when African American groups were formed for self-protection, these groups developed to combat the political culture of the Black Belt.

Located primarily in Louisiana, the Deacons for Defense was an armed group dedicated to self-defense. Responsible for many security details during protests, they employed weapons and participated in armed confrontations with the Klan, often proving successful. Ernest Thomas, a member of the Deacons stated, "I figured if the power structure would do that for the Klan, we'd better do something for ourselves."[3]

In Bogalusa, Louisiana, in 1965, the Deacons were described as being "reportedly armed with pistols, rifles, shotguns and even hand grenades.... In addition to their weapons, the Deacons have walkie talkies for instant communication, a fleet of ever-ready cars and a membership rumored to include about a tenth of the Negro adult male population (some 9,000 of Bogalusa's 23,000 residents are Negro)." This effort in Bogalusa also protected the members of the group Congress of Racial Equality (CORE) who were working in the area. James Farmer, CORE's national director, stated, "I am glad the Deacons exist." However, the Deacons were not the only group in the Black Belt dedicated to self-defense.[4]

The Black Panther Party of Lowndes County, Alabama, was another organization located in a very violent Black Belt community. Lowndes County, known also as Bloody Lowndes for its history of violence against African Americans, was overwhelmingly black and openly hostile to change. Viola Liuzzo, a white civil rights activitst, was murdered by the Ku Klux Klan during a peaceful march from Selma to Montgomery. Working in conjunction with the SNCC on civil rights issues in Lowndes County, these groups (the SNCC and the Black Panther Party) were often targeted for violence. They found it necessary to physically protect themselves during their work in the movement and were vocal about their self-protective ideology. The SNCC also worked in rural Georgia and Mississippi, which were dangerous and violent areas for civil rights workers. From his work in the Black Belt with the Lowndes County Freedom Organization, Stokely Carmichael began to espouse a more radical self-protection ideology he named "Black Power." Hine et al. describe Black Power as "promoting positive self-identity, racial pride, and the development of independent political and economic power. However, he and others acknowledged the impact the

---

[3] Hamilton Bims, "Leave the Protecting to Us, Deacons for Defense" in *Reporting Civil Rights Part Two American Journalism, 1963–1973* (New York: The Library of America, 2003) 439.
[4] Ibid., 430.

Black Belt had on their definition of Black Power. SNCC organizers first encountered rural black traditions of self-reliance and determination in the Magnolia state. Mississippi is also where they first became interested in independent politics."[5] According to scholar Hasan Jefferies,

> SNCC's brand of Black Power emerged as a direct result of organizing successes in Lowndes County.... [P]lacing SNCC's Alabama fieldwork in its proper context, and linking it to the demands for black political empowerment, allows us to begin to assess the continued change in political ideology within black people of the Black Belt and how the origins of the Black Power movement began there. It was the reality of SNCC's organizing campaign in Alabama that laid the basis for rhetoric of Black Power.[6]

The organizing experiences of SNCC field officers in Lowndes County ultimately gave form to the modern version of Black Power. It also continues the long tradition of Black Power strategies in Lowndes County and the larger Black Belt region.

Other political theorists promoted a more radical Black Belt self-defense ideology, such as Robert Williams, a former NAACP leader in North Carolina who moved to Cuba at the invitation of Fidel Castro and broadcast a radio show called *Radio Free Dixie*. Williams espoused the need for African Americans to arm themselves and promoted the Black Belt Nation thesis often discussed by Communist Harry Haywood and others and promoted liberation through armed struggle. As during slavery, post-slavery, and Reconstruction, twentieth century efforts to acquire social equality included varying political ideologies and strategies. However, change in the region employed nonviolent strategies most often. Yet these self-protective strategies included a clear

---

[5] Hines, Hines, and Harrold, *The African American,* 609. Hasan Jefferies, "SNCC, Black Power, and Independent Political Party Organizing in Alabama, 1964–1966," *The Journal of African American History* 91/2 (2006): 188. Timothy Tyson, "Robert F. Williams, 'Black Power,' and the Roots of the African American Freedom Struggle," *The Journal of American History* 85/2 (1998): 546.

[6] Hasan Kwame Jeffries, "SNCC, Black Power, and Independent Political Party Organizing in Alabama, 1964–1966," The Journal of African American History 91/2 (Spring 2006): 188.

understanding of the Black Belt culture and the often-present violent nature within.

With the *Brown v. Board of Education* (1954) court ruling and the passage of civil rights legislation, the political fortunes of blacks began to change. In addition, there were changes in the political parties within the region that greatly shifted party allegiances in civil rights and race relations. Table 4.0 and 4.1 shows partisanship in the House and Senate with regard to modern civil rights legislation and begins to highlight changes in partisan support within the South. In addition, it shows the hard stance Southern Democrats had against civil rights legislation.

Table 4.0 Partisanship in the House of Representatives on Civil Rights Law Passage

| Year | Southern Democrats | Nonsouthern Democrats | Southern Republicans | Nonsouthern Republicans |
|---|---|---|---|---|
| 1957 | 0-99 | 118-8 | 1-3 | 167-16 |
| 1960 | 5-82 | 174-12 | 2-3 | 130-12 |
| 1964 | 8-83 | 145-8 | 0-11 | 136-24 |
| 1965 | 22-59 | 199-2 | 1-15 | 111-9 |
| 1970 | 27-49 | 145-7 | 3-21 | 97-55 |
| 1975 | 49-23 | 198-4 | 10-17 | 84-26 |
| 1981-1982 | 62-6 | 167-1 | 23-13 | 137-4 |

Source: J. Morgan Kousser, *Colorblind Injustice Minority Voting Rights and the Undoing of the Second Reconstruction* (Chapel Hill: University of North Carolina Press, 1999) 40.

Table 4.1 Partisanship in the Senate on Civil Rights Law Passage

| Year | Southern Democrats | Nonsouthern Democrats | Southern Republicans | Nonsouthern Republicans |
|---|---|---|---|---|
| 1957 | 5-17 | 26-1 | 0 | 43-0 |
| 1960 | 4-18 | 38-0 | 0 | 29-0 |
| 1964 | 1-20 | 45-1 | 0-1 | 27-5 |
| 1965 | 3-17 | 44-0 | 0-2 | 30-0 |

| 1970 | 3-9 | 28-2 | 1-1 | 32-0 |
|---|---|---|---|---|
| 1975 | 9-5 | 40-1 | 2-5 | 26-1 |
| 1981-1982 | 11-0 | 31-1 | 6-4 | 37-3 |

Source: J. Morgan Kousser, *Colorblind Injustice Minority Voting Rights and the Undoing of the Second Reconstruction* (Chapel Hill: University of North Carolina Press, 1999) 40.

These tables show the realignment of the political parties behind racial issues and civil rights in modern politics during the twentieth century. Mobilization and activism throughout the Black Belt resulted in changes in the political system and birthed the modern civil rights legislation. As a result, black voter registration increased significantly in the Southern states and within the Black Belt. Table 4.2 shows the estimated voter registration within the region. In a short period, the numbers appear to have doubled or tripled in some states, as the decade of the modern civil rights movement put forth massive political change and proved blacks had a political voice.

Table 4.2 Estimated Black Voter Registration in the Southern States

| State | 1956 | 1960 | 1964 | 1968 |
|---|---|---|---|---|
| AL | 53,366 | 66,009 | 111,000 | 273,000 |
| AR | 69,677 | 72,604 | 95,000 | 130,000 |
| FL | 148,703 | 183,197 | 300,000 | 292,000 |
| GA | 163,389 | 180,000 | 270,000 | 344,000 |
| LA | 161,410 | 159,003 | 164,700 | 305,000 |
| MS | 20,000 | 22,000 | 28,500 | 251,000 |
| NC | 135,000 | 210,450 | 258,000 | 305,000 |
| SC | 99,890 | 58,122 | 144,000 | 189,000 |
| TN | 90,000 | 185,000 | 218,000 | 228,000 |
| TX | 214,000 | 226,818 | NA | 540,000 |
| VA | 82,603 | 100,000 | 200,000 | 255,000 |
|  | 1,238,038 | 1,463,203 | 2,164,200 | 3,112,000 |

Source: David Garrow, *Protest at Selma: Martin Luther King, Jr., and the Voting Rights Act of 1965* (New Haven CT: Yale University Press, 1978) 11, 19, 189.

After the Voting Rights Act of 1965, the number of African American lawmakers increased significantly, but the economic status of their constituents did not improve significantly with black representation. Tables 4.3 and 4.4 show the increase in black elected representation in the Southern region decades after the movement.

Table 4.3 Black Elected Officials as a Percentage of Total Officials in Southern State Covered by the Voting Rights Act. July 1980: Specific Categories

| State | % Black Population | % House Members | % Senate Members | % Municipal Boards | % County Board |
|---|---|---|---|---|---|
| AL | 25.6 | 12.4 | 5.7 | 5.3 | 6.6 |
| GA | 26.8 | 11.7 | 3.6 | 5.2 | 3.4 |
| LA | 29.4 | 9.5 | 5.1 | 9.4 | 13.2 |
| MS | 35.2 | 12.3 | 3.3 | 10.4 | 6.6 |
| NC | 22.4 | 3.3 | 2.0 | 6.0 | 3.7 |
| SC | 30.4 | 11.3 | 0 | 6.7 | 11.7 |
| TX | 12.0 | 8.7 | 0 | 1.4 | 0.5 |
| VA | 18.9 | 4.0 | 2.5 | 5.2 | 6.8 |

Source: The U.S. Commission on Civil Rights. "Voting Rights Act: Unfulfilled Goals" (Washington DC: Government Printing Office, 1981) 32.

Each of the states within the Black Belt had African American representation on all levels, national, state and local, after modern civil rights legislation was passed.

Table 4.4 The Number of African American Elected Officials in 1980

| State | No. of Black Elected Officials |
|---|---|
| MS | 387 |
| LA | 363 |
| GA | 249 |

| | |
|---|---|
| NC | 247 |
| SC | 238 |
| AL | 238 |
| TX | 196 |
| VA | 124 |
| Total | 2042 |

Source: The U.S. Commission on Civil Rights. "Voting Rights Act: Unfulfilled Goals" (Washington DC: Government Printing Office, 1981) 27.

*Local Government Control*

Historically, the political culture of the South gave enormous power to local political structures. Traditionally, very little local power rested in the hands of rural blacks. As a result, after the civil rights movement, the fight to keep the hierarchical, discriminatory power structure in place was continued by the community's elite, while African Americans fought for inclusion in local decision-making. This political infighting resulted in a lack of cohesive effort within these communities to bridge racial divides that were centuries in the making and crippled the communities socially and economically.

One example of this internal community struggle occurred decades after the civil rights movement. The importance of valuable elective power on the local level in the Black Belt has no clearer example than in the Black Belt of Alabama. Without true local accountability and local power, one rural black community fell victim to its own local inept and ineffective leadership. In 1978, Chemical Waste Management, a subsidiary of Waste Management, Inc., purchased a landfill permit for a 300-acre tract of land near Emelle in the center of Sumter County, Alabama. Sumter County is one of the country's most impoverished counties, and one-third of the residents live below the poverty level. More than 65 percent of the residents are black and more than 90 percent of the residents near the landfill are black. Local Emelle residents thought they were getting a brick plant when they learned of a "new factory" moving into their town.[7]

> In 1978, Chemical Waste Management (ChemWaste) opened the nation's largest hazardous-waste treatment, storage and disposal facility in Sumter County.... The hazardous waste operation was brought to the Emelle community without the input of local residents.... No blacks held public office or sat on governing bodies, including the state legislature, county commission, or industrial development board.... It was not until 1984 that blacks took the majority of seats.... Few residents knew that they were about to become the host community for the nation's largest hazardous-waste dump. Rumors circulated throughout the community about a "new industry coming to town."... *The Sumter County Record*...headline read "Unique New Industry Coming: New Use for Selma Chalk to Create Jobs."[8]

Since acquiring the landfill, the company has dumped millions of tons of hazardous waste on the rich Black Belt soil, creating the largest hazardous waste landfill in the United States, and possibly the world. The landfill is often tagged the "Cadillac of Dumps." Nearly 40 percent of the toxic waste disposed of nationwide between 1984 and 1987 under the federal Superfund removal program ended up in the landfill, which sits directly over the Eutaw Aquifer, which supplies water to a large part of Alabama.[9] This is just one example of unrepresentative local government victimizing their own community.

Presently, in many Black Belt communities, local officials characterize hazardous waste facilities as wonderful economic development opportunities. Yet besides the fact that they are extremely hazardous in most cases to the environment of the community and some have been linked to serious health crises, they often bring very few jobs. But because of the racial divisions within many Black Belt communities,

---

[7] Robert D. Bullard, "Environmental Racism in the Alabama Blackbelt" http://www.ejrc.cau.edu/envracismalablackbelt.htm, accessed 17 December 2012.

[8] Robert Bullard, *Dumping in Dixie: Race, Class and Environmental Quality*, 3rd ed. (Boulder CO: Westview Press, 2000) 60.

[9] "Emelle, Alabama: Home of the Nation's Largest Hazardous Waste Landfill." http://www.umich.edu/~snre492/Jones/emelle.htm, accessed 17 December 2012.

these communities in flux are in no condition to fight the companies as divided entities. Wendell Paris, an African American civil rights activist, states, "Our community needs jobs, but we also don't want to be poisoned. Jobs are scarce in this area. This trusting community was deceived. Of the 400–500 workers at the plant, roughly fifty Emelle and Geiger [another black community in the area] residents work at the plant. The large number of cars with out-of-state license plates at the plant tells the story of what this community is getting. We were promised jobs, but what we got was a giant hazardous-waste headache."[10]

Local decision makers did not utilize input from those who would be affected most by the facility, and this is just one example of the difficulty in the integration of political bodies and economic development efforts within the Black Belt long after the modern civil rights movement. Black Belt elites continued to control local politics in the Alabama Black Belt. This example reveals the importance of participatory democracy in elective politics. The necessity of having a mechanism in local decision-making through which the people can hold their leadership accountable is imperative in places like this, where transparency of decision-making is the only way forward.

## *Important Changes in Local Government Structure*

Alarmingly, recent developments within the Black Belt could result in a return to pre-civil rights power distribution in the region and threaten political legitimacy and transparency. Two important developments within the region weigh heavily upon the region's ability to progress and to remain democratic in nature. These include a reliance on nonelected, appointive decision makers on key community boards or authorities, particularly development authorities, and the changing transition from the mayor-council form of government to the council-manager form of government during the first terms of newly elected African American mayors. These factors threaten the legitimacy of electoral politics, social development, and decision-making processes in the region.

---

[10] Bullard, *Dumping in Dixie*, 62.

## Appointive Positions, Democracy, and a Lack of Inclusion

The increasing reliance on nonelected appointive positions for local-level leadership has the potential to hinder the progress of the region, particularly in issues of development and the allocation of resources, because it has resulted in an inability for local decision makers to be accountable to the people and to be transparent. Appointive positions tend to be held by traditional leaders within the community, deeply rooted in the establishment and the status quo. These appointees are rarely pulled from all aspects of the community and tend not to be diverse in race or socioeconomic status. It is important to note that these appointive positions do not allow for community inclusion in decision-making, and the people have very little say in who is appointed or the logistics of the work. These "public" entities often operate as very private entities with little accountability to the community. It is important to stress that these entities work autonomous to elected officials in many endeavors and, in some cases, work counter to the goals of elected officials. Although elected officials may have budgetary power over these groups, it is very difficult for elected officials to truly shape the agenda of the organization. Important decisions about community development and where money should be spent is meant to be rooted in democratic practices, yet these entities do not allow this. Many are left out of decision-making about how to develop their communities and how to access funds that may be available. Because of the history of the region, it is important that political structures be transparent and, more importantly, inclusive in nature. Allowing for appointive positions from already well-established groups clearly does not create an inclusive political or economic system for the region.

## Mayor-Council versus Council-Manager: Do I Have a Voice?

According to the International City/County Management Association (ICMA), the council-manager form of government is becoming increasingly attractive to many local governments. According to a 2010 report, "The council-manager form of government is the most prevalent form in five of the nine ranges. Fifty-four percent (54%) of municipalities with a population between 5,000 and 250,000 residents are governed under the council-manager structure (2,745 out of 5,124)."[11]

Yet the change from mayor-council government to council-manager government during the tenure of African American mayors proves to be another perplexing change in the region that threatens the legitimacy of the democratic processes there for many African American residents. Please note that the perplexity does not reveal itself simply by the structural change but rather, more importantly, the timing of the change. First, it is necessary to give a brief discussion of the two political structures.

Although local power distribution is ultimately the result of the city charter, the mayor-council form of government allows for the local government to be structured with the mayor of the community having executive power and the council having legislative power, hypothetically with the administrative power to be shared by the two. In this local governmental structure, the mayor has significant power in several areas, particularly budgeting and appointive powers to key positions within the city. This allows constituents the ability to influence government through their elected officials, which is basic to our representative democracy, and the mayor can be held accountable to the people through the electoral process. Contrastingly, the council-manager form of government is different in that the mayor is primarily not as powerful, and, depending on the configuration of the council, may be used as a tie breaker if the council is deadlocked. The council is responsible for the legislative functions and hires a manager to handle the administration of the city. The council can hire and fire the manager as needed. However, there is an opportunity for factions of the council to run the city through the manager with very little input from the community at-large, which is undemocratic. In addition, due to the lack of electoral accountability of the manager, this unelected person holds tremendous power within city

---

[11] Form of Government Statistics: "Council Manager versus Mayor Council in Specific Population Range." ICMA Municipal Yearbook 2010. http://icma.org/en/icma/knowledge_network/documents/kn/Document/9364/Form_of_Government_Statistics_CouncilManager_versus_MayorCouncil_in_Specific_Population_Ranges, accessed 17 December 2012.

government, particularly in small communities such as those found in the Black Belt. Even more troubling, the trend to change from the mayor-council to council-manager form of government during the term of a newly elected, first-time African American mayor tends to trouble many from within and outside of the region as a strategy of discouragement of black political participation within the community. Although many of these efforts are discussed within the context of progressing politics within the community, the timing of the effort is often a point of conflict.

According to many scholars, the rise of the transformation of governmental structures can be linked to the politics of race. According to Amy Bridges, the Progressive Movement was connected to the unfortunate legacy of racism, eugenics, and nativism through reform tools such as voter registration, literary tests, extended residency requirements, and poll taxes. Similarly, changing structures of government to stymie the political progress of blacks within the region would also fit these activities.[12] Others, such as Banfield and Wilson, found problems with the "businesslike model" of government because they found that this meant "getting rid of politics," thus weakening the power of low-status minorities. "In its early years the [council-manager] plan appealed to a good many people as a convenient means of putting the Catholics, the Irish, the Italians, the labor unions, and all other 'underdogs' in their places."[13]

Morone found that the reformers who promoted these changes in government "envisioned an 'idealized civilization' that was suspicious of, if not outright hostile towards, immigrants, populist farmers, blacks, and poor whites."[14]

Located in the Black Belt of Georgia, the city of Milledgeville gives us an example. Discussions about changing the structure of government from mayor-council to council-manager occurred for years

---

[12] Amy Bridges, *Morning Glories: Municipal Reform in the Southwest* (Princeton NJ: Princeton University Press, 1997) 8.

[13] Edward C. Banfield and James Q. Wilson, *City Politics* (Cambridge, MA: Harvard University Press, 1966) 171.

[14] James Morone, *The Democratic Wish: Popular Participation and the Limits of American Government* (New Haven CT: Yale University Press, 1998) 114.

but were not put into action until the first African American was elected mayor of the antebellum capital. This effort in Milledgeville resulted in years of legal filings as the first African American mayor, Floyd Griffin, found himself being stripped of power as the city decided to transition from a mayor-council system to a council-manager system during his first tenure. The fight to retain power resulted in his term as mayor being consumed by a fight to maintain the current governmental system. The mayor tried to stop the city from hiring a city manager.[15] City government was paralyzed and his tenure was marred by racial conflict as the fight to change the charter of the city was divided along racial lines, even though some African American council members were in support of the structural change. A physical altercation ensued between the mayor and a councilman and also hardened the divisions within the community.[16] This episode proved not to be an unusual case and has been occurring on a regular basis throughout the Black Belt region. It is questionable whether a community truly has representative government if unelected managers or appointive individuals make decisions rather than the elected mayor. So to rely strictly on electoral success as a test of real power in the present Black Belt region is unwise. To simply elect an African American official within an appointive power structure is no real power at all. Be advised however, that this author does not negate the positives of the council-manager form of government. To provide sound accountability in hiring and administrative practices in the Black Belt is a positive occurrence. There needs to be a push for merit-based hiring, accountability, and transparency of actions, as well as sound accounting practices and the elimination of patronage. Yet to only see the benefit of this system once newly elected African American mayors are in place is suspect, particularly in a region with such a torrid racial history in politics.

---

[15] Anonymous, "Milledgeville Mayor Suffers Another Loss In Campaign against Council" http://chronicle.augusta.com/stories/2003/09/26/met_391435.shtml, accessed 17 December 2012.
[16] Pam Beer, "Vance Files Police Report" http://thebaldwinbulletin.com/2004/April/pages/vance_0429.htm, accessed 17 December 2012. "Milledgeville Mayor Suffers Another Loss In Campaign against Council" http://chronicle.augusta.com/stories/2003/09/26/met_391435.shtml, accessed 17 December 2012.

## Voting Participation in the Black Belt: Fair and Equal?

"This has been a systemic problem of corruption. It is a culture problem, an elite believing they have the right to decide who holds office. Democracy itself is the victim of what is occurring here." —Attorney General Troy King in *The Tuscaloosa* (AL) *News*, 17 August 2007

Voter and election fraud are legendary factors in Black Belt politics. Historically, elections in the Black Belt have been stained by stolen election boxes, voter intimidation, and even murder. The present Black Belt political environment still includes allegations of voter fraud and intimidation. Many have linked recent voter fraud efforts by the Justice Department and state changes in local governmental structure as ways to diminish African American political power within the Black Belt. Yet many within the region will acknowledge that the new African American leaders are not the first in the Black Belt to use unscrupulous tactics to maintain power in the region and therefore the new sense of creating fraud-free politics in the Black Belt is timed perfectly with the rise of black political power. "When the majority finally took control in the Black Belt, a lot of the black politicians said to hell with you. But who do we have to blame for that? Us, the white political establishment, that's who. Some white leaders had a very big part in creating bad political leadership in this part of the South," stated Dr. Wayne Flynt, formally of Auburn University and a scholar of Southern culture.[17]

It is imperative that fraud, regardless of color, be eradicated from Black Belt politics if the region is to move forward and develop. Race politics will not develop the region in the twenty-first century, nor will it right the wrongs of past or present injustices. African American and white leaders must work to obtain fraud-free, race-neutral politics together, as these are not racially based values. However, there is great concern by many rural African Americans, who are the subject of this text, that there is a strategic assault on the power of the African American leadership within their community in both structural changes

---

[17] John Fleming, "Gone Time, Lives Anew in Alabama," *APF Reporter* 22/2 (2002). www.aliciapatterson.org/APF2202?Fleming/Fleming.html, accessed 17 December 2012.

and the unequal electoral fraud prosecution. In some mid-1980s efforts within the Black Belt of Alabama, prominent figures such as Albert Turner (a former chief aide to Dr. Martin Luther King, Jr.), his wife Evelyn, and coworker Spencer Hogue, Jr., all from Perry County, were targeted. Charged with changing the absentee ballots of a number of black voters in the Democratic primary election in 1984, they faced a twenty-nine-count indictment, a maximum of 115 years in prison, and $40,000 in fines. They were all acquitted of these charges, but the effect on the black community was immeasurable. Just two decades after the Voting Rights Act of 1965 provided them with the right to vote, many blacks felt they were again political targets of the establishment. Other black grassroots leaders were also targeted, including sheriff John Hulett of Lowndes County; school board chairman Wendell Paris and county commission employee Adeline Webster of Sumter County; Eutaw city council member Spiver W. Gordon and retired school teacher Rosie Carpenter in Greene County; and Rev. Thomas Threadgill and county commissioner Bobby Joe Johnson of Wilcox County.[18] Many of these leaders were known civil rights leaders and were vocal against the modern Black Belt power structure. These efforts went a long way to create the suspicion that the black leaders in the state were the only groups targeted of wrongdoing, which tainted these efforts for some.

These types of efforts were also active in the twenty-first century during the 2008 election, as, according to the Alabama media,

> Federal and state authorities are looking into accusations of voting fraud in three largely black counties of Alabama, including Perry and Lowndes counties, which played a historic role in the struggle for black voting rights in the 1960s.... The accusations have roiled this old plantation country of rich soil, impoverished people and unremitting distrust between black majorities and white minorities, where several trials and indictments in vote fraud cases have already occurred over the years—in 1985, 1997 and 2007—some of which resulted in convictions of county and city officials.[19]

---

[18] Allen Tullos, "Crackdown in the Black Belt," *Southern Changes* 7/1 (1985): 1–5.
[19] "Officials Investigate 3 Alabama Counties in Voter Fraud Accusations" http://www.nytimes.com/2008/07/10/us/10fraud.html, accessed 17 December 2012.

These activities continue a pattern of investigating these counties specifically. The pursuit of voter fraud-free elections must also be race neutral, and those who participate in these efforts should be cognizant of the racial history of the region. The 1970s and 1980s, many believe, was a period of regression in political power for African Americans in the Black Belt and a period in modern politics of a perceived increased political intimidation by others.

*Absentee Ballots*

The heart of many of these charges is the absentee ballot. Black Belt absentee ballots have often been factors associated with conflict because many voters in Black Belt counties are elderly and need assistance to the polls, or must work outside of the county and therefore must make alternative arrangements for voting. There has been little effort to hinder the use of absentee ballots historically, but recently there have been efforts to limit their use. Allegations of voter intimidation and prosecutions for voter fraud have become prevalent and strategically used, according to many residents in the Alabama Black Belt.

> There are ongoing efforts to pass laws that make voting more difficult, challenges to redistricting maps that have provided fairer representation, constant "investigations" of Black elected officials, and media reports that picture these officials as dishonest and incapable of managing government. Senator Hank Sanders notes that the many-faceted assault is ominously like the attacks that drove Blacks from office during the terror that followed Reconstruction in the last century.[20]

The actions in West Alabama—prosecutions of leaders and citizens, negative media attention—appear to have been successful, according to Hank Sanders, who wrote a legal briefing paper to Attorney General Reno and Assistant Attorney General Eric Holder, Jr., during the 1990s:

> Leaders pointed out that the Federal Bureau of Investigation (FBI) questioning of voters has produced a dramatic reduction in voter turnout. In the June 2, 1998, first primary election, overall voter turnout declined

---

[20] Anne Braden, "Voting Rights on Trial Again in Alabama," *Southern Changes* 20/2 (1998). http://beck.library.emory.edu/southernchanges/article.php?id=sc202_007&keyword=anne%20braden, accessed 17 December 2012.

to 3,928 from 4,691 in the comparable election in 1994, despite the fact that the number of registered voters increased during the four year period. Most striking was the decline in absentee ballots filed, from 1,118 in the 1994 first primary election, to 147 absentee ballots cast on June 2.[21]

As late as 2008, ongoing voter fraud investigations in the Alabama Black Belt continued. Efforts must be made to ensure that not only are elections carried out free of fraud, but also that in a region with such a discriminatory history, rural African Americans do not become victims of selective prosecution in voter fraud cases. This would be a continuation of the Old South tactics being employed in the New South.[22]

Table 4.5 Black Belt 2000 Voting and Registration Information

|  | Voting percent | Registration percent |
|---|---|---|
| United States |  |  |
| Black | 39.6 | 60.2 |
| White | 43.3 | 63.9 |
| Alabama |  |  |
| Black | 51.6 | 74.1 |
| White | 51.6 | 74.3 |
| Arkansas |  |  |
| Black | 45.0 | 51.8 |
| White | 31.1 | 65.9 |
| Florida |  |  |
| Black | 33.4 | 50.4 |
| White | 40.6 | 61.1 |
| Georgia |  |  |
| Black | 64.1 | 40.2 |
| White | 62.0 | 36.8 |

---

[21] Ibid.
[22] "Hale County Officials Worry Voter Fraud Is Back," Tuscaloosanews.com http://www.tuscaloosanews.com/article/20100528/news/100529584, accessed 17 December 2012

Abandonment in Dixie

| | | |
|---|---|---|
| Louisiana | | |
| Black | 46.0 | 69.5 |
| White | 35.7 | 75.2 |
| Mississippi | | |
| Black | 40.4 | 71.3 |
| White | 40.7 | 75.2 |
| North Carolina | | |
| Black | 38.2 | 57.4 |
| White | 40.5 | 65.6 |
| South Carolina | | |
| Black | 42.8 | 68.0 |
| White | 48.8 | 67.9 |
| Texas | | |
| Black | 35.5 | 62.1 |
| White | 33.5 | 59.7 |
| Virginia | | |
| Black | 23.4 | 53.6 |
| White | 32.4 | 63.5 |

Source: *Black Elected Officials: A Statistical Summary, 2001*. Joint Center for Political and Economic Studies, May 2002. Wwww.Jointcenter.org.

Table 4.5 shows voting and registration and political participation in the region in 2000. However, voting is not the only way to politically participate. In addition to voting, holding elective office is also an important form of political participation, and the number of black elected officials rose from 1,469 in 1970 to 9,101 by 2001, according to the Joint Center for Political and Economic Studies. Presently, African Americans are elected on all levels of government, as shown in Table 4.6, which shows the growing number of African American elected officials, ranging from 243 in the state of Florida to 892 in the state of Mississippi.

Underdevelopment in the Bible Belt

Table 4.6 2002 Black Elected Officials in the South

|  | Total | Congress | State Senator | State Rep. | County Officials | Mayors | Statewide Officeholder |
|---|---|---|---|---|---|---|---|
| United States | 9,101 | 39 | 155 | 442 | 820 | 454 | 41 |
| Alabama | 756 | 1 | 8 | 27 | 80 | 46 | 0 |
| Arkansas | 502 | 0 | 3 | 12 | 0 | 32 | 0 |
| Florida | 243 | 3 | 5 | 17 | 24 | 14 | 2 |
| Georgia | 611 | 3 | 11 | 36 | 95 | 30 | 6 |
| Louisiana | 705 | 1 | 9 | 22 | 131 | 33 | 1 |
| Mississippi | 892 | 1 | 10 | 35 | 105 | 54 | 0 |
| North Carolina | 491 | 2 | 7 | 18 | 57 | 30 | 6 |
| South Carolina | 534 | 1 | 7 | 24 | 74 | 28 | 0 |
| Texas | 460 | 2 | 2 | 14 | 17 | 34 | 2 |
| Virginia | 246 | 1 | 5 | 10 | 48 | 5 | 0 |

Source: *Black Elected Officials: A Statistical Summary, 2001* May 2002, Joint Center for Political and Economic Studies. Www.jointcenter.org.

Each of the tables above shows that even with perceived negative activities within the region, such as voter and electoral official intimidation and absentee ballot problems, there have been significant changes in the Black Belt political arena, and African Americans have made tremendous electoral progress. These numbers prove the success of democratic processes instituted in the region and the electoral success of the movement. Yet it is important to note that, just as in the period after Reconstruction, elective power does not automatically translate into economic and social power, which are key components to full citizenship within American society.

*African American Congressional Representation*

In addition to navigating the challenges of local and state politics, African Americans are also participating in a new era of national politics. Since the redistricting of the 1990s, the Southern region has sent record numbers of African Americans to Congress, and the Black Belt is no exception. Today, there is African American congressional representation in Alabama, Texas, Mississippi, Louisiana, Georgia, South Carolina, North Carolina, Virginia, Florida, and Maryland. Yet because of the way districts are drawn, these representatives typically represent a minority population and minority issues in a majoritarian system. In fact, the very reason for these record numbers of African Americans in Congress has created a hostile environment in which to do congressional work. Every ten years, based on the new census data, congressional districts are redrawn to address population shifts. This allows for the potential to reshape Congress and the agenda. During the 1990 redistricting efforts, decisions were made to increase the number of minorities within Congress, and as a result, majority-minority districts were drawn throughout the country, which allowed for increased African American representation. Yet simultaneously, because of the concentration of African Americans in a few districts in each state, extremely conservative districts were also drawn as a result. Thus, the political environment created very few opportunities for moderate districts or the election of moderate lawmakers. Therefore, Congress has been populated with African Americans and conservatives who typically represent different ends of the political spectrum, a truly difficult environment in which to address the differing concerns of their district constituents. Couple this with a racially based two-party system, and you have a very difficult work environment within which to address key Black Belt concerns.

*Democrats and Republicans: Changing Directions*

Beginning in 1948, the Democratic Party in the South began to splinter as a result of the growing support among progressive and liberal Democrats for civil rights legislation versus the Dixiecrats, a group of conservative Southern Democrats who opposed civil rights legislation. This split began as a third-party run for the White House by Dixiecrat Strom Thurmond of South Carolina and eventually resulted in conservative Southern Democrats joining the Republican Party. This effort was strongly aided by Richard Nixon's Southern Strategy, which purposely injected race into Southern elections to play on the fears and resentments of Southern whites against the national government and the

Democratic Party's support of civil rights. Only recently has the Republican Party, represented by Ken Melham, former chair of the Republican National Committee, apologized for the racist strategy.[23] Additionally, this strategy also influenced state and local governments as the Republican Party stood opposite the Democratic Party on social progress, increasing their power in the South.

By the mid-1990s, Republicans controlled the legislative processes at the national level, and because the African Americans in Congress from the South were members of the minority party, most were unsuccessful at implementing their policy agendas. The Republican Congress during the 1990s and early 2000s promoted a very conservative policy agenda, and consequently many of these policy concerns were not promoted by black representatives or their constituents. Therefore, although there were record numbers of African American in Congress, the political environment was not conducive to much legislative policy success on behalf of rural blacks. Table 4.7 shows present African American legislators in Congress during the 111th Congress.

In 2010, two black Republicans were elected from the South: Allen West of Florida and Tim Scott of South Carolina, both members of the Tea Party. The Tea Party is a group of extremely conservative people dedicated to limiting the size and scope of government. Unusual as these victories were, they were small since thirty-two blacks ran in Republican primaries in the election. According to prominent black talk show host Tavis Smiley, "If two is the highest number of black Republicans to win since Reconstruction, it's hard to call that a breakthrough."[24]

---

[23] Mike Allen, "RNC Chief to Say It Was 'Wrong' to Exploit Racial Conflict for Votes," *The Washington Post*, 14 July 2005, www.washingtonpost.com/wp-dyn/content/article/2005/07/13/AR2005071302342.html, accessed 17 December 2012.

[24] Jennifer Steinhauer, "Black and Republican and Back in Congress," *The New York Times*, 5 November 2010, www.newyorktimes.com/2010/11/06/us/politics/06house.html, accessed 17 December 2012.

Table 4-7 111th Congress African American Congressional Leadership

| State | House | Senate |
|---|---|---|
| Alabama | Artur Davis (D) | |
| California | Barbara Lee (D)Maxine Waters (D)Diane E. Watson (D)Laura Richardson (D) | |
| District of Columbia | Eleanor Holmes Norton (D) | |
| Florida | Corrine Brown (D)Alcee L. Hastings (D)Kendrick Meek (D) | |
| Georgia | Sanford D. Bishop, Jr. (D)John Lewis (D)Cynthia McKinney (D)David Scott (D) Henry "Hank" Johnson, Jr. (D) | |
| Illinois | Danny K. Davis (D)Jesse L. Jackson, Jr. (D)Bobby L. Rush (D) | Roland Burris (D) |
| Maryland | Elijah E. Cummings (D) Donna F. Edwards (D) | |
| Michigan | Carolyn Cheeks Kilpatrick (D)John Conyers, Jr. (D) | |
| Indiana | André Carson (D) | |
| Virginia | Robert C. Scott (D) | |
| Minnesota | Keith Ellison (D) | |
| Mississippi | Bennie Thompson (D) | |
| Missouri | William Lacy Clay, Jr. (D)Emanuel Cleaver II (D) | |
| New Jersey | Donald M. Payne (D) | |
| New York | Gregory W. Meeks (D)Yvette D. Clarke (D)Charles B. Rangel (D)Edolphus Towns (D) | |
| North Carolina | G. K. Butterfield (D) Melvin Watt (D) | |
| Ohio | Marcia L. Fudge (D) | |
| Pennsylvania | Chaka Fattah (D) | |
| South Carolina | James E. Clyburn (D) | |

| Texas | Al Green (D)Sheila Jackson Lee (D)Eddie Bernice Johnson (D) | |
| Virgin Islands | Donna M. Christensen (D)1 | |
| Wisconsin | Gwen Moore (D) | |

Source: www.house.gov and www.senate.gov, accessed 20 November 2010.

There have been few policy issues that Democratic African American officials have been able to partner with Republicans, and for the most part they have been in conflicting camps, resulting in few policies for the African American Black Belt residents. The political culture of the region, with its strict class structure and social hierarchy, has made it difficult for many incumbents to work across the aisles. One significant point of contention of political ideology between the two groups is the size and activity level of government or the appropriate role and responsibility of government in the lives of people. These issues are often broken down along class lines and not just racial ones. Blacks, though, are typically strong proponents of an activist government. An August 2011 Gallup Poll found 59 percent of blacks and 19 percent of whites believe government should play a major role in improving the socioeconomic circumstance of blacks.[25]

*African American Classism within the Black Belt Region*

Stringent classism within the region occurs between both races (black and white) and has historically controlled segments of Black Belt society. Even when the African American community is represented in arenas of power in the region today, representatives tend to come from the middle and upper classes. Although this is not unique to the Black Belt, because of the distinctiveness and history of this region, there must be room for impoverished people of both races to participate in remedy discussions in order to address poverty issues of the region. Yet most African American representatives in decision-making roles tend to be of a different class. In some cases, these African Americans have very little

---

[25] Frank Newport, "Blacks, Whites Differ on Government's Role in Civil Rights," *USA Today*/Gallup, 19 August 2011, 4–7 August 2011, www.gallup.com/poll/149087/blacks-whites-differ-government-role-civil-rights.aspx.

relationship with African Americans in the lower economic strata of the community, which creates alienation of poor blacks who do not view themselves as having a voice in decision-making.

Historically, ministers, educators, and business and landowners composed the leadership of the African American community in the Black Belt. This group in the rural Black Belt tended to form a distinct black leadership class, which proved beneficial to the community, because regardless of class, all African Americans were influenced by segregation and terrorism. Yet issues today are increasingly different, and many concerns of middle class blacks are not the same concerns of those in the lower class, and unlike in the past, group solidarity has been splintered based on class. African American middle and upper class leadership within the region often focuses on a preoccupation with upward mobility for their group at the expense of a collective consciousness and group identity that would result in real assistance to the black rural lower and working class in issues that affect their lives. Much of the social leadership responsibilities previously provided by black leadership within the community is now often performed by weak governmental institutions such as educational and social welfare agencies, resulting in a vacuum of real organic African American leadership. Some have argued that this vacuum has allowed present black leadership greater opportunity to make decisions based on their own economic interests at the expense of the black community as a whole. So ineffective policy, such as inadequate rural education, is not addressed because black middle and upper class leadership is vested in the present educational system, as teachers, principals, consultants, and representatives of the school board, and less-wealthy African Americans have little power or resources to combat it.

As a result, fewer lower-income African Americans participate politically. Low participation rates and trust by this group is linked to both history and symptoms of present inequity. As local governments rely on appointive rather than elective positions of power, lower-income blacks are locked out of the system not just by white elites, but also now by black elites. One may ask why rural black lower-income citizens do not participate in those positions that are elective. I argue that maybe no participation is just as rational as participation for this group. As history has shown, they have received few tangible benefits from participating in politics since their enormous sacrifices during the passage of the Civil Rights Act and the Voting Rights Act in the 1960s. Lower-income rural Black Belt residents were some of the first to participate in civil rights activities, with some middle-income African American community leaders playing catch up after movement activities had already begun within their communities. Without lower-income blacks and their efforts, the movement would have surely failed in many communities if it needed to rely on middle-income blacks alone. These issues must also be addressed when determining strategies of progress in the region. African Americans in the region are not a monolithic group. Yet the numbers reveal a significant population of lower-income blacks who are not represented in political decision-making roles today. Success within the region will include efforts to link political participation with economic benefit, and the elites of both races highlight a definite link between political participation and economic success, but rural lower-income blacks do not. Efforts must be made to use politics to achieve economic success on all levels, not just for those at the top of the economic spectrum, but also for those toiling at the bottom rungs of society. According to State Representative Yusuf Salaam of Selma, Alabama, "Politics don't put money in your pocket."[26]

Lower-income rural blacks, like other blacks nationwide, find themselves at a disadvantage within the political system because as a minority in a majoritarian society, it is very difficult to influence the political process. Our present political system requires organizational resources such as lobbying and mobilization strategies and financial contributions. These are not resources to which most lower-income people have access. In the past, middle- and upper-income African Americans within the Black Belt, also affected by segregation, could access Northern philanthropic organizations or articulate the evils of segregation in the media and in courts. Working together, lower-income African Americans contributed their bodies and minds to the movement and middle-income African Americans contributed their organizational skills and monetary resources. But today's struggle in the region is quite different. The needs of the two groups are not as similar as in the past. So

---

[26] Fleming, *Gone Time*.

to select blacks from middle-income ranks to serve on appointive boards that sponsor the same policy preferences as traditional power brokers has not proven beneficial to the Black Belt, or rural African Americans in particular. As stated, many of the issues affecting lower-income African Americans today are not necessarily the same issues that affect middle- and upper-income blacks. These issue—such as poverty, high unemployment or underemployment, no access to healthcare, inadequate housing, and lack of public transportation—typically are not issues that are the top priority for middle- and upper-income African Americans. In fact, except for race, they have the same policy preferences as middle- and upper-income whites, such as lower taxes, business regulation, and quality education for their children. However, regardless of race and class, a lack of development in the region influences the lives of everyone, as discussed by former Congressman Artur Davis, representing the Alabama Black Belt:

> Whether you are black or white in Perry County or Greene County or Sumter County, you are living in depressed conditions that needs changing. Even if you are a relatively affluent white person living in those areas, chances are your children are still going away to get jobs instead of coming back. Chances are that your children are going to a school system that is strapped for resources or you're spending thousands of dollars to send them to private school. You can't escape the conditions of the Black Belt based on your race or your economic status…. What we tried to do is to point out to many whites living in the Black Belt that their self-interest is bound up in the fates of the African Americans. The white community in the Black Belt cannot move forward without the Black community advancing as well, and both sides need to grow up and realize that.[27]

The 2008 presidential election proved a time of enthusiasm, as blacks in great numbers went to the polls to help elect the nation's first black president, Barack Obama. As shown in Table 4-8 the Black Belt region was actively involved in the election.

---

[27] Spencer, Thomas, "Politics of Color: Who Deserves to Lead?" *The Birmingham (AL) News*, 13 October 2002, http://www.al.com/specialreport/birminghamnews/index.ssf?blackbelt/blackbelt12.html, accessed 20 December 2012.

Table 4-8 Alabama's Black Belt 2008 Presidential Vote

| County | Obama Vote total | % of votes | McCain vote total | % of votes | Black pop. % | White pop. % | 2004 Kerry % | 2004 Bush % |
|---|---|---|---|---|---|---|---|---|
| Barbour | 5,697 | 49% | 5,866 | 49% | 46.3 | 51.4 | 45% | 55% |
| Bullock | 4,011 | 74% | 1,391 | 26% | 75.0 | 24.4 | 68% | 32% |
| Chambers | 6,799 | 46% | 8,067 | 54% | 37.3 | 60.4 | 41% | 59% |
| Choctaw | 3,636 | 46% | 4,223 | 54% | 43.5 | 54.9 | 46% | 54% |
| Clarke | 5,914 | 44% | 7,466 | 56% | 41.8 | 55.2 | 41% | 59% |
| Conecuh | 3,429 | 50% | 3,470 | 50% | 44.3 | 54.5 | 45% | 55% |
| Coosa | 2,273 | 41% | 3,248 | 59% | 32.5 | 66.3 | 41% | 58% |
| Dallas | 13,986 | 67% | 6,798 | 33% | 66.9 | 31.8 | 60% | 40% |
| Greene | 4,408 | 83% | 876 | 17% | 78.7 | 20.1 | 80% | 20% |
| Hale | 4,982 | 61% | 3,200 | 39% | 58.7 | 40.7 | 58% | 42% |
| Henry | 3,018 | 35% | 5,585 | 65% | 30.6 | 67.5 | 34% | 66% |
| Lowndes | 5,449 | 75% | 1,809 | 25% | 70.6 | 28.1 | 70% | 30% |
| Macon | 9,450 | 87% | 1,396 | 13% | 82.4 | 15.5 | 83% | 17% |
| Marengo | 5,926 | 52% | 5,516 | 48% | 52.8 | 46.5 | 49% | 51% |
| Monroe | 5,025 | 45% | 6,175 | 55% | 40.1 | 56.8 | 39% | 61% |
| Perry | 4,457 | 73% | 1,679 | 27% | 68.9 | 30.4 | 68% | 32% |
| Pickens | 4,594 | 46% | 5,434 | 54% | 42.5 | 56.9 | 43% | 57% |
| Pike | 5,879 | 42% | 8,0004 | 58% | 36.9 | 59.9 | 37% | 63% |
| Sumter | 5,264 | 75% | 1,731 | 25% | 70.9 | 26.7 | 71% | 29% |
| Wilcox | 4,612 | 71% | 1,868 | 29% | 72.6 | 27.2 | 68% | 32% |

Source: County Election results: CNN Election Results http://www.cnn.com/ELECTION/2008/results/county/#val=ALP00p6. U.S. Census Bureau. www.census.gov 2009, accessed 17 December 2012. CNN Alabama county results 2004. www.census.gov, accessed 17 December 2012.

The election of President Obama resulted in significant black political participation within the region among rural blacks. Voting results in the Alabama Black Belt during the 2008 election shows African-American voter enthusiasm. This trend was also seen in black voting trends nationwide as "96 percent of black voters supported Obama and constituted 13 percent of the electorate, a 2-percentage-point rise in their national turnout."[28] Yet this magnificent black political feat was amid a natural economic crisis that ravaged the black community as a whole and wreaked havoc on an already economically challenged people with the Black Belt region. Chapter 5 focuses on the lack of economic progress of blacks within the Black Belt region of the South.

---

[28] David Paul Kuhn, "Exit Polls: How Obama Won," 5 November 2008 http://www.politico.com/news/stories/1108/15297.html, accessed 17 December 2012

# 5

# RURAL AFRICAN AMERICANS AND PERSISTENT POVERTY

Historically, institutional racism as well as non-inclusive sociopolitical and economic institutions have negatively affected the lives of blacks within the Black Belt region. When blacks of this area are compared economically to blacks in other regions, they tend to fare worse than others, according to Falk and Rankin. This is particularly important since this is the region that has housed most blacks for the longest period of time and yet has not afforded the population many economic and social opportunities. Poverty and economic instability within the Black Belt region is not comparable to other regions around the country, and typically the Black Belt ranks very low on all economic indicators. Although rural places are among some of our country's poorest communities, the Black Belt region stands out as one of the poorest. When race is included in the analysis, African Americans in rural communities within the Black Belt region have historically been extremely impoverished, and this trend continues today.[1]

In Table 5.0 the historical trend of poverty within rural communities and racial differences are highlighted. In 1959, before the Civil Rights Act of 1964, African Americans who resided in nonmetro or farm areas were at least 70 percent impoverished compared to African Americans residing in nonfarm areas, who were roughly 45 percent impoverished. This also shows the extreme concentrations of poverty in rural areas from the 1950s up to 1980, particularly among African Americans. Poverty's connection to race and rurality is strong, particularly within the

---

[1] William Falk and Bruce H. Rankin, "The Cost of Being Black in the Black Belt," *Social Problems* 39/3 (August 1992): 299–313. Rosalind Harris and Dreamal Worthen, "African Americans in Rural America" in *Challenges for Rural American in the Twenty-First Century* edited by David Brown and Louis Swanson (University Park: Pennsylvania State Press, 2003).

Black Belt region. Although there has been a significant drop in poverty each decade, the percentage of African American rural dwellers living in poverty during this studied time period is staggering. Unfortunately, the trend of African American rural poverty continues. Although rural poverty affects all racial and ethnic groups, there is a strong historical connection to African American rural poverty within the Black Belt. This historical poverty influences the economic standing of many Southern states and the rural places within them today.[2]

Table 5.0 Percent of Rural Families below Poverty

| Year | Nonmetro Areas | White Nonfarm % | Farm areas | Nonmetro nonfarm | Blacks Nonfarm % | Farm |
|------|----------------|-----------------|------------|------------------|------------------|------|
| 1959 | 24.3 | 12.8 | 38.7 | 73.2 | 45.3 | 88.1 |
| 1969 | 12.0 | 7.3  | 15.1 | 49.0 | 27.1 | 56.4 |
| 1979 | 8.9  | 6.8  | 9.6  | 35.4 | 27.4 | 46.8 |

Source: *Dimensions of Poverty in the Rural South*, eds. Jogindar Dhillon and Marguerite Howie (Tallahassee: Florida A&M University: Center for Community Development and Research College of Engineering Sciences, Technology & Agriculture, 1986) 79.

*The Southern Region and Persistent Poverty*

The states within the Southern region consistently rank at the bottom of the most livable state rankings. In fact, in the 2008 edition of *State Rankings*, Mississippi ranked 50th and South Carolina ranked 49th. Arkansas, Louisiana, Alabama, North Carolina, and Georgia were ranked within the last forty states. Unfortunately, the Southern region has become synonymous with poverty, as historically it has been a place with high levels of poverty. There is a strong correlation between persistent poverty and the Southern region, with 280 of 444 persistent-poverty counties (counties with high levels of poverty for several decades) being located there. Joliffe finds comparatively that there are no nonmetro

---

[2] *Dimensions of Poverty in the Rural South*, eds. Jogindar Dhillon and Marguerite Howie (Tallahassee: Florida A&M University: Center for Community Development and Research College of Engineering Sciences, Technology & Agriculture, 1986) 79.

persistent-poverty counties in the Northeast. In addition to poverty, education level is also influenced by region, according to Robert Gibbs, who found that nine out of ten low-education counties (where at least one of four adults between the age of twenty-five to sixty-four has not completed high school) are located in the Southern region, particularly those counties with large populations of African Americans and Hispanics.[3]

*Geography of Poverty*, an Economic Research Service report from 2004, reveals that three-fourths of the high-poverty counties "reflect the low income of racial and ethnic minorities." Out of more than 400 high-poverty counties, 210 were identified as black high-poverty counties and, interestingly, all 210 black high-poverty nonmetro counties were located within the Black Belt region. The factors of race, class, and education are interconnected and have always tended to negatively define the South and the Black Belt within.[4]

Therefore, the importance of region in relation to quality of life cannot be overstated. Rural African American life is shaped by their region of residence, and a significant number of blacks reside in the Black Belt, making them particularly susceptible to poverty as well as a lack of quality education. As stated, African Americans living in rural nonmetro counties tend to be poorer than African Americans in other counties throughout the country. According to Rosalind Harris and Dreamal Worthem, "35 percent of the nation's poor, 43 percent of the rural poor, and 90 percent of poor rural African Americans reside in the

---

[3] Anonymous, "Which State Is the Most Liveable," *State Rankings 2008: A Statistical View of America* http://os.cqpress.com/StateRank2008_Rankings.pdf, accessed 17 December 2012. Dean Jollifee, "Persistent Poverty Is More Pervasive in Nonmetro Counties," *Amber Waves* (Washington, DC: US Department of Agriculture Economic Research Service). *From Rural Poverty at a Glance*, RDRR-100, USDA/ERS, 2004. Robert Gibbs, "Most Low-Education Counties Are in the Nonmetro South," *Amber Waves* (Washington, DC: US Department of Agriculture Economic Research Service, http://www.ers.usda.gov/AmberWaves/June05/Findings/LowEducationCounties.htm, accessed 17 December 2012.

[4] "Geography of Poverty," www.ers.usda.gov/topics/rural-economy-population/rural-poverty-well-being/geography-of-poverty.aspx, accessed 17 December 2012

Black Belt region. Within the Black Belt the deeply rooted connection between poverty of place and poverty of people is clear." It is clear that there is a historical connection between the predicament that African Americans in the Black Belt find themselves today and the high levels of poverty and lack of progress found in the past that limited blacks. These circumstances continue to impact the present and the future for this group.[5]

*Black Belt Poverty in Georgia*

During the early twentieth century, W. E. B. Du Bois studied the economic and social problems of the Georgia Black Belt. During the 1930s, Raper also focused on the Black Belt of Georgia, assessing the region for quality of life factors and finding similarly deplorable conditions as Du Bois, such as extreme poverty, economic intimidation, and little educational advancement. This chapter briefly focuses on the same Georgia Black Belt in the twenty-first century, specifically highlighting the most highly black-populated counties found there. In Table 5.1 the significant African American poverty in counties with black populations of 50 percent or more are shown. As revealed by the work of both Du Bois and Raper, African American poverty in the Georgia Black Belt is both prevalent and historical in nature. In addition to poverty, a lack of educational attainment has also been generational in scope and shows a deep connection between the Old and New South in Georgia. These counties show significantly higher poverty rates than the state average and show how the racial demographics of a county can influence other factors, as most of these highly black-populated counties also have large percentages of those blacks living in poverty compared to the white population. In fact, when comparing the poverty rates of whites

---

[5] Rosalind Harris and Dreamal Worthen, "African Americans in Rural America" in *Challenges for Rural American in the Twenty-First Century*, eds. David Brown and Louis Swanson (University Park: Pennsylvania State Press, 2003) 35.

and blacks, blacks have a three or four times higher poverty rate than their white counterparts in some counties.[6]

Table 5.1 African American High Population Counties in Georgia in 2000

| County | Population | Black % | White % | Overall Poverty rate | White poverty | Black Poverty | Bachelors Degree or higher |
|---|---|---|---|---|---|---|---|
| Baker | 4,248 | 50.4 | 47.4 | 23.4 | 9.1 | 36.1 | 10.7 |
| Burke | 23,189 | 51.0 | 46.9 | 28.7 | 13.8 | 42.1 | 9.5 |
| Calhoun | 6,102 | 60.6 | 38.3 | 26.5 | 10.8 | 37.1 | 11.7 |
| Clay | 3,317 | 60.5 | 38.4 | 31.3 | 5.5 | 48.5 | 10.1 |
| Dooly | 11,604 | 49.5 | 46.0 | 22.1 | 11.2 | 32.3 | 9.6 |
| Hancock | 9,811 | 77.8 | 21.5 | 29.4 | 35.5 | 25.0 | 9.8 |
| Jefferson | 16,883 | 56.3 | 42.1 | 23.0 | 11.1 | 31.9 | 9.1 |
| Macon | 13,935 | 59.5 | 37.4 | 25.8 | 16.4 | 30.7 | 10.0 |
| Randolph | 7,331 | 59.5 | 38.9 | 27.7 | 9.6 | 39.5 | 9.5 |
| Stewart | 4,981 | 61.5 | 37.1 | 22.2 | 8.3 | 30.1 | 9.3 |
| Talbot | 6,587 | 61.6 | 36.8 | 24.2 | 9.3 | 33.6 | 7.9 |
| Taliaferro | 1,896 | 60.3 | 38.2 | 23.4 | 11.2 | 32.0 | 8.4 |
| Terrell | 10,950 | 60.7 | 37.9 | 28.6 | 10.7 | 40.0 | 10.7 |
| Warren | 6,254 | 59.5 | 39.5 | 27.0 | 10.6 | 37.6 | 8.0 |
| Washington | 21,061 | 53.2 | 45.7 | 22.9 | 8.3 | 35.8 | 10.5 |
| Georgia | 8,829,383 | 28.7 | 65.1 | 13.0 | 8.2 | 23.1 | 24.3 |

Sources: US Census Bureau, State and County Quick Facts, www.census.gov. "The Georgia County Guide 2003," University of Georgia.

It must also be noted when compared to the state level, these counties have significantly higher poverty levels than the state average overall. In addition, educational attainment levels in these counties is

---

[6] W. E. B. Du Bois, *The Souls of Black Folks* (Chicago: A. C. McClurg,1903). Arthur Raper, *Preface to Peasantry A Tale of Two Black Belt Counties* (Chapel Hill: University of North Carolina Press, 1936).

Abandonment in Dixie

considerably low, and by focusing on the percentage of those with bachelor's degrees in the counties, the lack of education is truly publicized.

This chapter also focuses on other quality-of-life factors in the Georgia Black Belt in the twenty-first century. Factors such as family median income, median value of homes, access to higher education, access to health care, and other life issues reveal that the lives of residents within these counties is difficult. Median income shows a significant difference in income level between residents of these counties and the rest of the state, making it difficult for these residents to accumulate wealth, resulting in dire economic circumstances. The educational opportunities within these counties are also deemed limited, as shown in Table 5.2, since residents' ability to further their education is affected by the lack of institutions of higher education within these counties. In addition, the ability to access healthcare of any quality is limited by a lack of physicians and medical facilities.

Table 5.2 Quality of Life in Georgia Black Belt in 2000

| County | Median family income | Median value of home | Institution of Higher Education | No of Physicians 2000 | Hospital Facility |
|---|---|---|---|---|---|
| Baker | 30,338 | 62,700 | no | 1 | no |
| Burke | 27,877 | 59,800 | no | 13 | 1 |
| Calhoun | 24,588 | 48,200 | no | 7 | 1 |
| Clay | 21,448 | 53,600 | no | 3 | no |
| Dooly | 27,980 | 62,300 | no | 12 | no |
| Hancock | 22,003 | 53,000 | 2 year | 6 | no |
| Jefferson | 26,120 | 56,900 | no | 13 | 1 |
| Macon | 24,224 | 54,200 | no | 15 | 1 |
| Randolph | 22,004 | 48,600 | Private 2 year | 6 | 1 |
| Stewart | 24,789 | 44,000 | no | 1 | 1 |
| Talbot | 26,611 | 57,700 | no | 1 | no |
| Taliaferro | 23,750 | 40,300 | no | 1 | no |
| Terrell | 26,969 | 59,300 | no | 4 | no |
| Warren | 27,366 | 48,700 | no | 3 | no |
| Washington | 29,910 | 66,900 | no | 23 | 1 |
| Georgia | 42,433 | 111,200 | na | 15736 | na |

Sources: US Census Bureau, State and County Quick Facts, www.census.gov. The Georgia County Guide 2003, University of Georgia.

As during the time of Du Bois and Raper, Georgia's Black Belt counties are still impoverished, but more importantly for this work, the blacks living there are particularly poor. Unfortunately, like many of the blacks before them within these communities in centuries past, life revolves around poverty, little education, and few socioeconomic options.

These counties show the need for a focus on rural economic development policy in the region, but it is also a glaring example of why such policy must be innovative and comprehensive. The plight of these counties shows the inadequacy of addressing economic development by general nationalistic policy approaches without focusing on region and historical influences that continue to shape the future of these counties. Even when national economic indicators suggest that America is economically sound, this region is not economically vigorous and must therefore be treated as a distinct economy with special needs. In times of economic downturn, this region is hit the hardest and is most vulnerable. Since the beginning of the great recession of 2008, blacks have been particularly susceptible.

*Place-Based Development in Georgia*

Georgia, like many Southern states has had two economic realities for many decades: the Black Belt and the rest of the state. The metro Atlanta area is economically sound, yet the Black Belt region has not been a part of the economic success of the state. Georgia's rural economy has been weakened by the global economy with heavy losses in manufacturing, textile, and tobacco-related industries. Yet the state continues to invest in industry recruitment without truly developing comprehensive strategies for improving rural education and rural entrepreneurship. Rural areas of the state, such as the Black Belt region, need additional assistance to recover and grow. These unique places will require prescriptions for change, and relying on traditional industry recruitment techniques will not benefit many of these communities.

A 2007 article in *Georgia Trend* magazine highlighted Ken Stewart, commissioner of the Georgia Department of Economic Development, as he discussed Georgia's participation in the new global economy, focusing on the recruitment of the Kia plant and the state's investment in the project. He attributed $1.2 billion and 2,800 jobs associated directly with the plant and described the state's focus on international trade, stating,

> We have 10 international offices in place now around Europe, Asia, Canada, Mexico and South America; and we're very actively pursuing trade opportunities on all of those continents. We expect to open up, in the first quarter, a new office in China; and we are exploring opening an office in India. We have 1,600 foreign-owned facilities in the state from 43 companies. Twenty-five percent of our investment in Georgia is foreign-sourced.[7]

Stewart's discussion of economic development activity within the state focuses specifically on place-based development without much focus on people-based development, a needed strategy within the Black Belt specifically. Black Belt areas with low educational attainment and low physical infrastructural development may be ill prepared to attract global industry and investment to their communities. Special effort should be made to include this neglected area of the state in targeted innovative approaches to economic development, and educational goals should be established by the state to enrich and supplement educational opportunities within.

The state of Alabama is another Deep South state that has begun to focus specifically on the Black Belt region of the state. In April 2008, US Steel announced plans to invest $450 million in Sumter County, which is within the Black Belt of the state. In *The Birmingham News*, Alabama development office director Neal Wade noted, "This is one of the nation's top companies that is making a commitment to the Black Belt part of the state. I think that sends a very strong message to other companies that they should consider this type of investment in the Black Belt as well." According to the article, the state of Alabama provided a

---

[7] Susan Percy, "Marketing Georgia," *Georgia Trend*, www.georgiatrend.com/april-2007/marketing-georgia, . accessed 17 December 2012.

## Underdevelopment in the Bible Belt

$28 million incentive package for the deal, including tax abatements and worker training, while the Sumter County Industrial Development Authority donated the land for the project.[8]

However successful these projects are in Georgia and Alabama, though, they do not address the unique problems of the region as a whole. By focusing on the Black Belt region, demographic factors within the counties of the region warrant a more complex regional focused strategy instead of piecemeal state efforts. Although these efforts by the governors and states are necessary, welcomed, and should be applauded, a more comprehensive look at the Black Belt is needed as part of a regional-centered national strategy for change. The following section focuses specifically on Black Belt counties, as defined by this work, and the disturbing socioeconomic factors revealed by the 2000 census.

### *Black Belt High Black Population Counties*

The South has the largest concentrated black population in the country, and nine out of ten rural blacks live within the Southern region. So the political, economic, and socialization processes of the region are greatly influenced by the African American population located there. The following tables are statistical snapshots of the most heavily black-populated counties of the Black Belt region. Each of these counties has a black population of 40 percent or more, yet the Black Belt region, as a whole, has a 30 percent black population overall. This population greatly influences the economic condition of the counties, as this large black rural population often translates into high levels of poverty and low educational attainment. The connections between the lack of opportunities and missed opportunities within the history of the Black Belt are revealed there in the twenty-first century. The lack of investment in public education and training and the limited opportunities available significantly affect the large populations of rural people, particularly blacks within the region.

---

[8] Dawn Kent, "U.S. Steel to Invest in Alabama Black Belt with First-of-Its-Kind Coke Alternative Plant," *The Birmingham* (AL) *News*, www.al.com/news/birminghamnews/index.ssf?/base/news/1208592940164040.xml8ccoll =2, accessed 20 December 2012.

Table 5.3 Alabama's Black Belt Region

| Counties | Total Population | Black pop. Percentage | Rural Percentage | Black Poverty | % Whites w/o HS diploma | % Blacks w/o HS diploma |
|---|---|---|---|---|---|---|
| Barbour | 25,417 | 44.0 | 51.3 | 41.5 | 32.4 | 63.5 |
| Bullock | 11,042 | 72.3 | 64.0 | 45.8 | 34.1 | 59.9 |
| Butler | 21,892 | 40.2 | 65.8 | 3.1 | 39.7 | 62.5 |
| Choctaw | 16,018 | 44.2 | 100 | 48.4 | 37.1 | 59.0 |
| Clarke | 27,240 | 42.7 | 62.8 | 46.5 | 29.5 | 57.3 |
| Conecuh | 14,014 | 42.2 | 74.6 | 48.3 | 42.0 | 56.9 |
| Dallas | 48,130 | 57.8 | 42.7 | 55.2 | 26.0 | 54.6 |
| Greene | 10,153 | 80.6 | 100 | 54.7 | 28.1 | 52.4 |
| Hale | 15,498 | 59.5 | 80.3 | 50.9 | 32.9 | 56.8 |
| Lowndes | 12,658 | 74.1 | 100 | 49.8 | 22.9 | 53.4 |
| Macon | 24928 | 85.6 | 50 | 37.9 | 34.5 | 39.1 |
| Marengo | 11745 | 50.9 | 56.4 | 49.6 | 24.3 | 56.1 |
| Perry | 12759 | 64.4 | 67 | 57.9 | 31.8 | 61.5 |
| Pickens | 20699 | 41.8 | 89.6 | 54.2 | 34.3 | 61.4 |
| Sumter | 16174 | 70.3 | 58 | 50.4 | 22.7 | 60.2 |
| Wilcox | 13568 | 68.9 | 100 | 60.8 | 27.6 | 62.4 |

Source: Ronald C. Wimberley, Libby V. Morris, and Donald P. Woolley, *The Black Belt Databook*. TVA Rural Studies (Lexington: University of Kentucky, 2001).

*High school diploma data is for 25 or older population.

The Alabama Black Belt, as shown in Table 5.3, consists of sixteen rural counties with poverty percentage rates of roughly 50 percent, with the lowest being Macon County with 37.9 percent and the highest poverty rate being Wilcox County with a 60.8 percent poverty rate. The black population within these counties ranges from 41.8 percent in Pickens County to Macon County with 85.6 percent. By focusing on the factors identified in the chart, this region of the state is significantly impoverished with low educational attainment, which negatively influences the lives of the citizens of these communities and the economic stability of the state and the region. In addition, these factors reveal the importance of economically developing the Black Belt region and the need for strategic planning when coming up with economic development strategies that are creative and that address developing the people and the region as a whole.

Table 5.4 Arkansas's Black Belt

| Counties | Total population | Black pop. percentage | Rural percentage | Black poverty | % Whites w/o HS diploma | % Blacks w/o HS diploma |
|---|---|---|---|---|---|---|
| Chicot | 15,713 | 56.4 | 32.2 | 60.6 | 35.0 | 62.0 |
| Desha | 16,798 | 42.5 | 37.4 | 58.4 | 33.7 | 61.2 |
| Lee | 13,053 | 57.4 | 54.7 | 64.7 | 47.5 | 63.7 |
| St. Francis | 28,497 | 47.4 | 53.1 | 59.3 | 36.9 | 56.7 |

Source: Ronald C. Wimberley, Libby V. Morris, and Donald P. Woolley, *The Black Belt Databook*. TVA Rural Studies (Lexington: University of Kentucky, 2001).
*High school diploma data is for 25 or older population.

There are only four Black Belt rural counties in Arkansas with a black population of 40 percent or more, and like the Alabama Black Belt, poverty within these counties is extremely high, with little educational attainment. Sadly, for example, Lee County has an African American poverty level of 64.7 percent, which greatly influences the quality of black life within the county and influences the state. More disturbing is the significant percentage of blacks within these counties without high school diplomas, which limits their socioeconomic opportunities and the economic progress of the county and state as well as the quality of life for these individuals.

Table 5.5 Florida's Black Belt

| Counties | Total population | Black pop. percentage | Rural percentage | Black poverty | % Whites w/o HS diploma | % Black w/o HS diploma |
|---|---|---|---|---|---|---|
| Jefferson | 11,296 | 43.4 | 77.7 | 38.2 | 25.2 | 53.7 |
| Madison | 16,569 | 41.7 | 79.7 | 40.9 | 32.5 | 62.3 |

Source: Ronald C. Wimberley, Libby V. Morris, and Donald P. Woolley, *The Black Belt Databook*. TVA Rural Studies (Lexington: University of Kentucky, 2001).
*High school diploma data is for 25 or older population.

Florida, as shown in Table 5.5, has a small number of rural counties with black populations of at least 40 percent. But the poverty levels, the lack of educational attainment, and other factors are similar to the rest of the Black Belt region. Georgia, with its 159 counties, has a Black Belt region of 35 rural counties, with black population ranging from Hancock County's 79.4 percent to Turner County's 40.6 percent. These counties are highly impoverished, with an average poverty rate of 42.2 percent. Wilkinson County has the lowest poverty rate, with 25.8 percent, and Turner County has the highest, with 57.8 percent. These statistics reveal a difficult quality of life in the Georgia Black Belt. In addition, the lack of black educational attainment within these counties is alarming. For example, in Quitman County, almost 70 percent of blacks do not have a high school diploma, so competing in the twenty-first century global economy, which is based largely on knowledge, will be quite a challenge for these counties as they are ill-equipped to compete.

Table 5.6 Georgia's Black Belt

| Counties | Total Population | Black Population percentage | Rural Percentage | Black Poverty | % Whites w/o HS Diploma | % Black w/o HS Diploma |
|---|---|---|---|---|---|---|
| Baker | 3,615 | 51.5 | 100 | 35.0 | 37.7 | 56.6 |
| Baldwin | 39,530 | 42.3 | 42.7 | 31.6 | 24.9 | 51.8 |
| Brooks | 15,398 | 41.5 | 42.7 | 31.6 | 30.7 | 61.1 |
| Burke | 20,579 | 52.3 | 72.3 | 45.8 | 29.8 | 61.6 |
| Calhoun | 5,013 | 58.9 | 100 | 46.0 | 35.8 | 58.1 |
| Clay | 3,364 | 60.8 | 100 | 50.6 | 31.0 | 63.4 |
| Crisp | 20,011 | 40.7 | 48.4 | 52.9 | 33.0 | 66.0 |
| Dooly | 9,901 | 49.0 | 72.6 | 50.9 | 34.6 | 60.1 |
| Early | 11,854 | 44.1 | 52.8 | 51.5 | 36.1 | 62.4 |
| Greene | 11,793 | 49.9 | 75.7 | 37.6 | 38.7 | 62.8 |
| Hancock | 8,908 | 79.4 | 100 | 33.8 | 39.0 | 54.8 |
| Jefferson | 17,408 | 55.7 | 100 | 45.2 | 38.3 | 62.6 |
| Jenkins | 8,247 | 41.4 | 53.8 | 46.8 | 37.8 | 71.2 |
| Mcintosh | 8,634 | 43.1 | 100 | 31.5 | 34.1 | 56.5 |
| Macon | 13,114 | 58.7 | 65.6 | 39.8 | 33.2 | 57.3 |
| Marion | 5,590 | 41.3 | 100 | 42.9 | 38.0 | 57.9 |
| Meriwether | 22,411 | 44.6 | 82.3 | 32.3 | 38.4 | 64.4 |
| Mitchell | 20,275 | 47.6 | 56.2 | 45.3 | 32.4 | 63.5 |
| Peach | 21,189 | 47.5 | 61.3 | 43.6 | 21.1 | 48.4 |
| Quitman | 2,209 | 50.1 | 100 | 52.3 | 37.4 | 68.8 |

Underdevelopment in the Bible Belt

| Randolph | 8,023 | 57.9 | 53.5 | 53.0 | 35.7 | 64.6 |
|---|---|---|---|---|---|---|
| Screven | 13,842 | 44.9 | 79.3 | 37.6 | 31.6 | 56.2 |
| Stewart | 5,654 | 63.3 | 100 | 45.2 | 31.8 | 60.9 |
| Sumter | 30,228 | 46.5 | 45.4 | 41.8 | 22.8 | 58.0 |
| Talbot | 6,524 | 62.3 | 97.9 | 34.7 | 24.3 | 58.2 |
| Taliaferro | 1,915 | 60.9 | 100 | 44.1 | 32.9 | 65.6 |
| Taylor | 7,642 | 43.2 | 100 | 49.0 | 36.3 | 69.8 |
| Terrell | 10,653 | 59.9 | 50.3 | 42.4 | 28.0 | 65.3 |
| Turner | 8,703 | 40.6 | 44.5 | 57.8 | 35.9 | 64.3 |
| Twiggs | 6,078 | 45.9 | 100 | 40.7 | 43.3 | 63.0 |
| Warren | 6,078 | 60.2 | 100 | 44.0 | 45.3 | 68.0 |
| Washington | 19,112 | 51.7 | 67.1 | 33.0 | 28.0 | 57.1 |
| Webster | 2,263 | 50.0 | 100 | 37.1 | 36.0 | 65.2 |
| Wilkes | 10,597 | 46.3 | 59.6 | 37.1 | 29.2 | 62.0 |
| Wilkinson | 10,228 | 42.1 | 100 | 25.8 | 32.1 | 48.4 |

Source: Ronald C. Wimberley, Libby V. Morris, and Donald P. Woolley, *The Black Belt Databook*. TVA Rural Studies (Lexington: University of Kentucky, 2001).
*High school diploma data is for 25 or older population.

Table 5.7 Louisiana's Black Belt

| Counties | Total Population | Black Population percentage | Rural percentage | Black Poverty | % Whites w/o HS diploma | % Blacks w/o HS diploma |
|---|---|---|---|---|---|---|
| Bienville | 15,979 | 43.5 | 80.7 | 46.6 | 27.4 | 39.3 |
| Claiborne | 17,405 | 46.2 | 59.7 | 58.5 | 25.1 | 58.5 |
| De Soto | 25,346 | 44.0 | 78.7 | 53.7 | 25.6 | 51.5 |
| East Carroll | 9,707 | 64.8 | 44.6 | 74.2 | 36.0 | 62.6 |
| East Feliciana | 19,211 | 47.3 | 79.7 | 41.9 | 31.1 | 55.0 |
| Iberville | 31,049 | 46.3 | 76.9 | 42.7 | 34.4 | 49.4 |
| Madison | 12,463 | 59.5 | 31.6 | 63.1 | 33.4 | 58.7 |
| Pointe Coupee | 22,540 | 41.1 | 76.5 | 52.4 | 30.3 | 60.1 |
| St. Helena | 9,874 | 51.9 | 100 | 54.5 | 32.0 | 53.7 |
| St. James | 20,879 | 49.6 | 64.6 | 44.3 | 27.7 | 52.7 |
| Tensas | 7,103 | 53.3 | 100 | 66.5 | 30.2 | 54.6 |
| West Feliciana | 12,915 | 55.4 | 100 | 58.4 | 22.1 | 58.4 |

Source: Ronald C. Wimberley, Libby V. Morris, and Donald P. Woolley, *The Black Belt Databook*. TVA Rural Studies (Lexington: University of Kentucky, 2001).
*High school diploma data is for 25 or older population.

Louisiana, shown in Table 5.7, has twelve rural parishes within its Black Belt region, and these are heavily populated by African

Americans. From East Carroll Parish, with its 64.8 percent black population, to Pointe Coupee Parish, with 41.1 percent, these counties average a black poverty rate of 54.7 percent, with East Carroll Parish having the highest rate at 74.2 percent and East Feliciana Parish having the lowest at 41.9 percent. Again, these parishes show the importance of making the region a priority if those living there are to have a chance to succeed in the twenty-first century global economy and if the states in which these Black Belt counties are located are to be viable.

Table 5.8 Mississippi's Black Belt

| Counties | Total Population | Black Population percentage | Rural Percentage | Black Poverty | % Whites w/o HS diploma | % Blacks w/o HS Diploma |
|---|---|---|---|---|---|---|
| Adams | 35,356 | 48.7 | 45.0 | 48.8 | 21.7 | 46.8 |
| Amite | 13,328 | 45.3 | 100 | 50.7 | 31.4 | 60.9 |
| Bolivar | 44,175 | 62.9 | 50.4 | 59.2 | 27.9 | 58.3 |
| Claiborne | 41,875 | 62.9 | 100 | 51.2 | 23.7 | 48.1 |
| Clay | 21,120 | 53.3 | 59.8 | 40.2 | 25.1 | 57.4 |
| Coahoma | 31,665 | 64.6 | 37.7 | 63.9 | 26.7 | 60.8 |
| Copiah | 27,592 | 50.4 | 64.3 | 50.8 | 28.8 | 52.1 |
| Grenada | 21,555 | 41.4 | 49.6 | 41.6 | 31.0 | 65.8 |
| Holmes | 21,604 | 75.8 | 86.8 | 65.9 | 31.8 | 61.2 |
| Humphreys | 12,134 | 67.8 | 79.1 | 61.2 | 37.7 | 64.5 |
| Issaquena | 1,909 | 56.2 | 100 | 66.9 | 39.8 | 72.3 |
| Jasper | 17,114 | 50.8 | 100 | 43.7 | 30.6 | 52.1 |
| Jefferson | 8,653 | 86.2 | 100 | 52.8 | 26.5 | 51.8 |
| Jefferson Davis | 14,051 | 54.6 | 100 | 45.8 | 31.7 | 54.2 |
| Kemper | 10,356 | 55.4 | 100 | 53.8 | 27.7 | 59.3 |
| Leflore | 37,341 | 60.6 | 49.4 | 57.0 | 28.8 | 59.8 |
| Marshall | 30,361 | 50.7 | 76.1 | 45.2 | 41.8 | 56.5 |
| Montgomery | 12,388 | 43.9 | 53.9 | 55.4 | 37.5 | 53.5 |
| Noxubee | 12,604 | 68.1 | 100 | 55.9 | 31.9 | 61.8 |
| Panola | 29,996 | 48.4 | 78.7 | 53.6 | 36.0 | 60.2 |
| Pike | 36,882 | 45.7 | 68.6 | 52.3 | 27.4 | 57.5 |
| Quitman | 10,490 | 59.0 | 100 | 56.3 | 41.6 | 66.9 |
| Sharkey | 7,066 | 66.3 | 100 | 66.1 | 29.4 | 62.5 |
| Sunflower | 32,867 | 64.2 | 54.3 | 58.6 | 34.6 | 63.1 |
| Tallahatchie | 15,210 | 58.4 | 100 | 58.0 | 34.8 | 69.8 |
| Tunica | 8,164 | 75.3 | 100 | 70.7 | 30.7 | 65.8 |
| Walthall | 14,352 | 42.2 | 100 | 58.5 | 31.7 | 69.9 |
| Wilkinson | 9,678 | 67.5 | 100 | 56.1 | 31.8 | 63.5 |
| Winston | 19,433 | 41.7 | 63.1 | 44.5 | 33.2 | 55.4 |
| Yazoo | 25,506 | 52.7 | 51.3 | 60.5 | 31.6 | 64.7 |

Underdevelopment in the Bible Belt

Source: Ronald C. Wimberley, Libby V. Morris, and Donald P. Woolley, *The Black Belt Databook*. TVA Rural Studies (Lexington: University of Kentucky, 2001).
*High school diploma data is for 25 or older population.

Mississippi, as shown in Table 5.8, has another large Black Belt region, with thirty rural counties included. These counties range from Holmes County, with 75.8 percent black population, to Grenada County, with 41.4 percent. The poverty rates within the Mississippi Black Belt range from Clay County, with a 40.2 percent African American poverty level, to Tunica County, with a 70.7 percent black poverty level. These counties tend to be some of the poorest communities in the country.

Table 5.9 North Carolina's Black Belt

| Counties | Total Population | Black Population | Rural Percentage | Black Poverty | % Whites w/o HS Diploma | % Blacks w/o HS Diploma |
|---|---|---|---|---|---|---|
| Anson | 23,474 | 47.3 | 84.5 | 26.2 | 31.5 | 49.4 |
| Bertie | 20,388 | 61.5 | 100 | 34.4 | 32.1 | 55.4 |
| Caswell | 20,693 | 40.8 | 100 | 23.6 | 40.7 | 51.1 |
| Gates | 9,305 | 44.9 | 100 | 23.1 | 28.1 | 53.9 |
| Greene | 15,384 | 42.4 | 100 | 34.0 | 30.7 | 57.1 |
| Hertford | 22,523 | 57.6 | 68.7 | 34.0 | 29.2 | 53.0 |
| Hoke | 22,856 | 43.2 | 85.2 | 27.6 | 31.8 | 52.6 |
| Martin | 25,078 | 44.6 | 78.1 | 37.6 | 30.9 | 58.2 |
| Northampton | 20,798 | 59.3 | 100 | 33.8 | 32.1 | 59.6 |
| Tyrrell | 3,856 | 40.0 | 100 | 37.7 | 33.1 | 57.6 |
| Vance | 38,892 | 45.0 | 59.5 | 31.5 | 35.3 | 54.3 |
| Warren | 17,265 | 57.0 | 100 | 39.6 | 32.8 | 54.8 |
| Washington | 13,997 | 45.5 | 69.1 | 33.7 | 31.1 | 51.9 |

Source: Ronald C. Wimberley, Libby V. Morris, and Donald P. Woolley, *The Black Belt Databook*. TVA Rural Studies (Lexington: University of Kentucky, 2001).
*High school diploma data is for 25 or older population.

Although North Carolina, which is highlighted in Table 5.9, has been heralded as a wonderful example of Southern progress, with its top-notch universities and research centers, there are other places within the state that have not been as successful. North Carolina has thirteen Black Belt counties. The black population within these counties ranges from

Tyrrell County, with its 40 percent black population, to Bertie County, with a 61.5 percent black population. African American poverty levels within these counties range from Gates County, with a 23.1 percent rate, to Warren County, with a 39.6 percent population. It must be noted that these counties have the lowest poverty levels within the Black Belt region. This is possibly due to the technological advances within the state. Educational attainment has helped rural communities in North Carolina transition into the new global economy more successfully than other places in the Black Belt.

Table 5.10 South Carolina's Black Belt

| Counties | Total Population | Black Population | Rural Percentage | Black Poverty | % Whites w/o HS diploma | % Blacks w/o HS diploma |
|---|---|---|---|---|---|---|
| Allendale | 11,722 | 68.0 | 62.4 | 46.7 | 31.8 | 57.3 |
| Bamberg | 16,902 | 61.4 | 56.3 | 35.9 | 29.9 | 50.3 |
| Barnwell | 20,293 | 42.8 | 45.6 | 38.4 | 31.6 | 54.2 |
| Calhoun | 12,753 | 51.6 | 100 | 33.0 | 24.3 | 53.9 |
| Clarendon | 28,450 | 56.5 | 84.4 | 41.9 | 33.1 | 56.6 |
| Colleton | 34,377 | 45.0 | 84.0 | 40.0 | 29.8 | 50.2 |
| Dillon | 29,114 | 43.7 | 76.5 | 44.0 | 40.6 | 58.4 |
| Edgefield | 18,375 | 46.3 | 71.5 | 27.1 | 25.1 | 54.5 |
| Fairfield | 22,295 | 58.3 | 83.9 | 29.1 | 31.7 | 51.3 |
| Hampton | 18,191 | 54.3 | 83.1 | 39.2 | 30.7 | 52.4 |
| Jasper | 15,487 | 57.4 | 100 | 33.5 | 37.3 | 53.0 |
| Lee | 18,437 | 62.5 | 80.7 | 42.0 | 33.7 | 56.4 |
| McCormick | 8,868 | 58.5 | 100 | 31.5 | 35.1 | 58.4 |
| Marion | 33,899 | 54.6 | 60.0 | 41.6 | 35.4 | 54.4 |
| Marlboro | 29,361 | 48.5 | 59.0 | 37.3 | 42.6 | 57.0 |
| Williamsburg | 36,815 | 64.2 | 89.5 | 39.0 | 34.8 | 51.3 |

Source: Ronald C. Wimberley, Libby V. Morris, and Donald P. Woolley, *The Black Belt Databook.* TVA Rural Studies (Lexington: University of Kentucky, 2001).
*High school diploma data is for 25 or older population.

South Carolina, shown in Table 5-10, has sixteen Black Belt rural counties with black populations over 40 percent, and they range from the lowest population, Barnwell County, with 42.8 percent, to Allendale County, with 68.0 percent. These counties average 37.5 percent black poverty rate, with the lowest rate in Edgefield County, at 27.1 percent, and the highest in Allendale County, at 46.7 percent.

Table 5.11 Tennessee's Black Belt

| Counties | Total Population | Black Population | Rural Percentage | Black Poverty | % Whites w/o HS Diploma | % Black w/o HS Diploma |
|---|---|---|---|---|---|---|
| Fayette | 25,559 | 44.2 | 100 | 37.0 | 33.2 | 62.3 |
| Haywood | 19,437 | 49.7 | 48.5 | 39.0 | 40.2 | 55.0 |

Source: Ronald C. Wimberley, Libby V. Morris, and Donald P. Woolley, *The Black Belt Databook*. TVA Rural Studies (Lexington: University of Kentucky, 2001).
*High school diploma data is for 25 or older population.

Tennessee, shown in Table 5.11, like Florida and Arkansas, has very few Black Belt counties. In fact, Tennessee has only two rural counties that fit the criteria for this chapter. Yet they are similar to other counties throughout the Black Belt region in terms of poverty and educational attainment.

Table 5.12 Virginia's Black Belt

| Counties | Total Population | Black Population | Rural Percentage | Black Poverty | % Whites w/o HS Diploma | % Blacks w/o HS Diploma |
|---|---|---|---|---|---|---|
| Brunswick | 15,987 | 58.5 | 100 | 35.2 | 35.0 | 62.3 |
| Buckingham | 12,873 | 40.9 | 100 | 26.5 | 36.3 | 62.1 |
| Charles City | 6,282 | 63.2 | 100 | 21.3 | 28.5 | 51.6 |
| Greensville | 8,853 | 55.5 | 100 | 22.4 | 40.6 | 58.9 |
| King and Queen | 6,289 | 41.9 | 100 | 21.7 | 33.6 | 54.3 |
| Northhampton | 13,061 | 46.2 | 100 | 41.3 | 27.4 | 62.5 |
| Nottoway | 14,993 | 41.1 | 76.7 | 30.5 | 34.2 | 66.4 |
| Southampton | 17,550 | 44.8 | 100 | 32.8 | 26.2 | 62.5 |
| Surry | 6,145 | 55.5 | 100 | 21.1 | 28.1 | 55.6 |
| Sussex | 10,248 | 58.1 | 100 | 28.0 | 29.3 | 59.5 |
| Emporia City | 5,306 | 45.6 | 0 | 31.2 | 28.9 | 60.4 |
| Franklin City | 7,864 | 53.4 | 0 | 33.2 | 19.0 | 57.6 |
| Petersburg City | 38,386 | 72.1 | 0 | 24.0 | 29.5 | 41.8 |

Source: Ronald C. Wimberley, Libby V. Morris, and Donald P. Woolley, *The Black Belt Databook*. TVA Rural Studies (Lexington: University of Kentucky, 2001).
*High school diploma data is for 25 or older population.

Finally, the Virginia Black Belt, shown in Table 5.12, has thirteen rural counties with black populations ranging from Buckingham County's 40.9 percent to Petersburg County, at 72.1 percent. Virginia also has some of the lowest poverty rates in the region, which is likely attributed to economic opportunities such as public sector jobs provided by the federal government.

Each of the preceding tables focus on the Black Belt region and the 143 counties with the highest black populations in rural communities within the South. Most significant is the extreme black poverty rates within these counties at the turn of the twenty-first century, sometimes double or triple the state and national average, which suggests the uniqueness of the experience of rural blacks within the Black Belt and the need for public policy and development approaches that focus specifically on the needs of the region. In addition, each table shows that many rural blacks within the Black Belt tend to be ill equipped for the twenty-first century, with the lack of education playing a significant role in their ability to escape poverty and gain employment.

*The Importance of Regions*

According to Peter Dreier, John Mollenkopk, and Todd Swanstrom, "We have gotten so used to thinking in terms of a national economy that we have almost forgotten the importance of regions." Yet the key to economic success within the Black Belt is the promotion of regional economic development strategies, according to Barnes and Ledebur. Due to underdevelopment within the Black Belt, development approaches must address the socioeconomic ills of this unique place. The neglect of both the physical infrastructure and the people of the region have resulted in a dire situation, and, as a result, the economic future of these states and the nation is at stake. The reality of the economic problems revealed in the region highlights high unemployment, low educational attainment, and high levels of poverty. Yet by preparing people within

## Underdevelopment in the Bible Belt

the region to compete in open markets of the global economy, the region can break historical cycles of hopelessness and underdevelopment. This region, like other emerging economies around the world, can thrive within the new global economy through planning and investment opportunities. However, in order to participate in these global economic efforts, there must be an attempt to address the Black Belt's defining factors that have resulted in the stagnation in progress shown in the above tables. When assessing development opportunities, education is an important factor of social advancement, and we will discuss these factors within the Black Belt and the impact they have on the region.[9]

*Education in the Region*

The key to a successful transition into the new global economy for the Black Belt region starts with progress in education. The educational experiences of blacks within the South, as with their political experiences, have been shaped historically by the issue of race. In fact, segregation has left a legacy of low educational funding for public schools within the region, which has been disadvantageous to many rural blacks because of their reliance on public institutions. According to Kusimo, blacks in the Black Belt are likely to attend segregated schools and are less likely to graduate from high school and/or college than others. The Black Belt region built a system of segregation in public education and systematically assembled a dim educational future for blacks through decades of discriminatory law. As a result, the legacy of inadequate K-12 educational opportunities and limited access to higher education have resulted in a region with few people with advanced degrees and large numbers of people who are unemployed. The following tables focus on high black-population counties within the

---

[9] Peter Dreier, John Mollenkopk, and Todd Swanstrom, *Place Matters: Metropolitics for the Twenty-First Century* (Lawrence: University Press of Kansas, 2005). William Barnes and Larry Ledebur, *The New Regional Economies: The U.S. Common Market and the Global Economy* (Thousand Oaks CA: Sage Publications, 1998).

Black Belt and reveal the lack of advanced educational attainment by blacks and, subsequently, the high levels of unemployment there.[10]

Table 5.13 shows a significant difference between the educational attainment of blacks and whites within the Black Belt region in Alabama. It also reveals the high unemployment rates of blacks within the state, which is significantly higher than their white counterparts.

Table 5.13 Alabama's Black Belt Education and Unemployment in 2000

| Counties | % Whites with BA/BS degree | % Blacks With BA/BS degree | Unemployment % of Whites | Unemployment % of Blacks |
|---|---|---|---|---|
| Barbour | 16.6 | 3.9 | 4.4 | 12.5 |
| Bullock | 15.2 | 7.4 | 5.8 | 9.4 |
| Butler | 10.0 | 4.2 | 8.0 | 25.9 |
| Choctaw | 10.9 | 4.8 | 7.5 | 18.0 |
| Clarke | 14.5 | 4.3 | 4.4 | 13.8 |
| Conecuh | 8.0 | 3.7 | 6.5 | 20.1 |
| Dallas | 17.9 | 6.6 | 4.9 | 18.3 |
| Greene | 14.5 | 9.0 | 2.1 | 13.8 |
| Hale | 13.5 | 4.6 | 2.1 | 11.1 |
| Lowndes | 15.8 | 4.3 | 4.2 | 15.5 |
| Macon* | 14.7 | 18.3 | 6.7 | 15.7 |
| Marengo | 15.4 | 6.7 | 2.8 | 14.2 |
| Perry | 18.5 | 6.4 | 1.8 | 12.7 |
| Pickens | 8.5 | 3.2 | 4.5 | 15.5 |
| Sumter | 22.0 | 5.7 | 4.2 | 14.8 |
| Wilcox | 18.7 | 5.1 | 3.9 | 22.1 |

Source: Ronald C. Wimberley, Libby V. Morris, and Donald P. Woolley, *The Black Belt Databook*. TVA Rural Studies (Lexington: University of Kentucky, 2001).

* Macon County is the home of Tuskegee University

---

[10] Patricia Kusimo, *Rural African Americans and Education: The Legacy of the Brown Decision*. ERIC Clearinghouse on Rural Education and Small Schools (1999). http://www.ael.org/eric/digest/edorc984.htm, accessed 17 December 2012.

Underdevelopment in the Bible Belt

In Table 5.14, similar circumstances in the Arkansas Black Belt are revealed, as blacks fare far worse than whites in both educational attainment and unemployment within the state.

Table 5.14 Arkansas's Black Belt Education and Unemployment

| Counties | % Whites with BA/BS degree | % Blacks With BA/BS degree | Unemployment % of Whites | Unemployment % of Blacks |
|---|---|---|---|---|
| Chicot | 10.2 | 6.6 | 6.3 | 23.3 |
| Desha | 13.6 | 3.9 | 4.6 | 23.9 |
| Lee | 9.4 | 5.4 | 9.4 | 22.3 |
| St. Francis | 10.5 | 5.3 | 7.8 | 22.7 |

Source: Ronald C. Wimberley, Libby V. Morris, and Donald P. Woolley, *The Black Belt Databook.* TVA Rural Studies (Lexington: University of Kentucky, 2001).

Table 5.15 Florida's Black Belt Education and Unemployment

| Counties | % Whites with BA/BS degree | % Blacks With BA/BS degree | Unemployment % of Whites | Unemployment % of Blacks |
|---|---|---|---|---|
| Jefferson | 19.9 | 5.7 | 1.4 | 10.4 |
| Madison | 12.8 | 4.3 | 3.4 | 12.6 |

Source: Ronald C. Wimberley, Libby V. Morris, and Donald P. Woolley, *The Black Belt Databook.* TVA Rural Studies (Lexington: University of Kentucky, 2001).

Table 5.15 looks at Florida's Black Belt counties and finds tremendous differences in the educational attainment and unemployment between blacks and whites in the state.

Table 5.16 Georgia's Black Belt Education and Unemployment

| Counties | % Whites with BA/BS degree | % Blacks With BA/BS degree | Unemployment % of Whites | Unemployment % of Blacks |
|---|---|---|---|---|
| Baker | 13.5 | 4.7 | 4.0 | 13.0 |
| Baldwin | 18.6 | 4.8 | 4.0 | 12.8 |
| Brooks | 10.6 | 6.8 | 5.0 | 9.1 |
| Burke | 13.9 | 4.8 | 4.1 | 13.2 |
| Calhoun | 16.9 | 4.2 | 2.4 | 7.7 |
| Clay | 17.8 | 5.4 | 3.9 | 16.4 |
| Crisp | 12.9 | 4.1 | 4.1 | 9.0 |
| Dooly | 13.0 | 4.7 | 4.8 | 16.2 |
| Early | 12.1 | 4.8 | 2.8 | 13.5 |
| Greene | 13.0 | 3.1 | 3.8 | 11.5 |

| | | | | |
|---|---|---|---|---|
| Hancock | 9.3 | 5.9 | 3.3 | 9.4 |
| Jefferson | 9.8 | 2.5 | 5.2 | 10.6 |
| Jenkins | 10.0 | 3.7 | 4.9 | 12.8 |
| Mcintosh | 11.2 | 5.0 | 4.9 | 9.1 |
| Macon | 15.9 | 4.3 | 2.8 | 13.8 |
| Marion | 6.3 | 1.8 | 5.1 | 19.1 |
| Meriwether | 8.6 | 3.3 | 5.9 | 14.7 |
| Mitchell | 11.6 | 2.4 | 4.8 | 9.8 |
| Peach* | 16.0 | 14.0 | 3.1 | 17.0 |
| Quitman | 10.4 | 2.7 | 4.9 | 19.2 |
| Randolph | 9.9 | 2.4 | 4.5 | 15.8 |
| Screven | 12.3 | 2.3 | 3.8 | 11.2 |
| Stewart | 13.6 | 3.9 | 5.0 | 11.4 |
| Sumter | 23.1 | 4.7 | 3.7 | 16.1 |
| Talbot | 13.1 | 2.7 | 3.7 | 13.3 |
| Taliaferro | 10.8 | 1.7 | 3.7 | 12.6 |
| Taylor | 10.2 | 2.0 | 5.7 | 16.1 |
| Terrell | 16.3 | 2.7 | 3.5 | 15.5 |
| Turner | 8.5 | 4.4 | 5.1 | 24.3 |
| Twiggs | 5.5 | 3.7 | 6.8 | 12.8 |
| Warren | 7.0 | 1.7 | 3.2 | 14.4 |
| Washington | 15.2 | 3.9 | 2.6 | 12.9 |
| Webster | 9.6 | 0.9 | 1.6 | 7.5 |
| Wilkes | 15.4 | 3.4 | 2.6 | 13.7 |
| Wilkinson | 12.1 | 3.0 | 2.9 | 9.7 |

Source: Ronald C. Wimberley, Libby V. Morris, and Donald P. Woolley, *The Black Belt Databook*. TVA Rural Studies (Lexington: University of Kentucky, 2001).
*Peach County is the home of Fort Valley State University
*These counties either house institutions of higher education or are adjacent to counties that do

Georgia's Black Belt, as shown in Table 5.16, shows the same underdevelopment seen throughout the Black Belt, with the black population revealing significantly higher unemployment rates and lower education attainment than whites.

Table 5.17 Louisiana's Black Belt Education and Unemployment

| Counties | % Whites with BA/BS degree | % Blacks With BA/BS degree | Unemployment % of Whites | Unemployment % of Blacks |
|---|---|---|---|---|
| Bienville | 11.2 | 6.6 | 8.3 | 19.7 |
| Claiborne | 15.0 | 3.4 | 4.4 | 18.7 |
| De Soto | 11.1 | 7.3 | 8.0 | 22.3 |
| East Carroll | 16.0 | 5.5 | 4.8 | 40.1 |

## Underdevelopment in the Bible Belt

| | | | | |
|---|---|---|---|---|
| East Feliciana | 13.2 | 3.6 | 6.4 | 17.6 |
| Iberville | 10.9 | 6.1 | 7.2 | 16.6 |
| Madison | 11.0 | 7.6 | 5.4 | 25.9 |
| Pointe Coupee | 11.9 | 5.8 | 4.7 | 23.9 |
| St. Helena | 9.0 | 6.1 | 7.2 | 21.0 |
| St. James | 7.8 | 8.4 | 4.9 | 15.7 |
| Tensas | 17.1 | 5.9 | 4.8 | 22.7 |
| West Feliciana | 14.4 | 2.9 | 4.4 | 17.4 |

Source: Ronald C. Wimberley, Libby V. Morris, and Donald P. Woolley, *The Black Belt Databook.* TVA Rural Studies (Lexington: University of Kentucky, 2001).

Louisiana's Black Belt parishes are shown in Table 5.17, and Mississippi's Black Belt counties are shown in 5.18. Both reveal similar findings as the preceding tables of high unemployment and low educational attainment.

Table 5.18 Mississippi's Black Belt Education and Unemployment

| Counties | % Whites with BA/BS degree | % Blacks With BA/BS degree | Unemployment % of Whites | Unemployment % of Blacks |
|---|---|---|---|---|
| Adams | 18.8 | 9.5 | 5.5 | 20.9 |
| Amite | 10.7 | 5.6 | 5.1 | 15.2 |
| Bolivar | 23.9 | 8.5 | 3.9 | 23.4 |
| Claiborne* | 19.2 | 15.0 | 4.3 | 25.9 |
| Clay | 17.9 | 6.7 | 5.0 | 16.1 |
| Coahoma | 21.4 | 9.4 | 4.7 | 21.9 |
| Copiah | 13.0 | 4.8 | 5.3 | 15.0 |
| Grenada | 14.8 | 3.6 | 6.9 | 18.3 |
| Holmes | 18.0 | 5.8 | 3.7 | 21.9 |
| Humphreys | 14.1 | 7.8 | 2.5 | 10.5 |
| Issaquena | 8.7 | 2.7 | 5.1 | 15.3 |
| Jasper | 12.5 | 6.1 | 7.7 | 13.9 |
| Jefferson | 11.1 | 10.1 | 7.9 | 28.5 |
| Jefferson Davis | 10.4 | 7.2 | 8.6 | 14.8 |
| Kemper | 12.4 | 3.4 | 5.2 | 16.3 |
| Leflore* | 19.7 | 11.7 | 4.3 | 18.3 |
| Marshall* | 7.9 | 11.1 | 4.8 | 18.7 |
| Montgomery | 11.6 | 5.9 | 4.5 | 16.1 |
| Noxubee | 14.7 | 3.7 | 3.9 | 22.4 |
| Panola | 11.6 | 4.3 | 5.4 | 14.7 |
| Pike | 16.7 | 7.0 | 6.2 | 20.2 |
| Quitman | 13.0 | 5.1 | 3.3 | 20.5 |

| | | | | |
|---|---|---|---|---|
| Sharkey | 21.0 | 6.1 | 2.9 | 16.0 |
| Sunflower | 19.4 | 6.9 | 3.5 | 16.7 |
| Tallahatchie | 12.3 | 3.4 | 6.6 | 20.0 |
| Tunica | 18.4 | 3.6 | 2.0 | 23.8 |
| Walthall | 12.2 | 6.0 | 5.7 | 18.3 |
| Wilkinson | 15.1 | 5.2 | 2.8 | 25.3 |
| Winston | 12.8 | 7.2 | 5.3 | 16.3 |
| Yazoo | 16.8 | 6.2 | 4.4 | 15.9 |

Source: Ronald C. Wimberley, Libby V. Morris, and Donald P. Woolley, *The Black Belt Databook*. TVA Rural Studies (Lexington: University of Kentucky, 2001).

*These counties either house institutions of higher education or are adjacent to counties that do

The next four tables show North Carolina, South Carolina, Tennessee, and Virginia with their corresponding deficiencies in educational achievement and high unemployment, as seen in the preceding states.

Table 5.19 North Carolina's Black Belt Education and Unemployment

| Counties | % Whites with BA/BS degree | % Blacks With BA/BS degree | Unemployment % of Whites | Unemployment % of Blacks |
|---|---|---|---|---|
| Anson | 10.2 | 3.4 | 1.9 | 5.9 |
| Bertie | 10.6 | 6.0 | 2.9 | 10.0 |
| Caswell | 8.1 | 4.4 | 2.5 | 7.0 |
| Gates | 8.7 | 5.6 | 3.0 | 8.9 |
| Greene | 11.8 | 4.2 | 2.6 | 11.6 |
| Hertford | 13.7 | 8.1 | 1.5 | 10.4 |
| Hoke | 13.8 | 2.6 | 3.1 | 12.2 |
| Martin | 12.2 | 5.4 | 4.3 | 11.8 |
| Northampton | 13.0 | 5.3 | 2.0 | 11.4 |
| Tyrrell | 10.3 | 3.2 | 4.8 | 21.9 |
| Vance | 11.4 | 6.5 | 4.1 | 10.9 |
| Warren | 11.1 | 4.4 | 3.4 | 10.3 |
| Washington | 10.3 | 6.5 | 3.0 | 10.8 |

Source: Ronald C. Wimberley, Libby V. Morris, and Donald P. Woolley, *The Black Belt Databook*. TVA Rural Studies (Lexington: University of Kentucky, 2001).

Table 5.20 South Carolina's Black Belt Education and Unemployment

| Counties | % Whites with BA/BS degree | % Blacks With BA/BS degree | Unemployment % of Whites | Unemployment % of Blacks |
|---|---|---|---|---|
| Allendale | 16.8 | 5.2 | 5.5 | 14.8 |
| Bamberg | 14.5 | 8.4 | 4.0 | 14.1 |
| Barnwell | 16.9 | 3.5 | 3.9 | 19.7 |
| Calhoun | 17.7 | 4.9 | 3.9 | 9.6 |
| Clarendon | 15.0 | 5.6 | 2.3 | 13.7 |
| Colleton | 11.8 | 6.5 | 2.9 | 12.8 |
| Dillon | 10.7 | 4.8 | 5.0 | 11.6 |
| Edgefield | 15.2 | 4.4 | 3.1 | 9.2 |
| Fairfield | 15.2 | 4.4 | 3.1 | 10.5 |
| Hampton | 11.6 | 5.7 | 3.9 | 8.7 |
| Jasper | 7.3 | 2.5 | 4.2 | 8.0 |
| Lee | 9.8 | 5.5 | 4.3 | 12.7 |
| McCormick | 12.4 | 2.7 | 3.6 | 12.5 |
| Marion | 12.6 | 5.2 | 4.4 | 11.9 |
| Marlboro | 10.7 | 4.4 | 5.6 | 14.3 |
| Williamsburg | 14.3 | 6.8 | 2.5 | 11.0 |

Source: Ronald C. Wimberley, Libby V. Morris, and Donald P. Woolley, *The Black Belt Databook.* TVA Rural Studies (Lexington: University of Kentucky, 2001).

Table 5.21 Tennessee's Black Belt Education and Unemployment

| Counties | % Whites with BA/BS degree | % Blacks With BA/BS degree | Unemployment % of Whites | Unemployment % of Blacks |
|---|---|---|---|---|
| Fayette | 10.2 | 4.4 | 4.7 | 14.3 |
| Haywood | 12.4 | 4.3 | 5.3 | 12.9 |
| | | | | |

Source: Ronald C. Wimberley, Libby V. Morris, and Donald P. Woolley, *The Black Belt Databook.* TVA Rural Studies (Lexington: University of Kentucky, 2001).

Table 5.22 Virginia's Black Belt Education and Unemployment

| Counties | % Whites with BA/BS degree | % Blacks With BA/BS degree | Unemployment % of Whites | Unemployment % of Blacks |
|---|---|---|---|---|
| Brunswick | 9.0 | 5.3 | 2.5 | 10.0 |
| Buckingham | 10.9 | 3.4 | 4.0 | 5.9 |
| Charles City | 14.0 | 5.5 | 2.6 | 5.8 |
| Greensville | 4.5 | 6.0 | 2.7 | 7.7 |
| King and Queen | 10.6 | 3.2 | 2.5 | 6.7 |
| Northhampton | 18.1 | 5.1 | 3.5 | 11.5 |
| Nottoway | 12.2 | 3.4 | 3.0 | 6.7 |
| Southampton | 15.4 | 6.1 | 3.2 | 13.9 |
| Surry | 14.4 | 7.8 | 3.6 | 8.9 |
| Sussex | 15.4 | 3.1 | 2.7 | 7.3 |
| Emporia City | 17.0 | 8.2 | 2.5 | 13.2 |
| Franklin City | 25.3 | 3.5 | .9 | 12.4 |
| Petersburg City | 19.1 | 10.7 | 4.9 | 9.9 |

Source: Ronald C. Wimberley, Libby V. Morris, and Donald P. Woolley, *The Black Belt Databook.* TVA Rural Studies (Lexington: University of Kentucky, 2001).

The preceding tables reveal the devastatingly low education and high unemployment rates within the Black Belt's high black-population counties, which are legacies of ill-equipped secondary and postsecondary educational opportunities, limited access to higher education, and few economic and work prospects. This dilemma was built over decades of discriminatory and ill-fated efforts and will require efforts beyond these localities to address generations of educational and developmental neglect. This lack of educational attainment did not occur within this century nor is it independent of socioeconomic processes within the region. In addition, it is a reflection of the region's inability to transition from the manufacturing economy to the new, knowledge-based economy.

Educational inequality negatively influences targeted groups on many levels and is often successfully linked to both economic and political disenfranchisement. In order to participate fully in this capitalistic and democratic society, educational attainment becomes invaluable criteria as it translates into knowledge, political and economic freedom, and power. Traditionally, our governmental and economic institutions have tended to be composed and governed by those who are highly educated and vast opportunities are also afforded them.

*A Call for Progressive Leadership*

Strong black leadership and white leadership within the Black Belt region is just as important today as in the past in order to connect disadvantaged residents and the local power establishment to move the community as a whole forward. Today, more than ever, Black Belt communities are genuinely linked within a local economy that is in desperate need of change, development, and growth. Yet for many Black Belt communities, there is still a deep divide between the local power establishment and the rural blacks who make up a significant share of these rural communities. This divide has a long, complicated history that continues to influence present policy and socioeconomic relationships. However, education is an area that could address many problems within the region. All groups must work to develop viable solutions for excellence in order to advance their communities and connect them to the global marketplace. Today, the economy traps all residents within these communities with the same dilemma, and they will either regress or progress together. Progressing requires preparing communities for a twenty-first century economic development approach that is built on strong educational credentials and innovative approaches. Until creative and productive approaches to education are realized within the region, the ramifications of Black Belt African Americans attending "voluntarily segregated," ill-equipped schools—with Black Belt whites migrating to heavily white private schools—will continue to influence the future of rural Black Belt people and hinder their ability for economic opportunity. Successful twenty-first century education must go beyond traditional educational models to include vocational, high technology training, and entrepreneurial training opportunities.

In order to make changes, there must be a realistic assessment and definition of the region and its problems. Feasible solutions to generational poverty, low educational attainment, and a lack of opportunity are required. These factors reveal a region within the United States that is both underdeveloped and underproductive and will play a significantly negative role in the economy of twenty-first century America unless changes are made.

## A Landless People Is a Hopeless People

A landless people is a hopeless people. The Black Farmers and Agriculturalists Association motto epitomizes the experiences of blacks within the Black Belt. Yet there have been significant barriers to land ownership for blacks within the region, and unfortunately many of these barriers have come from governmental institutions. After the Civil War, blacks were eager for land, and the Freedmen's Bureau was created to serve their needs. Yet from the very beginning, the agency was understaffed and underfunded for such a large feat. Accordingly, "the Freedmen's Bureau never had more than 900 agents spread across the South from Virginia to Texas. Mississippi, for example, had twelve agents, in 1866. One agent often served a county with a population of 10,000 to 20,000 freedmen." The fact that the national government put so little effort in preparing the freedmen for independence shows possibly the most incompetent governmental response in American history. More sinister theorists would argue that it was not incompetence on the part of the national government but quite the opposite. The lack of assistance ensured African Americans would be forced to return to agricultural peonage and would then be used to rebuild the South and its economy, very cheaply. In addition, this arrangement guaranteed economic dependence for the freedmen and social control within the region by those with financial power. Or, more succinctly, a return to the power structure that was hierarchical and exclusive was assured. Efforts initially made by the feeble Freedmen's Bureau to ensure African American self-sufficiency were soon abandoned.[11]

However hopeless it seemed, Black Belt people strived to acquire land after slavery, and many succeeded but were unable to keep it. In Dougherty County, Georgia,

---

[11] Darlene Clark Hines, William Hines, and Stanley Harrold, *The African American Odyssey*, 4th ed. (New York: Pearson: Prentice Hall, 2008) 301.

W. E. B. Dubois found that most had lifted themselves out of the "submerged tenth" of sharecroppers and that somewhat more than an "upper tenth" had become cash renters and freeholders. Black owned acreage in the county had increased from 752 in 1875 to over 10,000 in 1900, while the value of all black property more than tripled. Three-quarters of the black landowners had purchased their holdings during the 1890s. However, this success was short lived. The land owned by black farmers has dwindled from roughly 17 million acres in 1910 to roughly 7 million today. And the number of black farmers has declined by 98 percent since 1920, compared with a 66 percent decline in white farmers over the same period.[12]

This trend of decline continued during the twentieth century. The 1999 Agricultural Economics and Land Ownership Survey (AELOS) reports that at the end of the twentieth century, there were 68,000 African American rural landowners owning about 7.7 million acres of land, meaning that at the dawn of the twenty-first century, blacks owned less than 1 percent of all privately owned rural land in the United States.[13] This lack of land ownership has greatly influenced the economic prospects of blacks within the region.

Cohen found that various laws burdened independent farming and economic independence within the Black Belt. Early on, for instance, historically enticement statutes made it criminal to hire a worker who was under contract with another employer while emigrant agent laws charged Northern labor recruiters enormous licensing fees. Other statutes criminalized breaking labor contracts and vagrancy and drunkenness ordinances resulted in involuntary servitude or crop lien laws, which

---

[12] Steven Hahn, *A Nation under Our Feet: Black Political Struggles in the Rural South from Slavery to the Great Migration* (Cambridge MA: Harvard University Press, 2003): 460. "USDA Black Farmers in America, 1865–2000: The Pursuit of Independent Farming and the Role of Cooperatives, Rural Business—Cooperative Service," Rural Business-Cooperative Service, RBS Research Report 194 (Washington DC: United States Department of Agriculture) 9. http://www.rurdev.usda.gov/rbs/pub/rr194.pdf, accessed 17 December 2012

[13] Miessha Thomas, Jerry Pennick, and Heather Gray, "What is African American Land Ownership? Federation/Land Assistance Fund." http://www.federationsouthern-coop.com/aalandown04.htm, 2004, accessed 17 December 2012

syphoned away a sharecroppers primary source of credit while trapping him or her into a cycle of continued debt and servitude.[14]

Even during the period of the Great Depression, when the government increased services to farmers, African Americans were at a disadvantage. "The New Deal also marked a significant increase of government services, for which distribution was controlled by politically connected groups in rural communities. For much of the South, this system resulted in diminished access to services for many blacks which, as alleged in recent lawsuits against USDA, persisted into recent years." These collective measures resulted in a legacy of debt, economic dependence, and few African American landowners. Many blacks within the region support the notion that this was a systematic, organized, and institutionally based process of inducing black economic dependence within the Black Belt region.[15]

*Farming Obstacles Today*

Agencies originally created to assist farmers eventually became impediments to success for many Black Belt African American farmers. Recently, there has been much discussion on the role of the United States Department of Agriculture (USDA) in the demise of many African American farmers. Many black farmers, politicians, and media professionals have charged that the agency has been discriminatory in its practices and processes, resulting in a legacy of debt and financial instability for black farmers. A report in *The Nation* found discrepancies in the USDA loan processes based on race: "The USDA lent a total of $1.3 billion to nearly 16,000 farmers to help them maintain their land during 1984–1985 during a farm crisis, of which only 209 of those farmers were black." For many, the USDA became a symbol of bureaucratic red tape, inefficiency, and ineffectiveness that was also

---

[14] William Cohen, "Negro Involuntary Servitude in the South, 1865–1940," *Journal of Southern History* 42/1 (February 1976): 31–60.
[15] "USDA Black Farmers in America, 1865–2000."

## Underdevelopment in the Bible Belt

discriminatory in its work against blacks and a governmental enabler of discrimination in the region.[16]

Often, many African American farmers have named the Farm Service Agency of the USDA as the major source of contention. John Boyd, a leader within the African American farm movement, stated in *Jet* magazine, in 1999, that, "It's time the USDA decided to end discrimination once and for all. The Farm Service Agency is at the heart of USDA's systematic pervasive discrimination.... This one organization...is responsible for about 95 percent of the discrimination." Boyd recalls discrimination against him firsthand: in 1994, the agency's county supervisor "tore up my [loan] application and threw it in the trash while I was sitting there."[17]

According to the Farm Service Agency (FSA) website, the agency administers and manages farm commodity, credit, conservation, and disaster and loan programs as laid out by Congress through a network of federal, state and county offices. State and county offices directly administer FSA programs."[18] Local elections select representatives for the county committee members. And they are "responsible for fairly and equitably resolving local issues while remaining dually and directly accountable to the Secretary of Agriculture and local producers through the elective process."[19] Yet the small number of votes cast in the 2006 election is problematic in that only 15 percent of eligible voters participated. In 2006, of more than 2 million eligible voters, only 307, 669 votes were actually cast, of which roughly 5,000 were cast by blacks, including Hispanic blacks. The small number of eligible black

---

[16] Habiba Alcindor, "Losing Ground," *The Nation* (20 March 2005). www.thenation.com/docprint.mhtml?i=20050404&s=alcindor, accessed 17 December 2012

[17] "Black Farmers Urge U.S. to Abolish Agriculture's Farm Service Agency," *Jet* (21 June 1999) is a brief article. "Black Farmers Look Forward to USDA Settlement" (25 February 2010) http://www.usatoday.com/news/nation/2010-02-24-black-farmers-usda-settlement_N.htm, accessed 17 December 2012

[18] "Welcome to Maryland State FSA," www.fsa.usda.gov/fsa/stateoffapp?mystate=md&area=home&<subject=landing&<topic=landing, accessed 20 December 2012.

[19] "About FSA," www.fsa.usda.gov/FSA/webapp?area=about&<subject=landing&<topic=sao, accessed 20 December 2012.

voters does not allow for descriptive representation and certainly does not support the inclusion of underrepresented groups in governmental decision-making. Supporting diversity among governmental agency decision makers is an important aspect within our democracy, as it adds legitimacy to the process. Because of the discriminatory history of the agency, it is necessary to revisit its decision-making structure to ensure that the democratic and equitable processes espoused are being practiced, particularly in a region with a history of noninclusive local control.[20]

In a commissioned study for the USDA in 1994, the treatment of minorities and women from 1990 to 1995 was highlighted:

> Few appeals were made by minority complainants because of the slowness of the process, the lack of confidence in the decision makers, the lack of knowledge about the rules, and the significant bureaucracy involved in the process. The study also found, (a) the largest USDA loans (top1%) went to corporations (65%) and white male farmers (25%); (b) loans to black males averaged $4,000 (or 25%) less than those given to white males; (c) 97% of disaster payments went to white farmers, while less than 1% went to black farmers.

The USDA itself found these findings troubling, with these factors representing impediments to African American farmer success. Yet there has been very little effort historically to correct these USDA problems with systematic changes within the agency. This has resulted in the continued extinction of the African American farmer and little economic independence for black farmers in the region.[21]

Insert 6-1 below shows recent demographic information about African American farmers. Most reside in the South, in the Black Belt region in particular. They are a small group within the agricultural industry and have very little financial support today, as in the past. Yet

---

[20] Farm Services Agency homepage: http://www.fsa.usda.gov/FSA/webapp?area=about&subject=landing&topic=landing. Election results for 2006. www.fsa.usda.gov/Internet/FSA_File/2006electionresults.pdf, accessed 17 December 2012

[21] Tadlock Cowan and Jody Feder, "The Pigford Case: USDA Settlement of a Discrimination Suit by Black Farmers," CRS Report for Congress, Congressional Research Service (Washington DC: The Library of Congress, 28 June 2007). http://www.nationalaglawcenter.org/assets/crs/RS20430.pdf, accessed 17 December 2012.

support for the black farmer in the Black Belt in particular could be an important economic development strategy that could employ local people and help sustain the local economy.

It has been obvious for some time that African Americans have been primarily disadvantaged within the present system. As a result of discriminatory evidence, many facets of American society, such as the media, watchdog groups, and civil rights groups began to focus on the plight of these farmers during the 1990s.

INSERT 6-1. DEMOGRAPHICS OF AFRICAN AMERICAN FARMERS

*Demographics*

—The 2002 Census of Agriculture reported 2.13 million farmers operated in the United States. Of this total 29,090 or approximately 1.4 percent of all farms were operated by African Americans.

—Over 74 percent (22,516) of African American farmers in the U.S. reside in Texas, Mississippi, North and South Carolina, Alabama, Georgia, Virginia, and Louisiana.

—Average annual market value and government payments for farms operated by African American farmers in 2002 were $18,060. The national average for all U.S. farmers was $97,320.

—Overall, the number of farmers operating in the United States decreased by 4.1 percent between 1997 and 2002. Farmers operated by African Americans increased from 18,451 to 28,090, a 36.6 percent increase over the five-year period.

—In 2002, 757 African Americans farmers received Commodity Credit Corporation loans amounting to a total of $7.6 million. This averaged $10,017 per African American farmer, about 28 percent of the national average ($36,122).

—National average government payments to African American farmers in 2002 ($3,457) were considerably lower than the national average government farm payment ($9,251).

—Total government payments of $6.55 billion were distributed to 707,596 farmers nationwide in 2002. Payments totaling $18.5 million (or three-tenths of one percent of all) were made to 5,344 black farmers.

> Source: "2002 Census of Agriculture, NASS," in Stephen Vina and Tadlock Cowan, "The Pigford Case: USDA Settlement of a Discrimination Suit by Black Farmers" (August 2005). CRS Report for Congress RS20430. http://assets.opencrs.com/rpts/RS20430_20050825.pdf, accessed 20 December 2012.

Black farmers also increased their political activism and actually marched in front of the White House in the late 1990s to demonstrate their frustration with the USDA and its discriminatory practices. Although dramatic, these events, led by John Boyd, Jr., the leader of the National Black Farmers Association, created media attention, yet proved of little consequence, since "black farmers received only 4% of the $1.9 billion in farm ownership loans issued by the USDA in fiscal year 1997. In addition, no black farmers received any of the 161 emergency loans doled out during that same time period. But according to a spokesman at the USDA…1.3% of those emergency loans went to African Americans farmers and 20% went to Hispanic farmers."[22]

With continued frustration, African American farmers decided to use the legal system for their grievances with the federal agency, and this effort culminated in the Pigford case settlements. A 1997 class-action civil-rights lawsuit, *Pigford v. Glickman*, was filed by three black farmers alleging the USDA had discriminated against them and other black farmers. Among other things, the farmers claimed they were systematically denied USDA loans and farm subsidies by agency officers. They also claimed that even if they were awarded a loan, the agency took so long to allot it that time ran out to plant that season's crop and they were unable to repay other debts. The Pigford case, which was

---

[22] Kelly Smith "Black Farmers Have Beef with the USDA: Loan Denials Spark Legislation Proposal to Protect African American Farmers-Proposed USDA Accountability and Equity Act," *Black Enterprise Magazine* 28/6 (January 1998) is a brief article.

filed in U.S. District Court for the District of Columbia, was settled in April 1999. Just over $1 billion was awarded to about 16,000 claimants.[23]

These settlements became a testament to the USDA's discriminatory practices. According to a *Washington Post* article,

> The deal is one of the largest racial discrimination settlements in federal history and puts to rest an issue that has long been a major embarrassment for the Agriculture Department. The vast agency derisively referred to as the "last plantation" by many black farmers and by many of the department's own minority employees who see it as a bastion of racial prejudice.... The black farmers alleged that for years they have been either denied government loans or given loans smaller than those awarded to white farmers who had similar credit histories and assets.

The process was complicated as, "Of the 94,000 Black farmers who sought relief as a result of the settlement, 81,000 were denied restitution—nearly nine out of 10—the report said. More than 75% of the denied claims were rejected because of a court-acknowledged mistake in which the plaintiffs' misinformed them of the deadline for filings." John Boyd noted, "This settlement was supposed to pay us back for unfairly denying us the same opportunities as everyone else, Instead, they have thrown up roadblock after roadblock."[24]

The settlement allowed two tracks to file a claim. Track A allowed for very little evidence to prove discrimination, which would result in a $50,000 settlement. Track B required for greater proof of evidence of discrimination but had no monetary cap. Most farmers were denied under Track B, as "40% of the 22,181 farmers who chose Track A were denied

---

[23] Lauren Etter, "Black Farmers, USDA Agree to $1.25 Billion Settlement" http://online.wsj.com/article/sb10001424052748704269004575073820593191804.html.

[24] Michael Fletcher, "USDA, Black Farmers Settle Bias Lawsuit," *The Washington Post*, 6 January 1999: A1. "Black Farmers Accuse Agriculture Department of Failing to Honor Bias Settlement," *Jet* 106/6 (9 August 2004) is a brief article. Www.nytimes.com/2004/07/21/us/black-farmers-accuse-agriculture-dept-failing-live-up-racial-bias-settlement.html, , accessed 20 December 2012.

compensation, and only 10% of 171 farmers who chose Track B received a favorable decision after a hearing."[25]

Many African American farmers felt these accommodations were too little too late. In a *Washington Post* 1999 article, an African American farmer expressed his experience with the USDA and its decision to offer $50,000 to black farmers who had been discriminated against. Bill Hillsman, Jr., who had been denied a loan to purchase a 290-acre farm, appealed the denial. Although the denial was reversed, it was too late for him to purchase the farm. It was eventually sold to a white farmer. "This settlement is not adequate for me. You can't put a price tag on your health, the disrespect, the embarrassment in the community," said Hillsman. Currently, he leases out his 400-acre cotton and peanut farm in Halifax County, North Carolina. "To have risked my life as a state police officer and then be a veteran for this country, then to have to go through this, is enough to make you hate people."[26]

Understandably, emotions ran high because of the history of discrimination within the region and the agency. Insert 6-2 shows another example of an African American farmer's experience with the USDA.

INSERT 6-2 A TALE OF WORKING WITH THE USDA

*Too Little Too Late*

Like many southern farmers, the Johnson brothers were plagued by the relentless drought and low crop yields of the 1970s and 1980s. In 1978, Leon began borrowing money from the Farm Services Agency (FSA)—local arm of the US Dept. of Agriculture (USDA)—for disaster assistance, operations and equipment. It was the worst move he ever made. Despite his large amount of land and collateral—and his uneventful credit history—the Halifax County FSA placed Leon on a

---

[25] Tamara Holmes, "Black Farmers Sue USDA for $20.5 Billion: Mismanaged 1999 Settlement Sparks Class Action Lawsuit," *Black Enterprise Magazine* (December 2004).

[26] Michael Fletcher, "USDA, Black Farmers Settle Bias Lawsuit," *The Washington Post* (6 January 1999).

"supervised" loan account, a time-consuming status that severely limited the farmer's ability to act in his own best interest. "You'd have to go to the farm supplier and have them write out a bill, and then go back to the FSA to sign a check for it," says brother, Milton. Since the checks were made payable to both Leon and his creditors, the farmer lost entire days in the field running between FSA and suppliers—something, the Johnsons later found, area white farmers with less land and worse credit were not required to do.

The ongoing drought and the mounting debt from supervised and chronically delayed loans—such delays are costly for farming due to its seasonal nature—put Leon in a financial bind. In March 1983, the desperate farmer sold a bin of corn outside of his supervised arrangement in order to make payments on his home and tractor. "The USDA sent federal marshals to my home and handcuffed me for selling mortgaged crops," recalled Leon, in a 2001 interview with Insight magazine. He was convicted a year later and spent four months in a federal prison, while FSA foreclosed, selling property and equipment.... The damage can never be undone. Upon the 1999 settlement, Leon, whose health had deteriorated since losing his farm, filed a claim under Track A. He died two years ago without receiving a penny. His brother fared no better. His brother Milton asked for $695,000 under Track B to cover his liquidated property. Seven months before his brother's death, he received a check for $140,000, the full amount of his settled case but an amount less than what he still owes the government from their bad loan practices. "They sold my house, they sold my equipment and everything, and they say I still owe them $162, 000," says Milton, of the debt the USDA could have written off in the settlement. "There ain't no way in the world that can be right."

Source: Damien Jackson, "40 Acres and a Mule, Denied," AlterNet. Posted 17 November 2004. http://www.alternet.org/story/20511/40_acres_and_a_mule,_denied, accessed 20 December 2012.

The Pigford case was reopened after black farmers argued that thousands of additional farmers hadn't been given the opportunity to make claims. The 2008 Farm Bill included a provision that restored those farmers' access to settlement awards. President Obama spoke on the issue in 2010, stating that a deal to accommodate late filers due to no fault of their own would bring "long-ignored claims of African-

American farmers to a rightful conclusion." According to Welch, "Agriculture Secretary Tom Vilsack said the agreement should close a 'sordid chapter' for the department, noting that blacks often lost their land or went deep into debt after being denied loans routinely awarded to white farmers."[27] To address the issue, the 2008 Farm Bill set aside $100 million of relief for the "late filers," and subsequently Congress appropriated another $1.15 billion for what could be as many as 70,000 claims. Yet there are still problems ahead for the black farmers, since they have been charged tremendous legal fees. For example, according to one black farmer interest group, "25 law firms involved in the lawsuit could make between 4.1 percent and 7.4 percent of the total amount appropriated for the settlement, minus the $22.5 million estimated for setting up the apparatus for evaluating claims. That's between $50.3 million and $90.8 million in attorneys' fees."[28]

This treatment of the black farmer has a far-reaching affect on many rural families within the region. Because the black farmer tended to be one of a few economically independent blacks within the Black Belt, his or her struggle is reminiscent of the African American experience in the Black Belt as a whole. The missed opportunity to promote black land ownership in the region weakened African American economic stability there. The lack of land ownership not only had economic ramifications, but also social and political ones. Because of a lack of land ownership, African Americans were subjected to economic dependency, political reprisals, and social exclusion within a region based on a land economy. This still influences the economic stability of many communities in the Black Belt today.

Efforts such as the creation of farming cooperatives and credit unions have been key to African American farm survival. The Federation of Southern Cooperatives (FSC) was founded in 1967, organized by

---

[27] William M. Welch, "Black Farmers Look Forward to USDA Settlement," 25 February 2010 http://www.usatoday.com/news/nation/2010-02-24-black-farmers-usda-settlement_N.htm, accessed 17 December 2012.

[28] Bartholomew Sullivan, "After USDA Discrimination, Black Farmers Await Settlement" 10 August 2011, http://www.independentmail.com/news/2011/aug/10/after-usda-discrimination-black-farmers-await-sett/, accessed 17 December 2012.

representatives from twenty-two cooperatives across the South, and still operates today as it promotes seventy-five cooperatives and credit unions in the South. A group of black farmers and other low-income people started the FSC with the assistance of civil rights organizations such as SNCC, SCLC, CORE, and the NAACP. Several cooperatives and credit unions were organized out of the civil rights movement to promote community-based economic development and business efforts in a strategy to develop an alternate economic structure within the Black Belt region, which had systematically excluded them. Due to economic reprisals of the civil rights movement, a cooperative was established as an alternate source of supply for people to utilize and support the boycott. For example:

> In 1965, a group of Black tenant farmers on several large plantations in north Sumter County, near the town of Panola, joined the Sumter County Movement for Human Rights, a local affiliate of the Southern Christian Leadership Conference (SCLC). These tenants filed suit against the plantation owners for their legal share of the government price support payment on cotton. The tenants won the lawsuit but almost a hundred families were evicted as of January 1, 1966....
>
> Many Black tenants and sharecroppers were being evicted across the South during this period for registering to vote, integrating schools and standing up for their civil rights. Some of the Panola families were forced to leave. One large group went to Chicago and another to Tuskegee but about forty families stayed behind in Sumter County and formed the Panola Land Buying Association (PLBA).[29]

By the late 1960s, a number of these cooperatives, associations, and credit unions that were created out of the civil rights movement were operating across the South. In spring 1966, the Southern Regional Council convened a meeting of about ten of these co-op groups at the Mt. Beulah Center, near Edwards, Mississippi, a mainstay in the civil rights movement. Several groups were represented, including low-income cooperatives such as the Southern Consumers Cooperative, Grand Marie

---

[29] Anonymous, "Federation/LAF History from the 25th Annual Report (1992)," http://www.federationsoutherncoop.com/fschistory/FSC25hist.pdf, accessed 17 December 2012.

Vegetable Producers, SWAFCA, Mid-South Oil Consumers, Greenala Citizens Federal Credit Union, Freedom Quilting Bee, and others from around the Black Belt, resulting in the development of the Federation of Southern Cooperatives. By 1968, the FSC had grown from twenty-two founding members to forty-five member groups encompassing over 10,000 low-income families, and by the second annual meeting there were seventy-two member groups and over 15,000 families. It also grew in prominence as legendary activist Fannie Lou Hamer was the guest speaker for the second annual meeting, and Rev. Ralph David Abernathy was the guest speaker for the third. By then, the federation had grown to 100 cooperative members and had 25,000 low-income families involved.[30] Although this effort is a testament to black self-determination and the quest for self-reliance, it also reveals the importance of white majority progressive efforts in the South such as the Southern Regional Council and its efforts for Southern development. As in the past, these activities are still needed in the region, since they serve as engines for creativity, innovation, and financial support to do needed work.

Table 5.23 below shows current African American cooperatives and credit unions. The work and effort of this federation has allowed for the sustainability of many African American farmers who fear their own extinction: "We're at a point right now where we're all but extinct. This is the last stand for black farmers. If we don't get a victory in the next six months, it's curtains for the black farmer. This is all a part of a conspiracy to get rid of us."[31]

---

[30] Ibid.
[31] *USDA Black Farmers in America.*[**Author? Place? Publisher?**] Darryl Fear, "Protesters Take Over USDA Office in Tennessee. Black Farmers Say Promised Loans Were Mishandled," *The Washington Post*, 2 July 2002.

Table 5.23 Black Cooperatives and Credit Unions in the South

| Location | Agricultural cooperatives | Credit Unions | Other Co-ops | Total |
|---|---|---|---|---|
| AL | 6 | 6 | 6 | 18 |
| MS | 11 | 3 | 3 | 17 |
| GA | 7 | 3 | 4 | 14 |
| SC | 11 | 0 | 3 | 14 |
| OTHER | 15 | 7 | 5 | 27 |
| TOTAL | 50 | 19 | 21 | 90 |

Source: Black Farmers in America, 1865–2000. The Pursuit of Independent Farming and the Role of Cooperatives. USDA RBS 194: 14. Http://www.rurdev.usda.gov/rbs/pub/rr194.pdf, accessed 20 December 2012.

Chapter 6 looks at other industries and economic development policy within the region and a need for unique economic development approaches.

The following counties compose the Black Belt region of the American South as defined by this author.

List of Black Belt Counties (30% African American population, non Metro and 35% rurality)

### Alabama

| | | |
|---|---|---|
| Barbour | Coosa | Macon |
| Bullock | Dallas | Marengo |
| Chambers | Greene | Monroe |
| Choctaw | Hale | Perry |
| Clarke | Henry | Pickens |
| Conecuh | Lowndes | Pike |
| | | Sumter |
| | | Wilcox |

### Arkansas

| | | |
|---|---|---|
| Bradley | Hempstead | Ouachita |
| Chicot | Lafayette | Phillips |

| | | |
|---|---|---|
| Columbia<br>Dallas<br>Desha | Lee<br>Lincoln<br>Monroe<br>Nevada | St. Francis<br>Union<br>Woodruff |

## Florida

Hamilton
Jefferson
Madison

## Georgia

| | | | |
|---|---|---|---|
| Baker<br>Baldwin<br>Ben Hill<br>Brooks<br>Burke<br>Butts<br>Calhoun<br>Candler<br>Clay<br>Cook<br>Crawford<br>Crisp<br>Decatur<br>Dooly<br>Early | Elbert<br>Emanuel<br>Evans<br>Grady<br>Greene<br>Hancock<br>Irwin<br>Jasper<br>Jefferson<br>Jenkins<br>Johnson<br>Lamar<br>Laurens<br>Liberty<br>Lowndes | McIntosh<br>Macon<br>Marion<br>Meriwether<br>Mitchell<br>Monroe<br>Morgan<br>Pulaski<br>Putnam<br>Quitman<br>Randolph<br>Schley<br>Screven<br>Seminole<br>Stewart | Sumter<br>Talbot<br>Taliaferro<br>Taylor<br>Telfair<br>Terrell<br>Thomas<br>Treutlen<br>Troup<br>Turner<br>Twiggs<br>Warren<br>Washington<br>Webster<br>Wheeler<br>Wilcox<br>Wilkinson<br>Worth |

## Louisiana

| | | |
|---|---|---|
| Assumption<br>Bienville<br>Claiborne<br>Concordia<br>DeSoto<br>East Carroll<br>East Feliciana<br>Franklin<br>Iberia<br>Iberville<br>Morehouse<br>Natchitoches | Pointe Coupee<br>Red River<br>Richland<br>St. Helena<br>St. Mary<br>Tensas<br>Washington<br>West Feliciana<br>Winn | |

# Underdevelopment in the Bible Belt

**Mississippi**

| | |
|---|---|
| Adams | Scott |
| Amite | Sharkey |
| Attala | Simpson |
| Benton | Sunflower |
| Bolivar | Tallahatchie |
| Carroll | Tate |
| Chickasaw | Tunica |
| Choctaw | Walthall |
| Claiborne | Warren |
| Clarke | Wayne |
| Clay | Wilkinson |
| Coahoma | Winston |
| Copiah | Yalobusha |
| Covington | Yazoo |
| Franklin | |
| Grenada | |
| Holmes | |
| Humphreys | |
| Issaquena | |
| Jasper | |

**North Carolina**

| | |
|---|---|
| Anson | Jones |
| Beaufort | Lenoir |
| Bertie | Martin |
| Bladen | Northhampton |
| Caswell | Pasquotank |
| Chowan | Pender |
| Columbus | Perquimans |
| Duplin | Person |
| Gates | Sampson |
| Granville | Tyrrell |
| Greene | Vance |
| Halifax | Warren |
| Hertford | Washington |
| Hoke | Wilson |
| Hyde | |

**South Carolina**

| | |
|---|---|
| Abbeville | Lee |
| Allendale | McCormick |
| Bamberg | Marion |
| Barnwell | Marlboro |
| Calhoun | Newberry |
| Chester | Orangeburg |

|  |  |
|---|---|
| Chesterfield<br>Clarendon<br>Colleton<br>Darlington<br>Dillon<br>Fairfield<br>Georgetown<br>Greenwood<br>Hampton<br>Jasper | Saluda<br>Union<br>Williamsburg |

**Tennessee**

Hardeman
Haywood
Lauderdale

## Virginia

|  |  |
|---|---|
| Accomack<br>Amelia<br>Brunswick<br>Buckingham<br>Caroline<br>Charles City<br>Charlotte<br>Cumberland<br>Essex<br>Greensville<br>King and Queen<br>King William<br>Lancaster<br>Lunenburg<br>Mecklenburg<br>Northhampton<br>Prince Edward | Richmond<br>Southhampton<br>Surry<br>Westmoreland |

# 6

## DEVELOPMENT POLICY AND THE REGION'S POLITICAL ECONOMY

As shown in the previous chapter, development of the Black Belt region has not been a high priority in most policy decisions, whether state or national, as "the unique history of the Black Belt has meant that it has suffered the most from the pattern of uneven development in the South." New Deal policies allowed for many new immigrant groups, and, to a larger extent, regions within the country, as well as many native Southern whites, to move up the economic ladder, aided by the federal government. Coupled with a Progressive-Era political ideology, many underprivileged ethnic groups were introduced into the American political and economic landscape. Racism, however, did not allow for these national remedies to solve the economic inequalities within the Black Belt region. Because of the unique racial experience of African Americans, their experience of chattel slavery and lawful segregation and discrimination, there were unusual challenges to overcome that were not experienced by other immigrant groups. This conflicting relationship between African Americans and Southern state and local governments and power structures has proven to be detrimental to the economic success of the rural South and the Black Belt region within.[1]

The patriarchal politics of the region was a direct result of the large black population within and the political and economic dominance by a small group. In addition, the region has also been characterized by four mechanisms of racial discrimination as discussed by Franklin and Resnick, which include,

---

[1] William Falk, Clarence Talley, Bruce Rankin, and Kathleen Little, "Life in the Forgotten South: The Black Belt," in *Forgotten Places: Uneven Development in Rural America*, eds. Thomas Lyson and William Falk (Lawrence: University Press of Kansas, 1993) 60.

—Covenants, statutes and practices, enforced by the apparatus of the state;
—Social preferences of the community that impinge upon the freedom of individuals in the dominant group who refuse or wish not to discriminate against blacks. This can be accomplished by group ostracism...
—Stereotypes derived from the culture and other sources that operate to produce generalizations about black character, work habits, and abilities.
—Market circumstances that make discrimination economically profitable to particular groups whose personal prejudices toward blacks may, in fact, nominal.[2]

Racial discrimination resulted in the formation and maintenance of split labor markets based on race, little funding for public assistance programs, and low funding for public education, as many Black Belt counties continue to have dual school systems separated primarily by race and now class. In addition, state and locally led economic development strategies have tended historically to neglect many of these majority-black rural counties. There is very little evidence that governmental officials have strategically planned to develop these Black Belt counties, and there is evidence that some officials have promoted existing economic development strategies or policies at the expense of the economic welfare of rural blacks within the region.[3]

Southern state politics historically were dominated by Black Belt politics, those areas of the state that were customarily ruled by a powerful landed elite who wielded tremendous power at the national, state, and local level. These powerful groups remained in control due to the maintenance of a political system that suppressed African American political participation and economic advancement. Tactics such as poll taxes, literacy tests, economic reprisals, violence, and lynchings were all

---

[2] Raymond S. Franklin and Solomon Resnik, *The Political Economy of Racism* (New York: Holt, Rinehart, Winston, 1973) 17.
[3] James, C. Cobb, *The Selling of the South: The Southern Crusade for Industrial Development 1936–1990*, 2nd ed. (Chicago: University of Illinois Press, 1993).

employed in the Black Belt region to continue the subordination of rural African Americans and preserve political leadership and economic dominance for a privileged few. Due to the structure of Black Belt society, African American economic dependence on this ruling class was in most areas absolute. New Deal policies, as part of a national economic remedy, should have represented welcomed support for blacks within the Black Belt, but they were not. Due, in part, to a history of exclusive approaches to economic development and economic oppression, the region continues to be one of the poorest regions in the country and with some of the poorest citizens within.

This historical legacy has ill-prepared the residents of the region for new transnational and global trends of the twenty-first century, as discussed by Falk, Tally, Rankin, and Little.

> No part of the United States has been more forgotten or overlooked than the Black Belt. It is a region like no other—here African Americans were first enslaved, were later freed, and remain in large numbers to this day; here political oppression was a way of life for blacks, a historical fact of life that is still slow to change; where poverty in nearly all aspects of life is normal for many people. Lacking substantial public and private efforts to improve Black Belt conditions, the region seems destined slowly to stagnate and decline.

John Fleming, in *Gone Time Lives Anew in Alabama*, points out, "Black leaders will point out that complex problems bedevil the Black Belt, including a changing global economy, the demise of the great plantations, lack of infrastructure, a poor public education system, a weak state government and the allure of a better life elsewhere that drains the area of great minds and leaders." Fleming has identified the major concerns of the region, and in order for the region to improve, these issues must be addressed.[4]

To combat the problems of the region requires lawmakers and community leaders to come up with comprehensive policies for equitable development. These policies must include remedies for complex social

---

[4] Falk et al., "Forgotten South," 73. John Fleming, "Gone Time, Lives Anew in Alabama," *APF Reporter* 22/2 (2002). www.aliciapatterson.org/apf2202?Fleming/Fleming.html, accessed 17 December 2012.

problems that exist within the region and must be inclusive of community participatory decision-making. Most importantly, developing this region forces the issues of race and poverty to be assessed as they relate to the socioeconomic composition and life within the region. This strategy has proven elusive in the past. Even after the civil rights movement, the South successfully negated the discussion or implementation of strategies of economic integration of blacks within Black Belt society. By only focusing on political integration, the region escaped the difficulty of coming up with a strategy to economically integrate rural African Americans into Southern society and economic power.

Traditionally, Southern development strategies have not included dealing with issues of race and class, issues that have always defined the region. James Cobb believes that the South sold itself and continues to sell itself as a place with abundant cheap labor without unions and with communities willing to provide large financial incentive packages. However, Black Belt residents were and are disadvantaged by this strategy, in the past as today. After all, predominately they were often the exploited labor source included in the large incentive packages used to lure industry to the region, ultimately suffering under the prescribed arrangement. For example, tax incentives or abatements often negatively influence rural school systems, since they limit the system's ability to develop and create physical infrastructure and other community amenities due to lower tax collections. The idea of policymakers assessing Southern rural places of persistent poverty in terms of race, place, and opportunity is a must for Black Belt residents to be equipped for twenty-first century opportunities. However, addressing other factors is also plausible in developing a strategy, such as the impact of globalization on regional economies as well as the issue of social exclusion. These could represent new exploration for development policy within this region. Yet the South and the Black Belt within have little tolerance for policies that address race and poverty. State leaders presently are adverse to governmental actions and approaches to economic problems that specifically address impoverished people, particularly minority people. So a region filled with impoverished minority people is a difficult region to acquire legislative remedy, particularly legislative remedy that is not traditional in scope.[5]

The country was forced to look briefly at Southern poverty—something we have not done for a long time—when Hurricane Katrina exposed to the world the ugly face of generational hopelessness, racism, poverty, and neglect in the South. Many of the faces exposed during Hurricane Katrina came from Black Belt areas of the South seeking refuge in the city, but were ill-equipped to participate in opportunities the city provided. There are similar circumstances in the Black Belt when compared to the urban blacks who are trapped in large isolated ghettos. It is hard to imagine that it has been less than fifty years or a little over four decades since blacks were afforded full citizenship consideration for a second time. Yet this historical transformation hardly touched their economic condition.

By assessing historical economic development strategies within the Black Belt region, it is evident that in many instances the opposite of economic development has been planned. Falk and Lyson found,

> Of all the counties in the South, the Black Belt counties are the most vulnerable. The economic bases of these counties are almost entirely slow growth, stagnating, or declaring industries with low wages and little upward occupational mobility especially for women and blacks. The better economic opportunities in these counties have been captured by white males. These counties have been at the end of the line as industries have shifted from higher wage industries North; now many of these industries are bypassing these counties entirely and shifting directly to the Third World. The Black Belt counties also have suffered from grossly inadequate attention to human resources development and the fact that out migration of younger, better educated people has left them with residual populations.[6]

---

[5] James, C. Cobb, *The Selling of the South: The Southern Crusade for Industrial Development 1936–1980* (Baton Rouge: Louisiana State University Press, 1982). James, C. Cobb, *The Selling of the South: The Southern Crusade for Industrial Development 1936–1990*, 2nd ed. (Chicago: University of Illinois Press, 1993).

[6] William Falk and Thomas Lyson, *High Tech, Low Tech, No Tech: Recent Industrial and Occupational Change in the South* (Albany NY: SUNY Press, 1988) x.

## Historical Economic Neglect

Historically, the economic well-being of the blacks within the region has been used as a tool for compromise in efforts to promote a difficult national harmony. Beginning soon after the Civil War and with the freedom of enslaved Africans, it became obvious that the national government would not pursue the socioeconomic or political equality of these new citizens, except for a brief moment. The withdrawal of federal troops from the Southern region after the Hayes-Tilden election began several historical negotiations among levels of government within our federal system in which the well-being of blacks was used as a pawn for a national calm. For decades, the national government has studied the South and its economic condition through various studies and projects. Each of these assessments has revealed that the South as a region is economically weaker than the nation, and the Black Belt South even weaker. As with the nation as a whole, most blacks have fared far worse than most whites in the region during any period, whether during economic success or economic downshift.

In 1938, President Roosevelt declared the South as the nation's number one economic problem. As he assembled twenty-three Southerners from educational institutions, business, and others in Washington D.C., he stated, "It is my conviction," he said "that the South presents right now the Nation's No. 1 economic problem—the nation's problem, not merely the South's.[7]

Within this troubled region resided a significant percentage of what W. E. B. Du Bois called the nation's other problem: "blacks." These two problems—poverty and race—are intrinsically linked in the South due to a lack of economic opportunity and a denial of economic protections by national and state governments, resulting in a socioeconomic quandary. A lack of economic opportunity for blacks provided an abundance of cheap labor and a favorable economic environment for a privileged few, and coupled with a traditionalistic political culture, a society was created in which economic options for blacks were limited. In the past, many

---

[7] Anonymous, "National Affairs: Problem No. 1," *Time Magazine* (18 July 1938) http://www.time.com/time/printout/0,8816,759988,00.html, accessed 17 December 2012.

"voted with their feet" and migrated to Northern cities for greater economic opportunity. "Nearly a half million left the South during or shortly after WWI. Chicago's black population jumped from 44,000 to 110,000 between 1910 and 1920 while Cleveland's more than quadrupled rising from 8,000 to 34,000." Yet the problems created by this distinctly regional predicament soon revealed a greater national problem as the northern and southern urban ghettos filled with poor, uneducated, and unskilled blacks, former residents of the Black Belt, looking for hope and opportunity.[8]

*No Rural Development Policy*

Those left behind continued to reside in a region with little development, and the lack of a national political focus on America's rural economies resulted in continued underdevelopment, high unemployment, and high poverty as well as an exodus from these communities of educated and middle-income residents. This trend is immense in the Black Belt region, as economic and social opportunities are few. In fact, nationally there has not been a comprehensive rural development policy initiated by the federal government since 1972, and this has put an unrealistic strain on states to reinvigorate these stagnant rural places or let them die. Many argue that due to dwindling populations within rural areas, development policy for these places should not be a high priority for national or state governments. Yet because of our participation in the new global, knowledge-based economy and the independence of not having to have businesses or individuals located in a certain place thanks to advanced technology, there should be a real effort on the part of national and state policymakers to ensure that rural communities play an active role in the new economy. Through education and technology, these communities can and should be linked as active participants in this new global economy with the enormous opportunity provided. This is more important than ever as society becomes more technologically advanced and can occur through broadband capabilities. According to John Horrigan, "Broadband is a distance killer, which can especially help rural

---

[8] August Meier and Elliot Rudwick, *From Plantation to Ghetto,* 3rd ed. (New York: Hill and Wang, 1976) 235.

Americans.... Broadband is not just an information source for news and civic matters, but it's also a pathway to participation."

Yet this transition to broadband has been difficult for many rural places.

> For the nation that pioneered the Internet, extending fast connections to small towns and rural areas has proved a daunting challenge. Carriers are loath to build networks where they can't sell service at a profit, and since 2003 more than $1.2 billion in federal loans aimed at helping private carriers serve remote areas has addressed only the most extreme cases. According to a study by the Pew Internet & American Life Project...only 38% of rural American households have access to high-speed Internet connections. That's an improvement from 15% in 2005, but it pales in comparison with 57% and 60% for city and suburb dwellers, respectively.[9]

In addition, rural and low-income communities were the last to get telecommunications infrastructure, and more than 60 percent of the zip codes in the Mississippi River Delta areas of Mississippi, Louisiana, and Arkansas still have no broadband provider well into the twenty-first century.[10]

This lack of technological infrastructure is exacerbated as rural communities tend to house more of the nation's persistently impoverished counties than metro areas around the country. Presently, 340 of 386 persistently poor counties in the United States (counties with 20 percent of their residents living in poverty over the past 30 years) were also defined as nonmetro counties or rural counties.

> From 1997 through 2003, over 1.5 million rural workers lost their jobs due to fundamental changes in industries that have historically been the mainstay of the rural economy. The rate of this job loss is increasing as firms seek to lower their costs through automation and the use of cheaper

---

[9] Arik Hesseldahl, "Bringing Broadband to Rural America," (18 September 2008). http://www.businessweek.com/technology/content/sep2008/tc20080917_797892.htm, accessed 17 December 2012.

[10] "Report Reveals Divisions between Rural, Urban South," (2 October 2002) http://southeastfarmpress.com/report-reveals-divisions-between-rural-urban-south, accessed 17 December 2012.

labor outside the U.S. In rural America, workers in manufacturing were hardest hit—from 2001 to 2003, one in ten displaced workers were employed in manufacturing. Looking ahead, the data show that workers with only a high school education, regardless of the industry in which they work, are especially vulnerable.[11]

When focusing on the dire situation that many rural communities find themselves, how can they play a role in the twenty-first century economy under such constraints? How do they develop their communities successfully while addressing the unique circumstances provided them? What development strategies would be most successful in the rural Black Belt region, with its unusual sociopolitical and economic circumstances?[12]

*Economic Development Strategy*

Traditionally, there have been two types of policy strategies designed for rural development. These strategies have been defined by Mark Drabenstott and Katherine Sheaff (2002) as "place-based development policy" and "people-based development policy." Place-based development policy focuses specifically on building up the physical infrastructure of a geographic area. The logic behind this kind of economic development policy is to build up the physical environment of an area and open it up to trade and commerce more effectively. The ability to connect rural areas to urban areas and aid in business success through industrial recruitment, the deliverance of goods, and the ability of citizens to travel to urban centers for employment and pleasure are all critical to the development and vitality of rural areas. People-based development policy is based on investment in the people of the region, promoting the human capital of the citizens. This policy initiates programs dedicated to improving the skills, education level, and quality

---

[11] Amy Glasmeier and Priscilla Salant, "Low-Skill Workers in Rural America Face Permanent Job Loss" (1 April 2006), policy brief 2, http://www.carseyinstitute.unh.edu/publications/PB_displacedworkers_06.pdf, accessed 17 December 2012.

[12] Dean Jolliffe, "Persistent Poverty Is More Pervasive in Nonmetro Counties," *Amber Waves* (September 2004). From Rural Poverty at a Glance. RDRR-100, USDA/ERS, 2004, www.ageconsearch.umn.edu/bitstream/129736/2/findings_ra_persistent.pdf, accessed 21 December 2012.

of life of the residents. Historically, this country has focused most of its few economic development efforts in rural America under the place-based development policy category. This effort was needed to provide these communities with the necessary physical infrastructure to develop their economies and make life better for the residents. However, little effort has been made to aid in the development of the residents themselves. Most of these efforts revolve around traditional educational structures.[13]

Most rural development policy physically changed rural America. Efforts such as the Rural Electrification Act of 1936 created the Rural Electrification Agency (REA), which provided loans to companies for electrical access to rural areas. By 1949, it also provided telephone service to rural areas. Rural economic development was also revisited with the Area Redevelopment Act of 1961, which focused on both cities and rural areas with chronic unemployment. This legislation promoted economic capabilities by providing features such as rural development loans, physical infrastructure loans, and debt forgiveness. Another rural development effort occurred with the passage of the Appalachian Regional Development Act of 1965, which established the Appalachian Regional Commission to focus on place-based development practices from a regional perspective, such as the Appalachian Regional Commission and the region's highway projects. As a result, "The Appalachian Development Highway System quickly became the cornerstone of the agency's strategy. The commission has spent nearly two-thirds of its money—$10.4 billion, after accounting for inflation—on the 3,025-mile network of roads. About 600 miles remain to be completed during the next 20 years."[14] However, this approach has some critics, as one article found that "after nearly 40 years and almost $10 billion in federal spending, only eight of the 410 counties in Appalachia

---

[13] Mark Drabenstott and Katherine H. Sheaff, "The New Power of Regions: A Policy Focus for Rural America," *Main Street Economists* (June 2002), http://www.kc.frb.org/publicat/mse/mse_0602.pdf, accessed 21 December 2012.

[14] Mark Ferenchik and Jill Riepenhoff, "Mountain Money, Federal Tax Dollars Miss the Mark in Core Appalachia," *Columbus* (OH) *Dispatch*, 26 September 1999, http://www.sullivan-county.com/info/dispatch/moun_money.htm, accessed 21 December 2012.

are equal to or better than the national average on indicators such as per-capita income, poverty and unemployment rates." Yet according to ARC chairwoman Anne Pope at the time, "the number of counties in the region that are considered 'distressed' have [sic] been reduced from 223 to 91 since 1965. Those are counties with poverty and unemployment rates that are at least one-and-a-half times the national average."[15]

Again, as with most rural economic development efforts, the main focus of the ARC was physical infrastructure. Finally, the Rural Development Act of 1972 authorized $500 million per year for rural development loans focusing on physical infrastructure and public works projects. However, there has not been a comprehensive policy on rural development since this act, and there have been tremendous changes since then in the world economy. Most rural development efforts are housed in the Department of Agriculture within the rural development title of the Farm Bill. Yet few rely on agricultural jobs, and many of the manufacturing opportunities rural residents depended on for work in the past are no longer available. The lack of rural development policy, coupled with an antiquated, general, broad-sweeping, nationalistic approach to economic policy has resulted in policymakers failing to properly develop rural economies or focus on regional approaches to development. In the 1990s, the Delta Regional Authority was created to address a lack of development in the Delta region of the Black Belt, but it has been assessed by many as inadequate in facing the challenges of the region because it is similar to the ARC in development approach.

Rural America has been mostly hidden for the last three decades in general national assessments of the economy, according to Drabenstott and Sheaff. However, the importance of regions and regional differences when analyzing the economic conditions of the nation is very important to rural development. The necessity of empowering regions has reengaged some lawmakers in a needed dialogue about rural areas and their economic well-being. It is imperative that more focus be placed on the concept of region, particularly if we are to change economic

---

[15] Anonymous, "Is Agency's Work to End Appalachian Poverty Done?," Associated Press, 24 May 2004. http://www.sullivan-county.com/nf0/june_2004/arc.htm, accessed 17 December 2012.

conditions within the Black Belt. We must look at the region as a whole, engage in strategic planning, and prescribe remedy that is reflective of the uniqueness of the Black Belt.[16]

This region has been hit very hard in the current economic downturn, and tables 6.0 and 6.1 show the quarterly unemployment rates for the Southern states overall as well as the rate for blacks. They also highlight the disproportionate impact the recession has had on blacks within the region.

Table 6.0 Overall Unemployment Rate by State and Quarter, 2007–2010

|    | 2007 Q4 | 2008 Q1 | 2008 Q2 | 2008 Q3 | 2008 Q4 | 2009 Q1 | 2009 Q2 | 2009 Q3 | 2009 Q4 | 2010 Q1 | 2010 Q2 | 2010 Q3 | 2010 Q4 | 2010 average |
|----|---------|---------|---------|---------|---------|---------|---------|---------|---------|---------|---------|---------|---------|--------------|
| AL | 3.7 | 4.0 | 4.5 | 5.2 | 6.5 | 8.4 | 9.7 | 10.3 | 10.4 | 10.2 | 9.5 | 9.1 | 9.1 | 9.5 |
| AR | 5.2 | 4.9 | 4.9 | 5.4 | 6.0 | 6.8 | 7.3 | 7.6 | 7.8 | 8.0 | 7.8 | 7.8 | 7.9 | 7.9 |
| DE | 3.7 | 3.9 | 4.4 | 5.3 | 6.2 | 7.3 | 8.0 | 8.2 | 8.6 | 8.7 | 8.4 | 8.3 | 8.4 | 8.5 |
| FL | 4.6 | 5.0 | 5.7 | 6.6 | 7.7 | 9.0 | 10.0 | 10.6 | 11.1 | 11.3 | 11.3 | 11.6 | 11.9 | 11.5 |
| GA | 5.0 | 5.3 | 5.8 | 6.6 | 7.6 | 8.8 | 9.6 | 10.2 | 10.4 | 10.3 | 10.0 | 10.2 | 10.4 | 10.2 |
| LA | 3.7 | 3.8 | 3.9 | 4.6 | 5.3 | 5.8 | 6.6 | 7.0 | 7.1 | 7.1 | 7.3 | 7.7 | 7.7 | 7.5 |
| MD | 3.6 | 3.6 | 4.0 | 4.7 | 5.5 | 6.5 | 7.1 | 7.4 | 7.6 | 7.6 | 7.4 | 7.4 | 7.4 | 7.5 |
| MS | 6.1 | 6.0 | 6.6 | 7.1 | 7.5 | 8.6 | 9.4 | 9.9 | 10.7 | 10.9 | 10.4 | 10.1 | 10.2 | 10.4 |
| NC | 4.9 | 5.1 | 5.7 | 6.6 | 7.9 | 9.8 | 10.9 | 11.0 | 11.2 | 11.4 | 10.8 | 10.1 | 9.8 | 10.5 |
| SC | 5.6 | 5.5 | 6.0 | 7.1 | 8.6 | 10.4 | 11.5 | 11.7 | 11.8 | 11.6 | 11.2 | 11.0 | 10.9 | 11.2 |
| TN | 5.3 | 5.6 | 6.2 | 6.9 | 7.9 | 9.6 | 10.7 | 10.8 | 10.5 | 10.3 | 9.8 | 9.4 | 9.4 | 9.7 |
| TX | 4.4 | 4.4 | 4.6 | 5.1 | 5.7 | 6.7 | 7.5 | 7.9 | 8.1 | 8.2 | 8.1 | 8.2 | 8.3 | 8.2 |
| VA | 3.2 | 3.3 | 3.7 | 4.1 | 4.9 | 6.1 | 6.9 | 7.1 | 7.1 | 7.2 | 7.0 | 6.8 | 6.6 | 6.9 |
| US | 4.8% | 5.0% | 5.3% | 6.0% | 6.9% | 8.2% | 9.3% | 9.7% | 10.0% | 9.7% | 9.6% | 9.6% | 9.6% | 9.6% |

Source: Algernon Austin "Depressed States Unemployment rate near 20% for some groups: Economic Policy Institute Policy Brief #299 20 April 2011, http://www.epi.org/page/-/IssueBrief299.pdf?nocdn=1, accessed 20 December 2012.

---

[16] Mark Drabenstott and Katherine H. Sheaff, "The New Power of Regions: A Policy Focus for Rural America." *Main Street Economists.* Center for the Study of Rural America. Federal Reserve Bank of Kansas City, http://www.kc.frb.org/publicat/mse/mse_0602.pdf, accessed 21 December 2012.

Underdevelopment in the Bible Belt

Table 6.1 Quarterly African American Unemployment
Rates by State* 2007–2010

|    | 2007 Q4 | 2008 Q1 | 2008 Q2 | 2008 Q3 | 2008 Q4 | 2009 Q1 | 2009 Q2 | 2009 Q3 | 2009 Q4 | 2010 Q1 | 2010 Q2 | 2010 Q3 | 2010 Q4 | 2010 average |
|----|---------|---------|---------|---------|---------|---------|---------|---------|---------|---------|---------|---------|---------|--------------|
| AL | 5.3 | 6.2 | 8.3 | 9.4 | 11.2 | 15.2 | 17.5 | 17.9 | 17.5 | 15.1 | 13.3 | 14.8 | 17.0 | 15.1 |
| AR | 8.8 | 10.3 | 9.3 | 10.3 | 10.8 | 12.3 | 13.6 | 13.6 | 13.8 | 13.6 | 15.8 | 16.1 | 14.4 | 15.0 |
| DE | 5.1 | 7.1 | 8.4 | 7.3 | 8.8 | 10.6 | 12.6 | 13.4 | 12.1 | 11.5 | 12.0 | 13.5 | 12.0 | 12.2 |
| FL | 6.1 | 7.0 | 7.5 | 9.3 | 11.0 | 12.7 | 14.4 | 15.2 | 16.9 | 18.2 | 18.2 | 17.4 | 17.1 | 17.7 |
| GA | 8.2 | 8.8 | 10.0 | 10.8 | 11.3 | 11.8 | 13.6 | 15.6 | 15.5 | 15.9 | 15.8 | 15.7 | 15.5 | 15.7 |
| LA | 8.0 | 7.3 | 6.8 | 8.1 | 10.6 | 11.3 | 10.8 | 10.4 | 9.4 | 10.2 | 11.7 | 11.6 | 11.7 | 11.3 |
| MD | 5.8 | 5.7 | 5.2 | 6.2 | 7.3 | 7.5 | 8.3 | 10.7 | 11.0 | 9.6 | 9.7 | 11.5 | 12.2 | 10.7 |
| MS | 10.7 | 12.0 | 11.5 | 11.6 | 12.8 | 13.1 | 12.9 | 13.7 | 17.8 | 20.0 | 17.7 | 16.9 | 17.3 | 18.0 |
| NC | 8.1 | 7.2 | 7.3 | 8.7 | 10.8 | 14.0 | 16.1 | 14.3 | 14.9 | 17.6 | 16.8 | 16.9 | 17.5 | 17.2 |
| SC | 10.8 | 9.8 | 9.8 | 11.5 | 12.6 | 15.1 | 17.7 | 20.6 | 20.7 | 17.5 | 18.0 | 20.2 | 18.7 | 18.6 |
| TN | 9.4 | 10.7 | 10.2 | 10.6 | 12.6 | 14.5 | 14.2 | 14.0 | 17.2 | 18.0 | 15.9 | 15.5 | 14.2 | 15.9 |
| TX | 8.1 | 9.4 | 10.5 | 10.5 | 10.4 | 10.7 | 12.8 | 13.6 | 12.0 | 12.9 | 14.8 | 14.4 | 12.4 | 13.6 |
| VA | 5.1 | 5.2 | 6.3 | 7.0 | 7.0 | 9.3 | 11.2 | 11.7 | 12.1 | 11.1 | 10.1 | 9.5 | 10.6 | 10.3 |
| US | 8.6 | 8.7 | 9.0 | 10.8 | 12.2 | 13.2 | 14.6 | 15.5 | 16.0 | 15.6 | 15.5 | 16.1 | 16.4 | 15.9 |

Source: Algernon Austin "Depressed States Unemployment rate near 20% for some groups: Economic Policy Institute Policy Brief #299 20 April 2011, http://www.epi.org/page/-/IssueBrief299.pdf?nocdn=1, accessed 20 December 2012. These estimates do not include black Hispanics.

As shown by comparing tables 6.1 and 6.2, blacks within the South have been severely influenced by the current recession. The twentieth century created several national policy remedies to combat economic inequality and to place economic equality on the national agenda. Yet the political culture of the Black Belt found it difficult to implement strategies of change. Governmental policies created in an effort to provide opportunities for improvement within the region have met many Black Belt institutional barriers that have hindered the implementation of many of these policies and the region's economic progress.

Previous research has found that national policies formulated to aid the economic conditions of the South in the twentieth century were never implemented equitably in the Black Belt region. For example, the Agricultural Adjustment Act of 1933 aided in the paternalistic dependence on whites by many rural blacks, which kept the stringent class structure of the Black Belt South in place. Instead of providing needed resources directly to black share croppers who needed economic assistance during the depression, this act instead gave landlords the federal monies to distribute to the tenants on their land as they saw fit.

This left tenants vulnerable to the whims of the landowners and the power structure.

In many instances, the sharecroppers never saw any relief, according to Meier and Rudwick. "As part of its general program for raising farm prices, the Agricultural Adjustment Administration paid farmers to restrict their acreage. Supposedly, tenant farmers were to receive a share of this money, but in practice they usually did not. In fact, because of acreage reduction, plantation owners had less need for workers. Many sharecroppers were forced off land and they moved to the urban ghettos."[17]

There were several discriminatory practices in the implementation of the New Deal policy on the local level within the South, including landlords who didn't distribute payments to lawful recipients, the partial distribution of payments, forcible theft of deserved payments, and eviction. Goldfield found the implementation of this policy resulted in about one-third of sharecroppers being evicted. Herein lies the problem of the Black Belt, today and in the past. The proposed recipients of progressive policy are often left out of the decision-making arena and are therefore unable to use help options for their benefit. If there had been some empowerment of the Black Belt residents to include them in the decisions of how monies would be distributed, or if there had been some assessment of the culture of the South, which was well-known, maybe the outcome could have been different. Yet just as during Reconstruction, the national government was unwilling to ensure adequate implementation of national policy, so rural blacks within the region suffered as a result.[18]

Although New Deal policies aimed to aid economic progress were quite successful for some, they were not for many. Many activities actually hindered African American progress in the South. As wages increased, previously unattractive jobs to white Southerners became

---

[17] Meier and Rudwick, *From Plantation to Ghetto*, 261.
[18] David R. Goldfield, *Black, White, and Southern Race Relations and Southern Culture 1940 to the Present* (Baton Rouge: Louisiana State University Press, 1990). Paul Mertz, *New Deal Policy and Southern Rural Poverty (*Baton Rouge: Louisiana State University Press, 1978).

more attractive at the cost of black employment. Several state officials were unwilling to participate in the New Deal policies if they required the inclusion of African Americans. Governor Talmadge of Georgia, for example, required that the federal government implement these policies in Georgia on its own with no help from the state. In fact, politicians such as Talmadge created very successful careers of fighting national measures that could promote opportunity for blacks and instead used these measures to flame racial discord and hatred by promoting the measures as "handouts to unworthy recipients" or national government's assault on states' rights. All of this occurred at the expense of the development of the Black Belt region and the development of its people.[19]

Many of the state official's constituents were concerned that blacks were benefiting unfairly from the programs and that many of these programs were taking "their" laborers from them by providing them wages the white landowners could not or would not provide. Some agencies such as the Civil Works Administration (CWA), which focused on public works projects, and the Works Progress Administration (WPA) tried to accommodate the region's rigid class structure by being very accepting of local culture, including adherence to a split-race workforce. However, the willingness of the national government to accept local discriminatory employment practices reveals how little economic protection African Americans had. Most of the New Deal policies were administered on the state and local level, which provided opportunities for racial discrimination and unequal implementation.

Instead of combating discriminatory practices within the region, many government agencies actually assisted the discrimination with lasting influence. According to Mertz, "In agreements with banks and other lending institutions, the Federal Housing Administration refused to guarantee mortgages on homes purchased by blacks in white communities. The United States Housing Authority, while providing public housing for many black families, financed separate projects for the two races." This allowed for several negative influences on black life. First, it provided African Americans with a clear understanding that the

---

[19] Mertz, *New Deal Policy*, 1978.

American political system, regardless of level, whether national, state, or local, would not treat them equitably. Second, it resulted in African Americans being relegated to communities with less overall property value, thereby influencing the economic independence and well-being of the group. It also created all-black impoverished enclaves of public housing that were then targeted for unique and discriminatory criminal justice and educational policies. These actions were unfortunately underwritten and supported by national governmental policies. This discrimination influenced all public sectors, particularly agriculture, which was and is a very important sector in the Black Belt region.[20]

Although significant in founding and developing the Black Belt economy, farming and agriculture were soon challenged for leadership of the Southern economy by other industries. These other development factors within the region included the textile and manufacturing industry.

*Split Labor Markets and Race*

After the Civil War, textile mills became a major influence in the Southern economy. However, early on, most often African Americans were not allowed to work in these Southern textile mills except for in the harshest, most dangerous positions. It has been noted that it was strategically planned for textile mills in the agricultural Black Belt to avoid competing with the Black Belt plantations for workers. In addition, the thought of African American males working in close proximity with white women went against the social norms of the Black Belt. Again, this decision was made by those in power, at the economic expense of the black masses of the Black Belt region. This also reinforced the racial and economic class structures of the South. African Americans were subjugated to the worst jobs in the region, and because of the lack of education and training of the residents, only low-wage, low-skilled jobs could locate there.

---

[20] Ibid.

## Underdevelopment in the Bible Belt

The exclusion of African Americans from textile production jobs—which had pervaded the industry since the late nineteenth century—ended in the 1960s and 1970s, and blacks entered the mills in large numbers, filling production positions that had previously been occupied by whites only." According to David R. Goldfield, "In South Carolina, for example, less than 5 percent of mill employees were black in 1964; by 1976, nearly one in three textile workers in the state was black" African Americans came into southern textile mills at a much faster pace than they came into other southern industries, and between 1960 and 1969 black employment in textile production increased four times faster than the national average for all manufacturing. By 1978 minorities held 18 percent of all American manufacturing jobs but around 25 percent of all production jobs in the southern textile industry.[21]

According to Thompson, the lack of innovation in the Black Belt can be attributed to the filtering-down theory. This theory states that industries are cyclical, with large high-tech businesses being the beginning of the industrial cycle and low-wage, low-skill industries being at the end of the cycle. For example, textile mills would be considered industries at the end of the cycle. Unfortunately, as in the past, most industries at the end of an industrial cycle find the Black Belt attractive and continue to do so. According to Falk and Lyson, "Of the nearly 400,000 new high-tech jobs added to the southern economy between 1977 and 1981…the rural white counties received only about 21,000 of these new jobs while the Black Belt received a meager 1,500."[22]

This data shows the neglect of the region in economic development plans of the Southern states and the importance of innovative education and training within the Black Belt region. Without the proper training,

---

[21] Wilber Thompson, *A Preface to Urban Economics* (Baltimore MD: John Hopkins Press, 1965). Timothy Minchin, "Black Activism, the 1964 Civil Rights Act, and the Racial Integration of the Southern Textile Industry," *The Journal of Southern History* 65/4 (November 1999): 810. William Falk and Thomas Lyson, *High Tech, Low Tech, No Tech, Recent Industrial and Occupational Change in the South* (Albany NY: SUNY Press, 1988).
[22] Falk and Lyson, *High Tech, Low Tech*, 45.

Black Belt residents are not equipped to take advantage of present-day opportunities nor are they equipped to work new high-tech jobs that are being created in the twenty-first-century economy. As a result, to entice any industry into the region, the community involved must provide unreasonable incentives to be competitive. These incentives are often at the expense of developing a strong local economy based on entrepreneurship and diversified industry. This strategy has a long history in the Black Belt region. Beginning with Mississippi's statewide "Balance Agriculture with Industry program" (BAWI), in 1937, which concentrated on industry recruitment, with the promise of cheap labor, tax credits, and other incentives, the South formed an interesting relationship with industry, mostly at the expense of its poorest citizens. Southern states were and are very good to industry with its "right to work" laws, allowing workers who work in plants that are unionized to have the option of not joining the union, even if the membership will benefit from the union activity, as well as, keeping taxation low and environmental regulations lax. But what is the ultimate price of this relationship? Table 6.2 shows the percentage of workers within the region in unions.

Table 6.2 Labor Union Membership as a Percentage of Nonagricultural Workers

| State/Region | 1964 (percentage) | 1984 (percentage) | 2002 (percentage) |
|---|---|---|---|
| All States | 29.3 | 19.1 | 13.2 |
| Confederacy | 14.75 | 10.0 | 6.3 |
| Alabama | 21.1 | 15.2 | 8.9 |
| Arkansas | 15.0 | 10.0 | 5.9 |
| Florida | 14.0 | 9.6 | 5.7 |
| Georgia | 11.9 | 10.3 | 6.0 |
| Kentucky | 25.0 | 17.3 | 10.0 |
| Louisiana | 18.1 | 11.1 | 8.1 |
| Mississippi | 15.4 | 9.7 | 6.1 |
| North Carolina | 8.4 | 7.5 | 3.2 |
| Oklahoma | 15.8 | 10.4 | 8.9 |
| South Carolina | 7.0 | 4.2 | 4.9 |
| Tennessee | 22.1 | 13.5 | 9.0 |
| Texas | 13.5 | 8.0 | 5.1 |
| Virginia | 15.8 | 10.8 | 5.9 |

Underdevelopment in the Bible Belt

Source: Alfred E. Eckes, "The South and Economic Globalization, 1950 to the Future," from *Globalization and the American South*, edited by James C. Cobb and William Stueck (Athens: University of Georgia Press, 2005) 43.

Union membership is just one indication of the pro-business environment of the region, and the strategy of anti-union has often been utilized as an important factor in Southern economic development strategies. Lyson stated that Southern states used tax-exempt industrial revenue bonds in the beginning to attract industry, yet they soon added free land, money, and other services such as extending sewage and water lines, roads, and railroad to industrial sites. In addition, tax breaks were given to businesses willing to locate in the South, yet these tax cuts often resulted in lower-level public services in a region that was in desperate need. According to Lyson, five southern states, Alabama, Kentucky, Louisiana, Mississippi, and South Carolina, provided tax exemptions worth over $140 million dollars during the late 1950s early 1960s.[23]

Cobb states,

> The South may have become the nation's most globalized region. It attracted more than half the foreign businesses drawn to the United States in the 1990s, and one in eight manufacturing workers in the South gets his or her paycheck from a foreign employer.... The South has become the apple of the international industrialist's eye primarily because of the continued willingness of its political leaders to serve up the huge subsidies and the more than ample pool of relatively cheap, overwhelmingly nonunion labor that have long been the cornerstone of its industrial development strategy.

Yet the tax breaks and the incentives provided industry are often at the expense of tax resources needed to develop the community and fund public education. Even when an industry locates within the region, there is no guarantee that the Black Belt masses will benefit from the location of the business. For examples, many Black Belt residents may not qualify for the positions available because of educational or skill deficiencies. As a result, many of the workers hired come from outside of the Black Belt region. Therefore, those who are employed may or may not

---

[23] Thomas Lyson, *Two Sides to the Sunbelt: The Growing Divergence between the Rural and Urban South* (New York: Praeger, 1989).

come from or reside in the community that provided the tax breaks and incentives in the first place. Many feeder or supplier companies who supply the larger industry may also receive significant tax breaks but may or may not remain in the location after the incentive-period concludes.[24]

During the 1970s and 1980s, several incentives were used to recruit industry to the South, as shown in Table. 6.3, including "right to work" laws, bond financing, and other elements.

Table 6.3 Selected Development Incentives Available in Eleven Southern States

|  | Year | AL | AR | FL | GA | KY | LA | MS | NC | SC | TN | VA |
|---|---|---|---|---|---|---|---|---|---|---|---|---|
| State Sponsored Industrial Authority | 1970 | X | X | X |  | X | X | X | X | X |  | X |
| State Sponsored Industrial Authority | 1984 | X | X |  |  | X | X | X |  | X |  | X |
| City or County Revenue Bond Financing | 1970 | X | X | X | X | X | X | X | X | X | X | X |
| City or County Revenue Bond Financing | 1984 | X | X | X | X | X | X | X | X | X | X | X |
| State Loans for Building Construction | 1970 |  |  |  |  | X | X |  |  |  |  |  |
| State Loans for Building Construction | 1984 |  |  | X |  | X | X | X |  |  |  |  |
| Corporate Income Tax Exemption | 1970 | X |  | X |  |  | X |  |  |  |  |  |
| Corporate Income Tax Exemption | 1984 | X | X | X |  |  | X |  |  |  |  |  |
| State Right to Work Law | 1970 | X | X | X | X |  |  | X | X | X | X | X |
| State Right to Work Law | 1984 | X | X | X | X |  |  | X | X | X | X | X |
| City or County Free Land to Industry | 1970 |  |  |  |  |  | X | X |  | X |  |  |

[24] James Cobb, "Beyond the 'Y'all Wall': The American South Goes Global" in *Globalization and the American South*, eds. James Cobb and William Stueck (Athens: University of Georgia Press, 2005) 1.

| | | | | | | | | | | | |
|---|---|---|---|---|---|---|---|---|---|---|---|
| City or County Free Land to Industry | 1984 | X | X | | | X | X | | X | | | |
| State Recruiting/Screening of Industry Employees | 1970 | X | X | X | X | X | X | X | X | X | X | X |
| State Recruiting/Screening of Industry Employees | 1984 | X | X | X | X | X | X | X | X | X | X | X |
| State Program to Promote Research and Development | 1970 | X | X | X | X | X | X | X | X | X | X | |
| State Program to Promote Research and Development | 1984 | X | X | X | X | | X | X | X | X | X | X |
| Tax Exemption for Research Development Activities | 1970 | | | | | | | X | | | | |
| Tax Exemption for Research Development Activities | 1984 | X | | X | | X | X | | X | | X | |

Source: Thomas Lyson, *Two Sides to the Sunbelt: The Growing Divergence between the Rural and Urban South* (New York: Praeger, 1989). Data from Site Selection Handbook, Geo-Political Index, 29/3 (September 1984) Conway Data Incorporated. 1970 Site Selection Handbook, vol. 2. Conway Research Inc., Atlanta.

In fact, the South's economic development strategy has been quite expensive. Mercedes was given a subsidy of $253 million to locate a plant in Alabama, and the 1,500 jobs may have cost the state in excess of $150,000 a piece. Cobb found that "Alabama has invested an estimated total of $874 million in subsidizing Mercedes, Honda, and the Korean auto manufacturer Hyundai."[25] As a result, more than 63,000 applications were submitted for less than 1,600 jobs at $167,000 to $200,000 each. Although Mercedes's starting wage was well above the state average for manufacturing, "it was still 30 percent lower than Germany even without the additional benefits." According to Cobb, these numbers raise the

---

[25] *Globalization and the American South*, eds. James Cobb and William Stueck (Athens: University of Georgia Press, 2005) 1–2.

question of whether the money spent actually benefited the residents of the state and communities that paid for the incentives. How many of those hired by Mercedes, Honda, and Hyundai came from the communities where the automotive giants are located? Could the money spent in incentives have been used to develop business from within the region? Or could money be invested in education to ensure that the residents from which the companies locate could be successful in gaining employment there? Some have argued that these strategies have been successful and these jobs are the foundation for the new Southern economy. The Alabama Development Office supports the expensive incentive packages by saying through these companies, Alabama's economy is thriving. "During the past four years, almost one half of the announced investment in the state and almost one third of the announced jobs were automotive-related."[26]

Yet not everyone has participated in these successes. For example, although the state of Alabama has been successful in attracting international companies with large tax abatements and other incentives, they have not connected with the masses of the unemployed in the Alabama Black Belt. Mercedes began production in 1997, and just one Mercedes supplier located in the Black Belt, that being tire and wheel assembly, which located in Greene County in the town of Boligee. It hired just thirty workers and left in 2001 for Birmingham, wanting to be closer to the new Honda plant east of the city. Bill Taylor, head of Mercedes in Alabama, stated that the problem with companies locating within the Black Belt is the low educational attainment and skill set within the region.[27]

Former governor Riley of Alabama was dedicated to improving the economics of the Black Belt region of his state and took a multifaceted approach to the effort. He developed the Black Belt Commission, in

---

[26] "The Drive to Move South: The Growing Role of the Automobile industry in the Southern Legislative Conference Economies" (November 2003) The Council of State Governments. http://www.slcatlanta.org/Publications/EconDev/TheDriveToMoveSouth.pdf, accessed 17 December 2012.

[27] John Archibald and Jeff Hansen, "Life Is Short, Prosperity Is Long Gone," *The Birmingham* (AL) *News*, 12 May 2002. http://www.al.com/specialreport/birmingham-news/index.ssf?blackbelt/blackbelt1.html, accessed 17 December 2012.

Underdevelopment in the Bible Belt

2005, to address issues of health, education, workforce development, and the economic development of the Alabama Black Belt. According to Margaret Bentley, chairwoman of the commission, the commission has recruited 1,400 jobs to the Black Belt and unemployment is down 6 percent.[28]

Yet this small number of jobs brought to the Black Belt is a miniscule piece of the development strategy for the state and the Black Belt as a whole. Even with these efforts, Southern states have been ranked low for industry competitiveness. Table 6.4 shows the ranking of these stated between 2005 and 2010, revealing low rankings for many of these states.

Table 6.4 BHI State Competitiveness Rankings for Southern States

| State | 2010 | 2009 | 2008 | 2007 | 2006 | 2005 |
|---|---|---|---|---|---|---|
| AL | 48 | 50 | 48 | 48 | 47 | 43 |
| AR | 38 | 38 | 43 | 46 | 6 | 8 |
| DE | 2 | 20 | 19 | 27 | 21 | 23 |
| FL | 12 | 25 | 32 | 33 | 27 | 28 |
| GA | 46 | 28 | 37 | 31 | 30 | 27 |
| LA | 39 | 41 | 49 | 50 | 48 | 50 |
| MD | 26 | 31 | 28 | 23 | 23 | 10 |
| MS | 50 | 49 | 50 | 49 | 50 | 49 |
| NC | 21 | 30 | 27 | 30 | 26 | 25 |
| SC | 42 | 45 | 46 | 42 | 37 | 29 |
| TN | 44 | 46 | 41 | 37 | 41 | 37 |
| TX | 25 | 24 | 23 | 20 | 22 | 20 |
| VA | 11 | 13 | 16 | 16 | 10 | 11 |

Source: "Tenth Annual State Competitiveness Report," Beacon Hill Institute, Suffolk University, 2010 http://www.beaconhill.org/Compete-10/Compete2010State.pdf, p. 6.

---

[28] Jason Morton, "Riley: Black Belt Initiative Will Help Rural Areas," *Tuscaloosa* (AL) *News*, 10 August 2007.

## Little Investment in Education

This reveals that there must be an expansion of economic development efforts beyond the reliance on cheap labor and industry recruitment. These efforts negate the importance of a diversified and skilled workforce that can be successful as the economy shifts from one sector-based economy to the next. The influence of the lack of investment in public education in the Black Belt has resulted in a captured, mostly unemployable populace in the twenty-first century. Historically, the Black Belt economy has been dependent on agriculture or low-end manufacturing, so human capital investment was not seen as necessary. However, as the global economy influences the twenty-first century economy of the Black Belt, human capital investment is imperative to wealth creation and economic development within the region.

For roughly fifty years, rural economic development has been based on industry recruitment and industry retention. However, this has proven very difficult recently as the economy has shifted to a global one. Now, economic development officials are focused on "growing business on Main Street." Yet developing entrepreneurship in rural areas is a time-consuming approach to economic development, and many areas resort to short-term, quick approaches. Entrepreneurship is very important in the twenty-first century economy, with two-thirds of the new jobs in the last twenty years stemming from entrepreneurship. This could be a wonderful opportunity to change the economic circumstances of the Black Belt if planned properly.[29]

## Economic Development in Other Rural Regions

Appalachia, for example, has historically relied on the strategy of industry recruitment and low-wage low skilled jobs to no great result, and we can learn from this region. According to sociologist Dwight Billings, as a result of their economic failure, community efforts have been made to combat funding economic industries from outside of the

---

[29] Mark Drabenstott, Nancy Novack, and Bridget Abraham, "Main Streets of Tomorrow: Growing and Financing Rural Entrepreneurs," *Main Street Economists*. Center for the Study of Rural America, Federal Reserve Bank of Kansas City, June 2003, www.kansascityfed.org/publicat/mse/mse_0603.pdf, accessed 23 December 2012.

area in an effort to stimulate economic growth within. The Democracy Resource Center, a member of the Kentucky Economic Justice Alliance, opposes grants and incentives given to out-of-area businesses to locate in the state while creating little job opportunity. According to the group, investing in creating local entrepreneurial opportunities makes better sense.

Drabenstott, Novack, and Abraham found that an ideal policy would create an entrepreneurial ecosystem. Elements of entrepreneurial ecosystems include policies and programs that create cultures of entrepreneurship, the creation of places where entrepreneurial behavior is encouraged by the community, and places where entrepreneurship education and training to facilitate business growth and development is successful. This effort has been established in some places in the Appalachian region and can be duplicated to fit the Black Belt region.

A key community-based organization in Appalachia, Appalachia Ohio Regional Investment Coalition (AORIC) utilizes partnerships to address problems in Appalachia, and partners work together on business development, community planning, and leadership development strategies. In addition, the group participates in arts and heritage as well as grant-making and networking. The AORIC is also dedicated to building economic and civic entrepreneurial capacity. These strategies can help rural communities thrive through local initiatives that promote a stable economic future, techniques that should be employed in the Black Belt region.

*Globalization, Trade, and Development*

As global influences significantly shape the economy of the Black Belt region, the region must adapt. For example, trade agreements are major developments in the global economy and have influenced job opportunities within the Black Belt region. The North American Free Trade Agreement, NAFTA, has been shown to have negatively affected many areas in the South. "It has been estimated that between December 1994 and February 2002, NAFTA cost 444,000 United States apparel jobs and 243,000 textile jobs. Seven states, Alabama, Georgia, Mississippi, North Carolina, South Carolina, Tennessee, and Texas, lost 385,000 of these positions." This negative influence on the Southern economy hurt the Black Belt and is the result of decisions made far removed from the area. Little planning went into preparing the people of the Black Belt for the impact of NAFTA and globalization at the national and state level. This created a precarious situation within the region with no easy solution. The future is economically bleak, according to Dr. Merle Black of Emory: "There is nothing going on for them. A state like Alabama has limited resources, so they are going to put it where it is going to have a return, not in the Black Belt. It's the same with industry. Additionally, of course you have an issue with leadership. Most of your quality leadership doesn't want to be there. The good leadership leaves the place."[30]

The regional history and culture has provided for the unique political economy of the Black Belt and its response to these changes.

> The interaction of the market and the state is geographically specific, because each locality consists of a distinct amalgam of economic, political and cultural relations—a historically accumulated social order—that influences how the market and state affect poverty. An example can be found in the Mississippi Delta, where the social order—shaped by a long agrarian history, a tradition of economic and political control by local elites, and a heritage of exploitive class, race and gender relations—influences the operation of the market and the state, constraining distributive mechanisms capable of addressing the region's entrenched poverty. Elsewhere, distinctly different social orders present geographically specific contexts in which the market and state function, generating variable chances for prosperity.[31]

This unique political economy has created a difficult case study for economic development, as the region's history has relied on very weak

---

[30] National Rural Funders' Collaborative Homepage, http://www.nrfc.org/ohio.asp, accessed 17 December 2012. Alfred Eckes, "The South and Economic Globalization, 1950 to the Future," in *Globalization and the American South*, eds. James Cobb and William Stueck (Athens GA: University of Georgia Press, 2005) 56.
[31] John Fleming, *Gone Time, Lives Anew in Alabama, APF Reporter* 22/2 (2002), www.aliciapatterson.org/APF2202?Fleming/Fleming.html, accessed 17 December 2012. Janet Kodras, "The Changing Map of American Poverty in an Era of Economic Restructuring and Political Realignment," *Economic Geography* 73/1 (January 1997): 67–93.

state structures and institutions and limited technological advances and innovation.

Below in Table 6.5 the important factors in state business competitiveness are highlighted, revealing the region's ill-preparedness in key areas such as human resources and governmental and fiscal policy as well as other issues that negatively influence the business environment in the region.

Table 6.5 Southern State Competitiveness Subindices Rank 2010

| State | Gov't and Fiscal Policy | Infrastructure | Human Resources | Technology | Business Incubator | Openness | Environmental Policy |
|---|---|---|---|---|---|---|---|
| AL | 25 | 35 | 49 | 32 | 39 | 39 | 19 |
| AR | 14 | 14 | 42 | 49 | 22 | 46 | 17 |
| DE | 6 | 32 | 27 | 19 | 3 | 10 | 49 |
| FL | 1 | 24 | 40 | 40 | 7 | 12 | 21 |
| GA | 15 | 19 | 47 | 35 | 12 | 28 | 43 |
| LA | 24 | 13 | 44 | 44 | 27 | 5 | 34 |
| MD | 35 | 45 | 12 | 2 | 23 | 24 | 47 |
| MS | 17 | 47 | 50 | 48 | 36 | 45 | 29 |
| NC | 21 | 9 | 39 | 21 | 8 | 32 | 37 |
| SC | 10 | 36 | 48 | 42 | 26 | 23 | 33 |
| TN | 9 | 20 | 46 | 39 | 18 | 29 | 42 |
| TX | 28 | 27 | 42 | 30 | 20 | 2 | 25 |
| VA | 5 | 26 | 24 | 10 | 9 | 30 | 26 |

Source: "Tenth Annual State Competitiveness Report," Beacon Hill Institute, Suffolk University, 2010 http://www.beaconhill.org/Compete-10/Compete2010State.pdf, p. 2, accessed 20 December 2012.

*Black Belt Poverty Trap*

Because of a lack of money, most local governments within the Black Belt cannot afford to invest in public goods and entities that are useful in development goods and fall into a "poverty trap," as defined by Humphreys, Sachs, and Stiblitz (2007). The poverty trap within the Black Belt region is realized in a system in which private investments in the area are contingent upon public physical infrastructure, educational systems, and quality-of-life factors. Unfortunately, in the Black Belt there is little money for investment in physical infrastructure, which results in a lack of private investment. Because of a lack of capital, Black Belt local governments cannot come up with matching funds for grants, qualify for loans, or afford to promote many economic development strategies due to the economic restrictions of the community. Within the Black Belt, poverty results in a lack of public investment, which then results in a lack of private investment and promotes continued poverty. In order to address the poverty trap of the Black Belt, efforts must be made to come up with alternative approaches to funding economic and development efforts. In addition, public investment incentives must benefit the public good and provide positive outcomes for the entire community and not just a few people within the community.

*National Economic Development Strategies*

National strategies of economic development have changed over time. According to the National Academy of Public Administration, during the 1930s national economic development strategies utilized direct federal action without input from state and local governments. During the 1940s and 1950s national strategies included a focus on business districts within urban areas, and specific areas of distress were targeted in the 1960s. Later, strategies included multifaceted economic development support programs that sometimes overlapped in service, programs, and jurisdiction. Today, economic development appears to be a policy area in flux—uncoordinated, without a clear national goal or strategy, which is part of the problem influencing the Black Belt. Unfortunately, most economic development efforts for rural areas are piecemeal and fragmented. According to a Government Accountability Office (GAO) 2000 study, ten agencies and twenty-seven subagency units administered seventy-three programs that performed national economic development activities. The GAO report also stated there was no commonly accepted definition for economic development, so definitions include terms such as job creation and capacity building and projects. The study identified six activities that are directly related to economic development: planning, constructing or renovating nonresidential buildings, establishing business incubators, constructing industrial parks, constructing roads and streets, and constructing water and sewer systems.

These activities were usually promoted through grants-in-aid programs, and most programs were funded at less than $50 million each. This GAO identification shows a narrow national definition of economic development and a reliance on place-based development activities.[32]

In addition, it shows the nationalistic uncoordinated activities under the label of economic development. There is a real need for a nationally funded, long-term regional strategy for economic development in the Black Belt region. In 1996, the National Academy of Public Administration proposed ten recommendations to improve economic development in America, theorizing that economic development was critical to America's competitiveness in the global economy and in the transformation of social policy from dependency to opportunity. These recommendations include three areas of importance for this chapter: provide incentives to local jurisdictions to design and implement regional economic development programs; encourage strategies that focus on long-term economic gains, rather than highly visible short-term projects; and invest in creating economic opportunities for residents of "distressed" communities.[33]

Each of these recommendations provides innovative and distinctive approaches to economic development strategies that could be useful within the Black Belt region. The focus on regionalism and sound long-term gains and the idea of providing opportunities for communities of distressed areas are very important, and if applied, could create effective strategies and benefits that go beyond ordinary efforts. Specifically, the development and implementation of regional economic development programs is truly needed. This would create an opportunity for our nation's definition of economic vitality to include the concept of regions, therefore revealing differences and the need for differences in remedy. In

---

[32] National Academy of Public Administration, "A Path to Smarter Economic Development: Reassessing the Federal Role," order 96-08 (Washington DC: US Economic Development Agency, 1996). "Economic Development: Multiple Federal Programs Fund Similar Economic Development Activities," United States General Accounting Office Report to Congressional Committees (September 2000) GAO/RCED/GGD-00-220.
[33] "A Path to Smarter Economic Development."

addition, it would allow for activities beyond just rebuilding physical infrastructure and include both human capital and education upgrades.

This concept of regional development has been utilized in the past in the Appalachian region with the development of the Appalachian Regional Commission (ARC). Table 6.6 shows the governance of the commission and its core priorities and decision-making structures. The desire to assist the impoverished Appalachian region resulted in the commission being funded by the national government, but although it has been successful in developing the region physically, it has not developed the people of the region as successfully. Many critics of the ARC find problems with the governance of the agency, as they believe by relying on local development districts, there is little input from community and the neediest people in the region.

Table 6.6 Appalachian Regional Commission Model

|  | Appalachian Regional Commission (ARC) Established: 1965 13 states |
|---|---|
| Governance | Federal Co-Chair appointed by the President with the consent of the Senate Governors of the participating states Resident of the state appointed by the Governor State Co-chair |
| Priorities/Core Areas | Infrastructure for economic and human resource development Development of industry Entrepreneurial communities Generating a diversified regional economy Making the regions industrial and commercial resources more competitive in national and world markets |
| Structure/Decision-making | Board Local Development Districts Local Municipalities |

Source: www.arc.gov

Other regional commissions and/or authorities are shown in Table 6.7. Each of these entities has specific geographic regions, governance, priorities, and decision-making structures. Most of these rely on the ARC model, and, as a result, these bodies are very limited in citizen participation. In fact, the Denali model is the only one that has limited direct citizen participation. The Delta Regional Authority, which covers some Black Belt counties, negates the opportunity for citizens to participate in decision-making regarding project funding or policy areas covered.

Table 6.7 Governmental Models of Development

|  | Governance | Priorities/Core Goals | Decision-making |
|---|---|---|---|
| Appalachian Regional Commission Established 1965 Total Population: 23 Million Coverage Area: 13 states | *Federal co-chair* appointed by the President with the consent of the Senate *Governors* of participating states *Resident* of the state appointed by the Governor State co-chair | Infrastructure for economic and human resource development Development of industry Entrepreneurial communities Generating a diversified regional economy Making the regions industrial and commercial resources more competitive in national and world markets | Board Local Development Districts or Planning Commission Local Municipalities |
| Delta Regional Authority Established: 2000 Total Population: 9.25 million Coverage Area: 8 states | Federal co-chair Appointed by the President *Governors* of participating States *Resident* of the state appointed by the Governor State co-chair | Basic public infrastructure Transportation infrastructure Business development/entrepreneurship Job training and education *Transportation and infrastructure projects receive at least 50% of the appropriate funds. | Board Local Development District Municipalities, Counties and Parishes |
| Denali Commission Established: 1998 Total Population: 625,000 | Federal co-chair Appointed by the President *State co-chair*/ Governor of Alaska Panel of five Commissioners Natives/Residents Organized labor | Energy Healthcare Facilities Training Intergovernmental Coordination Other Infrastructure | Board Citizen input through community-based comprehensive plans |

| Includes only the state of Alaska | University system/Education Construction contractors/Business Municipal managers/Local government | | |
|---|---|---|---|

Source: handout from statewide meeting.

This is a very important oversight in a region with such a colorful political environment. The Black Belt region cannot afford another effort with limited decision-making by citizens and input from the community. This would not be a useful strategy, so what would a regional or authority for the Black Belt look like? What unique factors would ensure needed citizen participation, transparency, and accountability to the community? How could there be a check on local authority and accountability, including the promotion of inclusion and race and class diversity? Chapter 7 discusses these complex ideas in depth.

# RECENT DEVELOPMENTS IN THE BLACK BELT

"Sometimes programs are handed down to persons, but they never reach the people who need the help most."—Rev. Curtis Bradley (Alabama Black Belt minister)

Recently, politicians, the media, and scholars have focused on the Black Belt in an effort to come up with successful strategies for substantial changes in the economic conditions of the area. The region has been hindered by conflicts of race, class, ineffective intergovernmental organization and cooperation, and insufficient private financial investment. Historically, the South and its economic condition have lagged behind the nation, and the Black Belt South has lagged even further behind. By assessing Southern economic development strategies over time, it is revealed that in many instances these strategies were not very helpful and in some cases harmful to African Americans because these strategies were not reflective of the unique characteristics of the South. Varied groups throughout the South began to promote the idea of a regional commission to address the economic problems of the Black Belt.[1]

The concept of creating a regional commission to combat a particular region's specific problems is not a new one. During the 1960s,

---

[1] Veronica Womack, "Continued Abandonment in Dixie: No More Policy as Usual," *Harvard Journal of African American Public Policy* 13 (Summer 2007): 41–53. Lynne Wilbanks Jeter, "Southern Black Belt Alliance: Will It Go Forward? Lack of Consensus May Sink Proposed Commission," *Mississippi Business Journal* 23[issue?] (5–11 November 2000). Jeffrey McMurray, "Miller Wants to Tackle 'Black Belt' Poverty," *Athens* (GA) *Banner- Herald,* 20 August 2001. Anonymous, "Artur Davis Makes Tour through Area," ANS272003, http://www.demopolistimes.com/2003/08/27/artur-davis-makes-tour-through-area, accessed 20 December 2012. Http://www.onlineathens.com/stories/082001/new_0820010010.shtml, accessed 23 December 2012. Samuel D. Calhoun, Richard Reeder, and Faqir Bagi, "Federal Funds in the Black Belt," *Rural America* 15/1 (January 2000): 20–27.

poverty was placed on the national agenda as featured by the national "war on poverty." In addition to urban ghettos, Appalachia and the rural or Black Belt South were targeted as areas in need of economic development assistance. In an effort to create economic opportunity and equality in the Appalachian region, the national government created the Appalachian Regional Commission, in 1965, to achieve these goals. Yet a comprehensive regional commission to address the problems of the Black Belt south was not produced.

Although a Southern regional commission or authority has been considered in the past, a twenty-first-century effort to create a Black Belt regional commission began with former Georgia senator Zell Miller in 2001. This group included former Alabama congressman Artur Davis, North Carolina congressman Mike Mcintyre, educational institutions such as the University of Georgia's Carl Vinson Institute, Eastern Carolina University, Tuskegee University, and several other Historically Black Colleges and Universities (HBCUs), together with input from over 300 community-based organizations in seven states throughout the old Confederate South, all hoping to make economic changes in the Southern region.

This distinctive effort involved an elaborate web of conflicting groups dissimilar in political experience, occupational background, race, class, and life experiences yet linked by the common goal of improving the economic conditions of the Black Belt South. Unfortunately, in the end, issues of race and class could not be overcome and the effort proved fruitless.

In 2001, several steps were taken within a seven-state region to promote federal legislation for the creation of a Southern regional commission to address the region's economic woes. Senator Zell Miller of Georgia received $250,000 from the Energy and Water Development Appropriations Act to study the practicability of a Southern Regional Commission. Funds were provided to study the Black Belt region to decide whether there was a need for a regional commission and if the Appalachian Regional Commission could be a realistic model to imitate. This study was labeled the Persistent Poverty Feasibility Study. Senator Miller clearly stated that the study should not be defined by race but rather by poverty stating, "Poverty—not race—should be the guiding principle in my opinion, and I hope those doing this study will take that into consideration." Miller named the University of Georgia, under the Carl Vinson Institute of Government, lead research agent in the study, and the university partnered with Tuskegee University to achieve the goals of the feasibility study. The study was divided into two components. The University of Georgia focused on business community stakeholders, state agencies, 1860s historically white land-grant institutions, and census statistics of the region. Tuskegee University focused on community-based organizations, 1890s land-grant Historically Black Colleges and Universities, and citizen stakeholders within the region. After completing the research and holding statewide meetings in six states (Alabama, Georgia, Florida, Mississippi, Virginia, and South Carolina), the two institutions of higher education combined their research into a final report to provide a comprehensive and in-depth look at the Black Belt region and the feasibility of a regional commission. In addition, Tuskegee University, along with its community partners, published a second report entitled "Persistent Poverty in the South: A Community Based Perspective," which discussed the desires of the Black Belt community with regard to a regional commission. Tuskegee University, its partner HBCUs, and its community partners all felt it was important for community voices on the topic to be heard.[2]

Concurrently, a group of individuals calling themselves the Black Belt Initiative convened to also focus on the Black Belt region. A fact sheet provided by the Black Belt Initiative (BBI) describes it as being composed of "individuals, communities, organizations, educational institutions and government agencies which seek to improve social, economic, health and educational standing of the Black Belt Counties of the South." A small, close-knit group met in Atlanta, in May 2001, and met again at Tuskegee University, in October of the same year. Individuals, organizations, and institutions involved in the Miller study were loosely connected with the BBI, and the group continued to grow. By the time the Black Belt Initiative met for what would become the most significant meeting of the group, in October 2001, representatives

---

[2] Walter Hill and Southern Food Systems Education Consortium, *Persistent Poverty in the South: A Community Based Perspective* (Tuskegee AL: Tuskegee University, 2002).

from state agencies and community-based organizations from North Carolina, South Carolina, Georgia, Alabama, Mississippi, and Louisiana had also joined the group.

The October 2001 meeting was deemed a planning session on what role the Black Belt Initiative organization could occupy in the quest to improve the Black Belt. However, the meeting proved heated as groups clashed over the direction of the Black Belt Initiative and its role. There were disputes between community-based organizations and institutions of higher education. There were also disputes over how race, in a region with such a significant African American population, and, more importantly, a region with such a dreaded history in race relations, would play a role in the makeup and leadership of regional efforts. No exchange was more heated, though, than the exchange between a community-led segment of the Black Belt Initiative group and representatives of a group from North Carolina calling for the Southeastern Crescent Authority (SECA). However, it was revealed that the proposed SECA steering committee was composed of all white males at the time, although the group stated it was making efforts to include diversity within the group later.

However, community-based representatives of the Black Belt Initiative were not optimistic about this diversity effort being a successful one due to the fact that SECA had not diversified prior to the meeting. This October 2001 meeting included groups that differed in their beliefs about what the goal of a regional commission should be, differed in how they thought economic development could be successful in the region, differed about which entities or approaches should be used to accomplish economic development success, and differed in their approaches to how race should be addressed and how the people of the Black Belt should be involved in the decision-making process of the authority/commission. All of these differences eventually resulted in the representatives of this momentous October meeting forming three separate alliances and sponsoring three separate and unique bills in the 108th Congress. This effort shows the deep race, class, and economic divisions of the region and how difficult they are to overcome. Although well intentioned, the effort could not overcome generations of mistrust and hostility. Here again, in this most noble effort, the Old South continued to manipulate and control the future of the region.

This complicated network would eventually fracture, but the goal of an effective economic policy for the Black Belt region would remain a focus for all involved. These separate rural partnerships were different in political ideology and political experience and savvy but alike in the goal of their sponsored bills. Remarkably, even with three separate bills on this one region, along with extraordinary support from various interest groups stretching from Mississippi to Virginia, and the sponsorship of several popular lawmakers, all of the bills floundered. What a missed opportunity to change the region for the better. These pieces of legislation were introduced by three Southern politicians, each with their own prescription for the unique problems of the region. Interestingly, only one bill even mentioned the term "Black Belt" in its title, and one can only speculate that this term was believed to have negative connotations and might have negatively affected the successful passage of the bill. Even on a national level, race is often seen as a negative factor, and national policy is reflective of the fact.

*Possible Economic Development Legislation: A Case Study in Community Decision-making*

As part of the feasibility study for a Black Belt regional commission, Tuskegee University conducted focus groups in six Southern states with community-based organizations and community leaders to discuss the feasibility of a national commission for Black Belt region issues. These groups voiced their eagerness for a Black Belt region commission but also their concerns about the Appalachian Regional Commission Model's governing structure. They created a governing structure with more community-based and direct resident participation in governance (SOFSEC, 2002). This was realized in a 108th congressional bill sponsored by Artur Davis of Alabama, which became the Delta Black Belt Regional Authority (DBBRA). As proposed by the bill, this authority would continue and expand the preexisting Delta Regional Authority's duties, including the Delta Regional Authority's original states of Alabama, Arkansas, Illinois, Kentucky, Louisiana, Mississippi, Missouri, and Tennessee, but also add Florida, Georgia, North Carolina, South Carolina, Texas, and Virginia. Table 7.0 shows the unique proposed governing structure, which included greater participation from residents and community-based organizations than other created or proposed entities. The Delta Black Belt Regional Authority created a Constituency Representation Board, which consisted of representatives from each congressional district in the authority. Representatives were to be selected by the governor of the state after being nominated by their congressional representative. They would have to represent community-based, faith-based organizations or institutions of higher learning and reside in distressed areas of the district, have experience as a community and economic development practitioner, and have direct contact with the impoverished population.

Finally, this board would provide Congress with an annual report on the activities of the funded projects. Although passage of the bill was unsuccessful, groups in the community felt their participation made a difference in this piece of legislation. Each previously discussed proposed initiative from former Senator Miller, Representative McIntyre, and former Congressman Davis offered suggestions for combating some of the ills of the Black Belt region, with common issue areas in healthcare, housing, education, and economic development. While Miller's and McIntyre's bills also proposed decision-making structures similar to those in other regional models, the Black Belt region is unique, and any structure created to address its problems must address its history of class and race exclusion. It must also reflect the weak political institutions within the region and the disconnect between governmental institutions and many rural African American residents.

Table 7.0 Governmental Structure Models

|  | Appalachian Regional Commission (ARC) Established: 1965 13 states | Proposed Characteristics of a DBBRA Proposed 2002 Included 14 states |
|---|---|---|
| Governance | Federal Co-Chair appointed by the President with the consent of the Senate Governors of the participating states Resident of the state appointed by the Governor State Co-chair | Federal Co Chair appointed by the President with the consent of the Senate Governors of participating States Constituency Representative |

| Priorities/Core Areas | Infrastructure for economic and human resource development | Develop comprehensive plans, establish priorities, and approve grant proposals |
|---|---|---|
| | Development of industry | Facilitate and coordinate interstate relations |
| | Entrepreneurial communities | |
| | Generating a diversified regional economy | Review the needs and assets of the region and support State government and Local Development Districts with economic development strategies |
| | Making the regions industrial and commercial resources more competitive in national and world markets | |
| | | Assist private investment in the region |
| Structure/Decision-making | Board | Board |
| | Local Development Districts | Constituency Representation |
| | Local Municipalities | Board |
| | | Comprehensive Strategic Plan developed by local communities to prioritize community needs |

Source: http://www.arc.gov. Appalachian Regional Commission. HR 5082, 109th Congress, Southern Empowerment Act to Authorize the Delta Black Belt Regional Authority, http://www.govtrack.us/congress/bills/109/hr5082/text, accessed 23 December 2012.

Most proposals for regional authorities or commissions utilize conventional decision-making structures that rely heavily upon local development districts in conjunction with local governments and planning commissions. These governmental institutions have historically been exclusionary, and in most localities in the Black Belt they are controlled and operated with very little participation from the African American population. Even with the inclusion of one or two African American local leaders, it is inadequate. The black community needs to play an active role in any successful economic development strategy formulated, and unfortunately there is little opportunity for them to do so presently within existing structures.

Because of weak state and local institutions, a history of exclusion, an elitist political environment, and the social class structure of the Black Belt region of the South, it is only logical that these factors would be evaluated and addressed in any proposed progressive economic development strategy for the region. Race and its impact on Black Belt society is a very authentic issue and should be a focus within any rural Southern regional economic development policy. Specific guidelines need to be in place to ensure that vulnerable Black Belt residents receive their fair share of any provided economic development funding. More specifically, there needs to be an effort made to require transparency in the operations of local policy and decision-making. Efforts should be made to include community participation in decision-making regarding the development of these rural communities. This will not be an easy feat, as the Black Belt resides in a very traditional political culture dedicated to limited government.

*Political Culture and the Power of Local Interests*

As discussed in previous chapters, the Black Belt region has a traditional political culture built on the beliefs that social and family relationships are key to political power. Communities tend to have prominent families or a small group that controls politics by relying on traditional social networks to sustain a hierarchical political structure and institutions. In this traditional political culture, government is limited in scope and is mostly used to maintain the existing social order. There are very little innovative approaches to social programs, and those in power tend to play a largely conservative and paternal role, with politics being dominated by a few people.

Historically, development activities in the Black Belt have been problematic for many. Lawrence Hanks found many African American residents of the Black Belt cynical about local economic development efforts, stating, "Through the rural South, it is common to find blacks who feel that their local officials are not interested in attracting industry to their area. This alleged practice keeps wages low, work scarce, and the environment intimate. These conditions also lay the groundwork for economic intimidation." Many scholars, including Hanks, have labeled this economic intimidation as the "empowerment trap." According to this premise, many residents of the Black Belt find themselves in an empowerment trap in which they are socially and economically impoverished, yet they have empty political rights. They need the favor of those in economic and political control of the community for work and/or security, but by accepting the work and/or security, they become beholden to the strict, local hierarchical system and are not able to speak out about unfavorable conditions in their community for fear of economic retaliation. All racial, economic, and political strata of the small, close-knit Black Belt community fear this retaliation.[3] Even though many residents, regardless of color or class, are well aware of the empowerment trap within their community, they are all locked into a system in which they are unwilling or unable to break the economic and social chains that keep them in control and their communities stagnant.

During the twentieth century, as our society shifted to become more industrial and mechanically based, local authority players became vital in the development of the Black Belt region. As early as the 1940s, Satterfield found local governments in the South assuming powers in several policy areas, including rural housing, libraries, planning, recreation, agriculture, forestry, and many other services. This concentration of power at the local level influenced the lives of African Americans in the South during this time, as it does today. One reason for this concentration of power is that these rural counties tend to be geographically smaller than other counties in the country. The smaller the area, the more direct control local governments have over the lives of their constituents. It is not difficult in these small communities to reveal those who speak out against authority, which makes the empowerment trap all too applicable and real. These counties have traditionally been led partly by influential county commissioners who control the counties' planning and fiscal affairs. This cannot be underestimated, because those who control planning also control the direction of growth or lack of growth in the community. Selection of growth sites and purchasing and hiring decisions are heavily linked to those in control of these small, rural counties and the local officials employed there. Local authority drastically influences the quality of life for people of the Black Belt, and the powerbrokers' ability to reward and punish based on loyalty and

---

[3] Lawrence Hanks, *The Struggle for Black Political Empowerment in Three Georgia Counties* (Knoxville: University of Tennessee Press, 1987) 92.

dissent is assisted by the closeness and size of the county and the intimate relations there.[4]

This local control strategy and its manipulation of the Southern rural African American community continued even past the civil rights movement era. Johnson, Parnell, Joyner, Christman, and Marsh found in the twenty-first century that local governmental officials used their authority to victimize African American residents in a small North Carolina community. Although outside of the Black Belt, this example reveals the vulnerability of rural Southern blacks. They found local officials were able to "manipulate zoning and land-use regulation to: (1) systematically deny African Americans political involvement in community and economic development decision-making; (2) needlessly expose African Americans to public health risks by denying them access to critical infrastructure resources like sewer service; and (3) intentionally targete African American communities for locally unwanted land-uses like highway re-routing." This is just one example of recent research revealing continued usage of existing political structures to systematically target African Americans and limit their economic and political opportunity.[5]

Charles Aiken looked at the Mississippi Delta region within the Black Belt in the twentieth century and the lack of political advancement in the area. He found strategic redistribution of the African American population resulting in political limitations in local politics in the Mississippi Delta, a critical area of the Black Belt region's post-civil rights movement. This is an example of tactics discussed by Kousser earlier in the text, in which the population concentration dictated a specific tool for taking power away from the group. According to Aiken, federal housing programs allowed for African Americans to be relocated

---

[4] M. H. Satterfield, "Trends in Rural Local Government in the South," The Journal of Politics 10/3 (August 1948): 510–35.

[5] James Johnson, Jr., Allan Parnell, Ann Moss Joyner, Carolyn J. Christman, and Ben Marsh, "Racial Apartheid in a Small North Carolina Town," *The Review of Black Political Economy* 31/4 (June 2004): 104.

to "fringe" communities outside of city limits, resulting in no voice in local politics.[6]

> Several factors contribute to the location of much of the new, federally sponsored housing in the Yazoo Delta on the fringes rather than within municipalities.... The major factor, however, has been fear by white controlled municipal governments that increases in housing for blacks within the corporate limit are a compromise. Even dwellings built beyond the corporate boundaries require a degree of approval by municipal governments, for water and sewer lines must be extended to them. Persons who work to improve housing of blacks in the Yazoo Delta have accepted the fringe locations because they realize that insistence that projects be located within municipal boundaries will merely result in new dwellings not being constructed. For merchants, who also are among the political leaders, a principal motivation for acceptance of new housing in the fringe is that increases in the local black population mean growth of retail sales without growth of black political power.[7]

These decisions are not only politically and morally reprehensible; they are also economically irrational. In the Delta, these municipal areas provide water and sewage lines, some fire protection, and garbage collection to these fringe areas and have to pay more for the services than for in-city residents, including two times the water rate of city residents, according to Aiken. Still, the enormous fiscal burden is not addressed because holding onto political power is more important, keeping residents outside the city limits is more important than fiscal considerations. Yet the importance of maintaining local political autonomy and control usurps any concern for fiscal conservatism in controlling local government within the Black Belt.

This local control affects the rural African American population even if black citizens have managed to acquire some political representation, because economic control remains impossibile. The reality of empty political rights is evident in the Black Belt in many

---

[6] Charles S. Aiken, "Race as a Factor in Municipal Underbounding," *Annals of the Association of American Geographers* 77/4 (December 1987): 573–74. J. Morgan Kousser, *Colorblind Injustice: Minority Voting Rights and the Undoing of the Second Reconstruction* (Chapel Hill: University of North Carolina Press, 1999).
[7] Aiken, "Race as a Factor," 573–74.

ways, particularly as African-American-elected officials compose part or in some cases many of the elected officials in Black Belt communities yet are unable to translate political power into real economic change for their constituents. Therefore, many local African American lawmakers are unable or unwilling to fight the economic leaders of their communities, and in some cases the state, because they remain economically dependent on these entities for jobs, or the task is simply too great to resist. Many have found that strategies of resistance have proven futile. Through centuries of generational experience, they have learned that there is often little internal or external protection for them if they go against the local power structure. As a result of this regional empowerment trap, unfortunately, many Black Belt residents continue to be subjected to public policy created within an exclusive political and economic environment. There must be an acknowledgement of the generations-old, embedded political elitism that has ruled local, state, and regional governmental systems, a labor pool based on a plantation caste system, and, yes, the real problem of race and racism. It is important that an agency or strategy is not created with institutional barriers that exclude the people targeted by the strategy from receiving support, but even more importantly, from participating in the decision-making process itself. The lessons learned by the Appalachian Regional Commission in establishing mechanisms to target the rural distressed areas in Appalachia should be noted when creating any commission/authority or strategy. When assessing the ARC, consider the following:

> This governing structure has already proven to be inadequate in the Appalachian region where the issue of race has not been a historical problem. After several decades of funding, there are mixed opinions of how successful the ARC has been at aiding the poor in the region. Early in its existence, there was criticism that a significant portion of the money was being spent on physical infrastructure in more affluent areas and very little money was invested in equipping the people with needed skills and resources.[8]

---

[8] Veronica Womack, "Continued Abandonment in Dixie: No More Policy as Usual," *Harvard Journal of African American Public Policy* 13 (Summer 2007): 41–53.

The lesson learned is that focusing just on placed-based development without developing the people of the region is not a successful strategy. Coming up with nontraditional intergovernmental, multicounty, community-based, public-private relationships may be necessary to successfully implement economic development initiatives in this region. Relying solely on preexisting, weak governmental structures and institutions may prove unproductive because these structures may be part of the institutional barriers that have not benefited the targeted communities initially.

Some strategies also tend to focus specifically on developing the physical infrastructure of the targeted area, thus ignoring the region's most valuable assets, its people. For example, in 2005, the Fourteenth Amendment Interstate, or SR 2735, in the 108th Congress was initiated by lawmakers from Mississippi and Georgia to create an interstate highway from Augusta and Macon, Georgia, to Natchez and Meridian, Mississippi, and to Montgomery, Alabama. According to this legislation, Congress found that the eleven-state region in the Southeast known as the Southern Black Belt was in need of the "same regional economic development plans as modeled by the ARC." It found that the African American population in the region doubled the national average, due to the history of the region. It also found that "the disparity in transportation infrastructure investment has been a key contributing factor to the persistent poverty and social ills of this region. The lack of adequate east-west Interstate Highway access has provided a significant impediment to travel throughout the region, served as a severe obstacle to the attraction of industry and jobs, and has been a detriment to public health and transportation safety."[9]

The proposed interstate would be called the Fourteenth Amendment Highway, and the legislation is said to protect the constitutional rights of regional residents—"particularly the descendants of free slaves"—to

---

[9] HR281, 109th Congress, 1st session, http://www.gpo.gov/fdsys/pkg/bills-109hr281ih/html/biccs-109hr281ih.htm, accessed 30 December 2012. "To require a study and report regarding the designation of a new interstate route from Augusta, Georgia and Natchez, Mississippi," 108th Congress, 2nd session, S. 2735, http://www.govtrack.us/congress/bills/108/s2735/text, accessed 30 December 2012.

equal treatment under the law." The legislation went on to say, "despite the Fourteenth Amendment, that region and the residents of that region...remain characterized by low employment, low incomes, low education levels, poor health and high infant mortality. Disparity in transportation infrastructure has been a key contributing factor to the persistent poverty and social ills of that region." As impressive as it is for a national policy to address the ills of the region, this type of economic development strategy is not conducive to targeting the disadvantages faced by the descendants of the enslaved Africans. It is more favorable to assist businesses within the region instead, as efforts to assist the descendants of the enslaved would need to go beyond just the development of a highway system and address the issues raised in the legislation. In addition to the highway system, the development strategy should include educational opportunities unique to the region and populace, job creation for these descendants, healthcare, and adequate housing and quality-of-life issues.

Strategies that exploit the present-day conditions of the residents of the Black Belt with little concern for remedying the problems are not beneficial to the region. For example, present-day agricultural policy does not assist African American farmers in the region:

> The Southern Rural Development Initiative conducted a study that shows that those 107 nonmetro counties with a majority population are also the ones whose farmers received more than $9 Billion in agricultural subsidies from 2001–2003. At most, 5 percent of those governmental payments went to African American farmers. The rest went to large farmers owned by a rather small number of white farmers and reveals the continued domination of national resources by a privileged few in rural Southern communities.

Simply setting up additional programs without changing the distribution processes of these programs will not yield needed results. The structure must be unique and reflective of the regional power distribution and existing inequities.[10]

---

[10] Cornelia Butler Flora and Jan Flora, *Rural Communities Legacy and Change*, 3rd ed. (Boulder CO: Westview Press, 2008) 86.

*Social Policy as Economic Development Policy*

Since the 1960s, American social commentary has favored the idea that poverty can be explained by certain social and psychological *defects* of the impoverished, such as the theory of a "culture of poverty." This theory, which was widely publicized during the 1960s, focused on alleged defective cultural traits within impoverished people, such as low ambition, a focus on instant gratification, and the lack of planning for the future. The theory was revised to include the factors of race, lack of intelligence, and place as explanations of poverty during the 1970s. The association between the "culture of poverty" and race has deeply influenced how poverty and development policy have been shaped in this country, and the Southern region is not an exception.[11]

Over the past two decades, social policy for the poor has often been caught up in discussions of race, slothfulness, morality, and fraud. This "culture of poverty" theory was challenged in the literature by works that tried to explain poverty in terms of place and opportunity. The idea that where you reside dictates your opportunities found a voice in sociological literature as it addressed urban poverty, but, unfortunately, it did not find its way into public policy in a major way. This has been particularly detrimental to discussions of economic development strategy as it relates to extreme rural poverty.[12]

The idea of policymakers assessing Southern rural places of persistent poverty in terms of place and opportunity would be a new exploration of development policy in this country. Interestingly, according to Hall and Midgley, this idea has been acknowledged by European lawmakers, who have focused on the idea of social exclusion as a factor of persistent poverty and have included it as a component of European development policy. "The idea of social exclusion accompanied growing concern about the way de-industrialization, global competitiveness and other economic difficulties emanating from the 1970s had produced a large number of unemployed people who were

---

[11] Anthony Hall and James Midgley, *Social Policy for Development* (Thousand Oaks CA: Sage Publications, 2004).

[12] William Julius Wilson, *The Truly Disadvantaged: The Inner City, The Underclass and Public Policy* (Chicago: University of Chicago Press, 1987).

increasingly marginalized from mainstream society." Successful economic development policy in the Black Belt must include the concepts of place, race and social exclusion, and opportunity as well as prescriptions for these factors.

Life for Black Belt residents is harsh, and an economic development policy based on status quo factors is clearly incompatible for the region. General approaches to economic development will not be successful in the Black Belt because of several factors. According to Whitener and McGranahan, "Rural economies are both diversified and diverse, so tried-and-true economic development strategies applied nationwide may be less successful now than 40 years ago. Prosperity for today's rural communities requires educational upgrades to reflect changing market conditions and innovative marketing of natural amenities and other income-generating strategies to attract people and jobs."[13]

An exclusive reliance on placed-based development policy will not aid the region in the new knowledge-based, global economy, and in many cases the Black Belt community does not have the capital to promote public investments. The reliance on a surplus of cheap, unskilled labor, tax incentives, and a low cost of living will not ensure private investment or successful industry recruitment in the new global economy as it did in the manufacturing-based economy of the past. Today, industry wants to locate in communities with large, educated workforces, good public school systems, and high quality of life standards. These are the keys to successful economic development strategies. Yet they require capital for investment, and often Black Belt communities are unable to offer this.

There must be an effort to strengthen weak governmental institutions within the region so that any actions made on the part of the community are democratic, promote equality, and benefit the community as a whole. However, development of these rural amenities will require twenty-first century strategies and development.

---

[13] Leslie Whitener and David McGranahan, "Rural America: Opportunities and Challenges," *Amber Waves* 1/1 (February 2003). http://ageconsearch.umn.edu/bitstream/130677/2/feature-rural%20america.pdf, accessed 17 December 2012

This chapter revealed that there is an acknowledgement that the Black Belt region is in desperate need of governmental response, and yet the old embedded issues of race, class, and exclusion still continue to play a significant role in the lack of development. However, unlike in the past, there is a sincere effort to bring change into the region by some, even though there is still reluctance to admit the damage racism and elitism continue to do in the Black Belt society. The lack of trust and unwillingness by all groups to move beyond the past appears to still render the Black Belt helpless and hopeless to change the downward spiral that is affecting all aspects of the society. However, it is imperative that government and the citizens of the Black Belt acknowledge and accept the past, learn from the experience, and begin to work together to change the direction of the region for future generations of Black Belt residents. Yet in accepting the past, it is nevertheless critical that governmental responses do not reenact the past.

# 8

# CONCLUSIONS

*Prescriptions for the Black Belt*

The problems of the Black Belt region are great and they will require several developments in order to make progress. For example, there is a need for an increased role by the national government and a revisiting of how rural communities are funded. According to Flora and Flora, although local, state, and national monies fund rural governments, 65 percent of their budget comes from the local communities themselves, increasing since the 1970s due to federal cutbacks and tax cuts. As a result, "Federal funds for programs with a primarily rural community or economic development focus (administered by the U.S. Department of Agriculture, the Environmental Protection Agency, and the Department of Health and Human Services) declined about 8 percent (plus inflation) between fiscal year 2003 and fiscal year 2007."[1]

The lack of funding for needed development must be addressed as well as the creation of innovative approaches to development and a commitment from members of the region to assist in moving the community forward if there is to be change. Regardless of strategy and approach, certain factors require immediate attention, such as education, governmental structure, community participatory governance, and national rural policy.

*Reforming the Black Belt*

So what would education reform need to look like in the Black Belt in order to prepare its students for the twenty-first century's knowledge-based global economy? The Black Belt needs to be recognized as a national economic priority along with an assessment of the lost

---

[1] Flora and Flora, *Rural Communities*, 332.

productivity growth within the region due to a lack of educational attainment and how this influences national and state economies. The fact that the Black Belt is connected with the economies of several states and the nation should serve as an impetus for change. Yet there should be a specific effort to focus on the development of the people of the region for change and not just the physical infrastructure as many proposals suggest. Regional education and training should be used as major change agents. As a national priority, regional efforts should be made to invest in the educational opportunities for the people of the region, with a significant focus on the need for resources for equipment, additional teachers, and physical infrastructure.

There must also be an effort to provide Black Belt students with needed training in advanced technology, business creation, and economic development. It is imperative that communities use existing rural community colleges as centers of education, knowledge, and training. This would also include the promotion of collaborative efforts between existing rural community colleges and secondary education. In addition, in places where there are no rural community colleges, efforts must be made to fund the provision of high technology opportunities within the secondary educational system, such as community broadband capabilities, with science and technology serving as regional priorities in education. It is important to note that this national effort should focus on regionalism and use it as the basis for any decisions made.

*Transforming Education*

Existing educational paradigms developed for the "old economy" must be restructured to encompass new-economy innovations and techniques. Future national and global market outcomes require job applicants to have more advanced education, and the trend continues to move toward greater education, knowledge, and training. Machin found that in the U.S., labor market outcomes have moved in favor of the most educated citizens. However, "better educated" specifically means greater skills in technology, science and mathematics.[2]

A better educated populace demands more of the workforce in today's economy, with technological changes resulting in a workplace where employers are willing to pay higher wages for skilled workers, while less-skilled workers either are retrained or left behind. These are very important factors when developing strategies to develop the Black Belt South and show the critical need for innovative education and changes to the system. Because most of the Black Belt region's workforce is comprised of low-skilled workers with limited education levels, their ability to acquire many of the jobs developing in the knowledge-based economy is challenged. It is important to address needed structural changes in K-12 education that will allow for innovative approaches to education and training. In addition, developing partnerships with the private and public sector to create training opportunities for the region's people for successful economic development is necessary and could be realized through the linkage of rural community colleges and high schools in the region and training efforts specific to a particular industry. Linking education and training to economic development is the only solution for a region that is in desperate need of economic restructuring for survival.

*Funding Quality Education*

At issue is the funding system of public education in the country, which has not changed in roughly seventy years. Karp finds that the school-funding system was created for an industrial economy with minimum education requirements. As a result, it is not equipped to prepare students for the twenty-first century's new knowledge-based global economy, which is grounded in quality education. Beginning with *Rodriguez v. San Antonio* (1973), the Supreme Court ruled that education was not a right provided by the Constitution, so the concept of equality of education has had little legislative or judicial support. Because education tends to rely

---

[2] Stephen Machin, "Skill-Biased Technical Change and Educational Outcomes," in *International Handbook on the Economic of Education*, eds. Geraint Johnes and Jill Johnes (Northampton MA: Edward Elgar Publishing, 2004).

on property taxes and the tax base of a community, the inequalities within communities and the U.S. at large are visible throughout the educational system. Unfortunately, the funding system serves as a mechanism for arranging education based on class membership. So there must be changes in funding that do not require already financially strapped taxpayers to increase their taxes for additional educational resources, because this choice often becomes a mandate against taxation itself and not the educational needs of the community. Most current school finance systems are based mostly on minimum education standards and not goals, outcomes, or quality. In the Black Belt region, the funding system must be restructured for high-quality education and not minimum standards. It is also important to recognize that increasing the Black Belt's share of the funding equation is impossible, since it is where some of the poorest Americans reside.[3]

*Education Reform Must Be Innovative*

Transforming education in the region will not be an easy task. Educational reform is often difficult to implement. Chubb and Moe suggest that education reform is institutionally flawed and will never work as long as it is implemented within the present organizational structures, including elected school boards, hired school administrators, federal and state departments of education, teachers and their unions, the textbook industry, etc., because everyone at every level is more interested in his or her interests than improving public education. This concept also includes politicizing educational funding. Education must be transformed into a truly public, apolitical entity, as education in the Black Belt must meet the new challenges that face our society. The development of a twenty-first century curriculum for the Black Belt must be a priority for the people of the region, the states of the Black Belt, and the nation. Education must be looked upon as a means to an end. Asking students to perform without providing a quality education standard suitable for an industrialized nation often proves to be a futile effort. An

---

[3] *San Antonio Independent School District v. Rodriguez*, 411 U.S. 1 (1973). Stan Karp, *Money, Schools and Justice* 18/1 (Fall 2003) http://www.rethinkingschools.org/ProdDetails.asp?ID=RTSVOL18N1&d=etoc, accessed 17 December 2012

effective effort must be a national priority supported by appropriate resources.[4]

*India as a Model of National Commitment*

Efforts to include Black Belt residents in the new knowledge-based economy must focus on successful models such as the transformation of India. The recent success of India as a world economic contender and producer of advanced technology did not occur by happenstance. After India's independence, there was a move to socially and economically develop the country through science and technology. This was made a national priority and was achieved through the creation of the Indian Institutes of Technology (IITs). Beginning in 1951, seven engineering and technology-oriented institutes of higher education were established by the government of India to train scientists and engineers in order to develop a skilled workforce. The national government saw this as the creation of a new future for the country, and they were right. Today, the world looks to India for technology and innovation, and they are key participants in the new knowledge-based economy. In a December 2007 article in *The Economist*, it was revealed that India boasted annual growth rates of nearly 30 percent in the past ten years, with revenues now nearing $50 billion, about 5.4 percent of India's GDP.[5]

Although some have speculated that this boom will slow down, no one can quantify the socioeconomic benefits of this progress. Another significant component of the IITs is the caste-based reservation policy, which sets aside positions for those with membership in India's lower castes. This policy was the result of leadership developing the country and its transformation for the future. The inclusion of formerly socially excluded groups into development can only benefit the entire community and should be looked upon as a benefit, not as competition. Properly funding public education must be seen as an apolitical decision that can

---

[4] John Chubb and Terry Moe, *Politics, Markets & America's Schools* (Washington DC: Brookings Institute Press, 1990).
[5] "Gravity's Pull. Is India's Computer Services Industry Heading for a Fall?" *The Economist* (13 December 2007), http://www.economist.com/node/10286436, accessed 30 December 2012.

only benefit the entire community. To provide historically excluded members of the Black Belt community significant training and quality educational opportunities can only benefit the Black Belt region, Southern states, and the nation. The Black Belt region's development will require a difficult acknowledgement of the social damages instituted by historical and present circumstances and will require a national and state governmental priority of education. This priority, as in the case of India, must result in a needed focus on innovative educational funding and delivery and an effort to include the region as a whole in economic development processes.

There is significant evidence, particularly in the Appalachian region, that when economic development efforts focus on physical infrastructure without upgrading the education levels of the people, the people may not benefit from the efforts. By investing in the people by focusing on education, the region can be assured that needy residents will be beneficiaries of the development efforts. Any investment in education will result in economic growth within the community and economic development strategies will benefit.

*Community-Based Participatory Decision-Making*

In addition to innovations in education, there must also be innovations in local governance. Efforts must be made by rural Black Belt residents and lawmakers to make local government in the region inclusive, not just in elective offices but also appointive ones. The Rochester participative governance process may serve as a model that could work in the Black Belt region, which entails engaging the people of the community in decision-making activities. The Rochester process was an effort in participative governance allowing citizens to become active participants in governance and relying on the knowledge of the citizens to address the needs of their community.

> In anticipation of the process that would ensue, the city especially sought to do four things to help meet these objectives: 1) use more community resources to solve community problems; 2) facilitate active resident participation despite the changes increased participation might bring; 3) deliberately redesign the existing networks of power through which

things got done in the city; and 4) encourage the development of those skills citizens need to meaningfully participate in community planning.[6]

Participatory community decision-making could open up centuries-old, exclusive governing processes within local communities and provide transparency and accountability on the local level. Local leadership is key to success. However, efforts to economically develop Black Belt communities require all levels of government, private investment, and public support. Even with significant inclusion on the local level, there must also be changes in the national rural development policy.

*National Legislative Rural Initiative*

In 2002, the Federal Reserve Bank of Kansas City organized a conference that focused on rural America, in which Jim Moseley, deputy secretary of Agriculture, identified four changes in the direction of rural policy, including technological changes that will innovatively change agriculture, shifting from commodity markets to specialty markets, advances in telecommunications and logistics that allow local businesses to go beyond local community, and the mobility of rural people. This new direction, according to the conference, should include a flexible rural policy to facilitate regional partnerships. This conference also identified challenges in developing regional strategy and discussed the importance of intergovernmental cooperation. This focus on intergovernmental cooperation also proposed developing additional innovative institutional structures to make the strategies feasible. There was a recognition that existing institutions may not be successful in creating successful strategies for the twenty-first century.

The Black Belt, with its exclusive weak institutional structures, is surely not currently equipped to succeed. In addition, the importance of the private sector in the development of strategy, with nonprofit and

---

[6] Sydney Cresswell, Jordan Wishy, and Terrence Maxwell, "Fostering Social Equity and Economic Opportunity through Citizen Participation: An Innovative Approach to Municipal Service Delivery." A discussion paper prepared for the National League of Cities. Intergovernmental Solutions program, June 2003, 8, Nelson A. Rockefeller College of Public Affairs and Policy, University at Albany, http://www.albany.edu/igsp/pdf/nlsfinal.pdf, accessed 30 December 2012.

governmental institutions assisting the private sector, is also important, as public-private partnerships are critical in developing rural communities; the Black Belt is no exception. Finally, there should be a focus on the assistance of rural businesses and the ability of these businesses to access funds to create new rural opportunities. Creating entrepreneurial opportunities in the region would develop these rural places socially, economically, and politically, as these efforts would empower local people by providing them with ownership opportunities, new leadership, and the community with tax revenues.

The Black Belt region has traditionally been defined as being populated by rural, largely poor African Americans and as a region of discrimination, social exclusion, and hardship. Yet the twenty-first century can create a new definition with innovation, creative leadership, and successful approaches to governance.

Finally, the 2008 Farm Bill provided for a Southern regional development commission that could be used to address some of the region's issues. However, the effort was based on the "policy as usual" ARC model and does not provide opportunities for decision-making by local people. Although this is not the model that most of the community efforts recommended, if properly implemented, policies from this governmental initiative could be used for positive change. However, if it continues the tradition of elitism and exclusion, it will be yet another example of a bureaucratic institutional barrier. In order for the Black Belt region to move forward and take advantage of twenty-first century opportunities, change must be transparent, open, innovative, and inclusive.[7]

---

[7] The Food, Conservation and Energy Act of 2008 PL 110–246.

# SOURCES

Aiken, Charles S. "Race as a Factor in Municipal Underbounding," *Annals of the Association of American Geographers* 77/4 (December 1987): 564–79.

Alcindor, Habiba. "Losing Ground." *The Nation* (20 March 2005). www.thenation.com/docprint.mhtml?i=20050404&s=alcindor, accessed 30 December 2012.

Anderson, John. "Black Vocational Education." In *Historical Perspectives in Vocationalism in American Education*, edited by Harvey Kantor and David B. Tyack. Palo Alto CA: Stanford University Press, 1982.

Appalachian Regional Commission Assessment. Http://www.whitehouse.gov/omb/expectmore/summary.10002330.2005.html, accessed 30 December 2012.

Archibald, John and Jeff Hansen, "Land Is Power, and Most Who Wield It Are Outsiders," *The Birmingham* (AL) *News* (13 October 2002) http://www.al.com/specialreport/birminghamnews/index.ssf?blackbelt/blackbelt/4.html, accessed 30 December 2012.

Barnes, William and Larry Ledebur. *The New Regional Economies: The U.S. Common Market and the Global Economy*. Thousand Oaks CA: Sage Publications, 1998.

Becker, Gary. *Human Capital: A Theoretical and Empirical Analysis with Special Reference to Education* 3rd ed. Chicago: University of Chicago Press, 1993.

Berlin, Ira. *Slaves Without Masters: The Free Negro in the Antebellum South*. New York: New Press, 1974.

Billings, Dwight. *Economic Representations in an American Region: What's at Stake in Appalachia?* Http://www.nd.edu/~econrep/essays/EconomicRepresentations.pdf, accessed 30 December 2012.

"Black Farmers Accuse Agriculture Department of Failing to Honor Bias Settlement," *Jet* 106/6 (9 August 2004): 15

"Black Farmers in America, 1865–2000: The Pursuit of Independent Farming and the Role of Cooperatives." Rural Business: Cooperative Service RBS Research Report 194. USDA. Http://www.rurdev.usda.gov/rbs/pub/rr194.pdf, accessed 30 December 2012.

"Black Farmers Urge U.S. to Abolish Agriculture's Farm Service Agency," *Jet* 96/3 (21 June 1999): 55.

Blalock, Hubert M. "Economic Discrimination and Negro Increase," *American Sociological Review* 21/5 (October 1956): 584–88.

———. "Percent Nonwhite and Discrimination in the South," *American Sociological Review* 22/6 (December 1957): 677–82.

———. *Toward a Theory of Minority Group Relations*. New York: John Wiley, 1967.

Blauner, Robert. *Racial Oppression in America*. New York: Harper, 1972.

Blumer, Herbert. "Race Prejudice as a Sense of Group Position," *The Pacific Sociological Review* 1/1 (Spring 1958): 3–7.

Bond, Horace Mann. "Negro Education: A Debate in the Alabama Constitutional Convention of 1901," *The Journal of Negro Education* 1/1 (April 1932): 49–59.

*Booker T. Washington and his Critics Black Leadership in Crisis* 2nd ed. Edited by Hugh Hawkings. Lexington MA: D.C. Heath and Co., 1974.

Braden, Anne. "Voting Rights on Trial Again in Alabama," *Southern Changes* 20/2 (Summer 1998): 2.

Bradshaw, Michael. "Public Policy in Appalachia: The Application of a Neglected Geographical Factor?" *Institute of British Geographers New Series* 10/4 (1985): 385–400.

Brown, David and Glenn Fuguitt. "Percent NonWhite and Racial Disparity in Nonmetropolitan Cities in the South," *Social Science Quarterly* 53/3 (December 1972): 573–82.

*Brown v. Board of Education*, 347 US 483 (1954). *United States Supreme Court Reports*.

Bullard, Robert. *Dumping in Dixie: Race, Class and Environmental Quality* 3rd ed. Boulder CO: Westview Press, 2000.

Calhoun, Samuel D., Richard Reeder, and Faqir Bagi. "Federal Funds in the Black Belt," *Rural America* 15/1 (January 2000): 20–27.

Card, David and Alana B. Krueger. "School Quality and Black-White Relative Earnings: A Direct Assessment," *Quarterly Journal of Economics* 107/1 (February 1992): 151–200.

———. "School Resources and Student Outcomes: An Overview of the Literature and New Evidence from North and South Carolina." In *Education Matters*, edited by Alan Krueger. Northampton MA: Edward Elgar, 2000.

Chubb, John E., and Terry Moe. *Politics, Markets & America's Schools*. Washington DC: Brookings Institution, 1990.

Clark, Kenneth. "The Negro Elected Official in the Changing American Scene." In *Black Political Life in the United States: A Fist as the Pendulum*, edited by Lenneal J. Henderson, Jr. San Francisco: Chandler Publishing Company, 1972.

Clay, William. *Just Permanent Interests Black Americans in Congress 1870–1992*. New York: Amistad, 1993.

Cleaver, Kathleen and George Katsiaficas. *Liberation, Imagination, and the Black Panther Party: A New Look at the Panthers and Their Legacy.* New York: Routledge, 2001.

Cobb, James C. *The Selling of the South: The Southern Crusade for Industrial Development 1936–1980.* Baton Rouge: Louisiana State University Press, 1982.

———. *The Selling of the South The Southern Crusade for Industrial Development 1936–1990* 2nd ed. Chicago: University of Illinois Press, 1993.

Cobb, James and William Stueck. *Globalization and the American South.* Athens: University of Georgia Press, 2005.

Cohen, Cathy and Michael Dawson. "Neighborhood Poverty and African American Politics," *American Political Science Review.* 87/2 (June 1993): 286–302.

Cohen, William. "Negro Involuntary Servitude in the South: 1865–1940," *Journal of Southern History* 42/1 (February 1976): 31–60.

Colclough, Glenna. "Uneven Development and Racial Composition in the Deep South 1970–1980," *Rural Sociology* 53/1 (Spring 1988): 73–86.

Collins, Patricia Hill. *Black Feminist Thought: Knowledge, Consciousness, and the Politics of Empowerment* 2nd ed. New York: Routledge Press, 2000.

———. "Toward a New Vision: Race, Class and Gender as Categories of Analysis and Connection." In *Privilege: A Reader*, edited by Michael Kimmel and Abby Ferber. Cambridge MA: Westview Press, 2003.

Corzine, Jay, James C. Creech, and Lin Huff-Corzine. "Black Concentration and Lynchings in the South: Testing Blalock's Power Threat Hypothesis," *Social Forces* 61/3 (March 1983): 774–96.

Cotton, Jeremiah, "Opening the Gap: The Decline in Black Economic Indicators in the 1980s," *Social Science Quarterly.* 70/4 (December 1989): 803–19.

Cowan, Tadlock and Jody Feder. *The Pigford Case: USDA Settlement of a Discrimination Suit by Black Farmers.* 28 June 2007. Washington DC: Library of Congress.

Cresswell, Sydney, Jordan Wishy, and Terrence Maxwell. "Fostering Social Equity and Economic Opportunity through Citizen Participation: An Innovative Approach to Municipal Service Delivery." Paper presented at the National League of Cities, Intergovernmental Solutions program, June 2003.

Davis, Theodore. "Income Inequities between Black and White Populations in Southern Nonmetropolitan Counties," *The Review of Black Political Economy* 22/4 (Spring 1994): 144–58.

Delia, Albert A., S. Richard Brockett, and Malcolm Simpson. *Southeastern Crescent Authority: A Proposal for Economic Growth in the Southeastern United States.* Greenville SC: East Carolina University Regional Development Institute, 2002.

Devey-Tomaskovic, Donald and Vincent J. Roscigno. "Racial Economic Subordination and White Gain in the US South," *American Sociological Review* 61/4 (August 1996): 565–89.

———. "Uneven Development and Local Inequality in the US South: The Role of Outside Investment, Land Elites, and Racial Dynamics," *Sociological Forum* 12/4 (December 1997): 565–97.

*Dimensions of Poverty in the Rural South*. Edited by Jogindar Dhillon and Marguerite Howie. Tallahassee FL: Rose Printing Company, 1986.

Drabenstott, Mark and Katherine Sheaff. *The New Power of Regions: A Policy Focus for Rural America—A Conference Summary*. Economic Review (second quarter 2002) Http://www.kc.frb.org/publicat/econrev/pdf/2q02drab.pdf, accessed 30 December 2012.

Drabenstott, Mark, Nancy Novack, and Bridget Abraham. "Main Streets of Tomorrow: Growing and Financing Rural Entrepreneurs. A Conference Summary" 88/3 *Economic Review* (third quarter 2003): 73–84.

*Dred Scott v. Sanford*, 60 US 393 (1857). *United States Supreme Court Reports*.

Dreier, Peter, John Mollenkopf, and Todd Swanstrom. *Place Matters: Metropolitics for the Twenty-First Century*. 2nd ed. Lawrence: University Press of Kansas, 2004.

"The Drive to Move South: The Growing Role of the Automobile Industry in the Southern Legislative Conference Economies." A Special Series Report of the Southern Legislative Conference. Council of States. November 2003. Www.slcatlanta.org/publications/econdev/nashville_auto_remarks.html, accessed 30 December 2012.

Du Bois, W. E. B. *The Conservation of Races*, A Penn State Electronic Classics Series Publication: The American Negro Academy Occasional Papers. 2 (1897) 1–15. Www2.hn.psu.edu/faculty/jmanis/webdubois/duboisconservationraces.pdf, accessed 30 December 2012.

———. *The Souls of Black Folk*. Chicago: A. C. McClurg & Co., 1903.

Duncan, Cynthia. *Worlds Apart: Why Poverty Persists in Rural America*. New Haven CT: Yale University Press, 1999.

Dunning Art, James G. Ledbetter, and Joseph Whorton. *Dismantling Persistent Poverty in the Southeastern United States It's a Matter of Wealth*. Athens: Carl Vinson Institute of Government at the University of Georgia, 2002.

Edwards, William James. *Twenty Five Years in the Black Belt*. Electronic edition. Chapel Hill: University of North Carolina, 1869. Http://docsouth.unc.edu/fpn/edwards/edwards.html, accessed 30 December 2012.

Elazar, Daniel J. *American Federalism: A View from the States*. 2nd ed. New York: Thomas Y. Crowell, 1972.

Falk, William and Thomas Lyson. *High Tech, Low Tech, No Tech, Recent Industrial and Occupational Change in the South*. Albany NY: SUNY Press, 1988.

Falk, William and Bruce H. Rankin. "The Cost of Being Black in the Black Belt," *Social Problems* 39/3 (August 1992): 299–313.

Fear, Darryl, "Protesters Take Over USDA Office in Tennessee. Black Farmers Say Promised Loans Were Mishandled," *Washington Post*, 2 July 2002, http://www.commondreams.org/headlines02/0702-04.htm, accessed 30 December 2012.

Ferenchik, Mark, "A Sharpened Focus Ohio Governor Pledges for 29 Appalachian Counties," *The Columbus* (OH) *Dispatch*, 30 September 1999, 01A.

Ferenchik, Mark and Hill Riepenhoff, "Mountain Money, Federal Tax Dollars Miss the Mark in Core Appalachia," 26 September 1999, http://www.sullivan-county.com/nfo/dispatch/moun_money.htm, accessed 30 December 2012.

Fitzgerald, Michael. "'To Give our Votes to the Party': Black Political Agitation and Agricultural Change in Alabama, 1865–1870," *The Journal of American History* 76/2 (September 1989): 489–505.

Fletcher, Michael, "USDA, Black Farmers Settle Bias Lawsuit," *Washington Post*, 6 January 1999.

Fleming, John. "Gone Time, Lives Anew in Alabama." *APF Reporter* 22/2 www.aliciapatterson.org/APF2202?Fleming/Fleming.html, accessed 30 December 2012.

Flora, Cornelia Butler and Jan Flora. *Rural Communities Legacy and Change*. 3rd ed. Boulder CO: Westview Press, 2008.

Foner, Philip. *American Socialism and Black Americans: From the Age of Jackson to World War II*. Westport CT: Greenwood Press, 1977.

Fredrickson, George. *White Supremacy A Comparative Study in American & South African History*. New York: Oxford University Press, 1981.

Friedman, Thomas L. *The World Is Flat: A Brief History of the Twenty-First Century*. New York: Farrar, Straus and Giroux, 2006.

Gauthier, Howard. "The Appalachian Development Highway System: Development for Whom?" *Economic Geography: Societal and Policy Perspectives*. 49/2 (April 1973): 103–108.

*The Ghetto Underclass: Social Science Perspectives*. Edited by William Julius Wilson. Newbury Park CA: Sage Publications, 1993.

Gibbs, Robert. "Most Low-Education Counties Are in the Nonmetro South." Amber Waves. U.S. Department of Agriculture Economic Research Service, 2005. http://ageconsearch.umn.edu/bitstream/129509/2/loweducation.pdf, accessed 30 December 2012.

Gibson, J. Sullivan. "The Alabama Black Belt: Its Geographic Status" *Economic Geography* 17/1 (January 1941): 1–23.

Glenn, Norval. "Occupational Benefits to Whites from the Subordination of Negroes," *American Sociological Review* 28/3 (June 1963): 443–48.

———. "The Relative Size of the Negro Population and Negro Occupational Status," *Social Force* 43/1 (October 1964): 42–49.

Goldfield, David R. *Black, White, and Southern Race Relations and Southern Culture 1940 to the Present.* Baton Rouge: Louisiana State University Press, 1990.

*Gomillion v. Lightfoot*, 364 US 339 (1960). *United States Supreme Court Reports.*

"Gravity's Pull: Is India's Computer Services Industry Heading for a Fall?" *The Economist* (13 December 2007) www.economist.com/node/10286436, accessed 30 December 2012.

Gray, Rhyllis. "Economic Development and African Americans in the Mississippi Delta," *Rural Sociology.* 56/2 (June 1991): 238–46.

Hahn, Steven. *A Nation under Our Feet: Black Political Struggles in the Rural South from Slavery to the Great Migration.* Cambridge MA: Harvard University Press, 2003.

Hall, Anthony and James Midgley. *Social Policy for Development.* Thousand Oaks, CA: Sage Publications, 2004.

Hanks, Lawrence. *The Struggle for Black Political Empowerment in Three Georgia Counties.* Knoxville: University of Tennessee Press, 1987.

Harrington, Michael. *The Other America: Poverty in the United States.* Baltimore MD: Penguin Books, 1963.

Harris, Fredrick, Valeria Sinclair-Chapman, and Brian McKenzie. *Countervailing Forces in African-American Civic Activism: 1973–1994.* New York: Cambridge University Press, 2006.

Harris, Rosalind and Dreamal Worthen. "African Americans in Rural America." In *Challenges for Rural American in the Twenty-First Century*, edited by David Brown and Louis Swanson. University Park: Pennsylvania State Press, 2003.

Harris, Rosalind, and Julie Zimmerman. "Children and Poverty in the Rural South," SRDC Policy Series 2 (November 2003).

Haywood, Harry. *Negro Liberation.* New York: International Publishers, 1948.

Hill, Walter. *Persistent Poverty in the South a Community Based Perspective.* Southern Food Systems Education Consortium. Tuskegee AL: Tuskegee University, 2002.

Hines, Darlene Clark, William Hines, and Stanley Harrold. *The African American Odyssey.* 4th ed. New York: Pearson: Prentice Hall, 2008.

Holmes, Tamara. "Black Farmers Sue USDA for $20.5 Billion: Mismanaged 1999 Settlement Sparks Class Action Lawsuit," *Black Enterprise*

(December 2004). Www.blackenterprise.com/mag/black-farmers-sue-usda-for-205-billion/, accessed 30 December 2012.
Holmes, William. "The Leflore County Massacre and the Demise of the Colored Farmer's Alliance," *Phylon*. 34/3 (third quarter 1973): 267–74.
———. "The Demise of the Colored Farmer's Alliance," *The Journal of Southern History*. 41/2 (May 1975): 187–200.
Humphreys, Macartan, Jeffery D. Sachs, and Joseph E. Stiglitz. *Escaping the Resource Curse*. New York: Columbia University Press, 2007.
Jackson, Damien. "Southern Black Farmers: Targets of USDA Racism 40 Acres and a Mule Denied," *AlterNet* (17 November 2004). Http://www.alternet.org/story/20511, accessed 30 December 2012.
James, David. "The Transformation of the Southern Racial State Class and Race Determinants of Local State Structures," *American Sociological Review*. 53/2 (April 1988): 191–208.
Jeter, Lynne Wilbanks. "Southern Black Belt Alliance: Will It Go Forward? Lack of Consensus May Sink Proposed Commission," *Mississippi Business Journal* 23 (5–11 November 2000) Http://msbusiness.com/blog/2001/11/05/southern-black-belt-alliance-will-it-go-forward/, accessed 30 December 2012.
Johnson, Andrew. First Annual Presidential Address, 4 December 1865. 39th Congress, 1st Session. Appendix, page 3. (December 1865). *Annals of the Congress of the United States*.
Johnson, James, Jr., Allan Parnell, Ann Moss Joyner, Carolyn J. Christman, and Ben Marsh. "Racial Apartheid in a Small North Carolina Town," *The Review of Black Political Economy* 31/4 (Spring 2004): 89–107.
Jolliffe, Dean. "Persistent Poverty is More Pervasive in Nonmetro Counties." 1 September 2004. Http://ageconsearch.umn.edu/bitstream/12973612/findings_ra_persistent.pdf, accessed 30 December 2012.
Karp, Stan. "State-by-State Battle for Funding Equity Gets Mixed Results," *Money, Schools and Justice*. 18/1 (Fall 2003).
Keith, Jeanette. *The South: A Concise History*. Volume 2. Upper Saddle NJ: Pearson Education, 2002.
Kennedy, Renwick. "Black Belt Aristocrats: The Old South Lives on in Alabama's Black Belt," *Social Forces* 13/1 (1934–1945): 80–85.
Kent, Dawn. "U.S. Steel to Invest in Black Belt Plant It Will Make Alternative to Coke—A First," *The Birmingham* (AL) *News* (19 April 2008). Http://www.al.com/news/birminghamnews/index.ssf?/base/news/1208592940164040.xm/&coll=2, accessed 30 December 2012.
Key, V. O., Jr. *Southern Politics in State and Nation*. New York: Knopf, 1949.
———. *Politics, Parties and Pressure Groups*. 5th ed. New York: Thomas Y. Crowell Company, 1964.

Kindig, David, Christopher Seplaki, and Donald Libby. "Death Rate Variation in US Subpopulations," *Bulletin of the World Health Organization.* 80/1 (2002): 9–15.

Kodras, Janet. "The Changing Map of American Poverty in an Era of Economic Restructuring and Political Realignment," *Economic Geography.* 73/1 (January 1997): 67–93.

———. "Restructuring the State: Devolution, Privatization, and the Geographic Redistribution of Power and Capacity in Governance" in *State Devolution in America: Implications for a Diverse Society*, 79–96. Edited by Lynn Staeheli, Janet Kodras, and Colin Flint. Volume 48 of *Urban Affairs Annual Reviews.* Thousand Oaks CA: Sage, 1997.

Kousser, J. Morgan. *Colorblind Injustice Minority Voting Rights and the Undoing of the Second Reconstruction.* Chapel Hill: University of North Carolina Press, 1999.

Kusimo, Patricia. *Rural African Americans and Education: The Legacy of the Brown Decision* ERIC EDO-RC-98-4, 1999. Http://www.eric.ed.gov/pdfs/ed425050.pdf, accessed 30 December 2012.

Ledbetter, James G., and Joseph Whorton. *Dismantling Persistent Poverty in the Southeastern United States It's a Matter of Wealth.* Athens: Carl Vinson Institute of Government at the University of Georgia, 2002.

Lee, Alston and Joseph Ferrie. *Southern Paternalism and the American Welfare State: Economics, Politics, and Institutions in the South 1865–1965.* New York: Cambridge University Press, 1999.

Lewis, David Levering. *W. E. B. Du Bois: The Fight for Equality and the American Century 1919–1963.* New York: Henry Holt & Company, 2002.

Lewis, Oscar. "The Culture of Poverty," *Scientific American.* 4/215 (October 1966): 19–25.

Lieberman, Robert and John Lapinski. "American Federalism, Race and the Administration of Welfare," *British Journal of Political Science.* 31/2 (April 2001): 303–29.

Lyson, Thomas. "Two Sides to the Sunbelt." In *The Growing Divergence between the Rural and Urban South.* New York: Praeger, 1989.

Lyson, Thomas and William Falk. *Forgotten Places: Uneven Development in Rural America.* Lawrence: University Press of Kansas, 1993.

Machin, Stephen. "Skill-Biased Technical Change and Educational Outcomes." In *International Handbook on the Economic of Education*, edited by Geraint Johnes and Jill Johnes. Northampton MA: Edward Elgar Publishing, 2004.

Mandle, Jay. "Continuity and Change: The Use of Black Labor After the Civil War," *Journal of Black Studies.* 21**[need issue]** (June 1991): 414–27.

*McCulloch v. Maryland*, 17 US 316 (1819). *United States Supreme Court Reports.*

McMurray, Jeffrey. "Miller Wants to Tackle 'Black Belt' Poverty," *Athens (GA) Banner-Herald* (20 August 2001). Http://onlineathens.com/stories/082001/news_0820010010.shtml, accessed 30 December 2012.

Meier, August and Elliot Rudwick. *From Plantation to Ghetto.* 3rd ed. New York: Hill and Wang, 1976.

Mertz, Paul. *New Deal Policy and Southern Rural Poverty.* Baton Rouge: Louisiana State University Press, 1978.

Minchin, Timothy. "Black Activism, the 1964 Civil Rights Act, and the Racial Integration of the Southern Textile Industry," *The Journal of Southern History.* 65/4 (November 1999): 809–44.

Minor, Bill. "Grand Opening: The Mississippi Sovereignty Commission. *Southern Changes.* 20/2 (Summer 1998): 20–22.

Moger, Allen. "The Origin of the Democratic Machine in Virginia," *Journal of Southern History.* 8/2 (May 1942): 183–209.

Molnar, Joseph and William Lawson. "Perceptions of Barriers to Black Political and Economic Progress in Rural Areas," *Rural Sociology.* 49/2 (Summer 1989): 261–83.

Morton, Jason. "Riley: Black Belt Initiative Will Help rural Areas," *The Tuscaloosa News* (10 August 2007). Www.tuscaloosanews.com/article/20070810/news/708100349, accessed 30 December 2012.

Mosley, Jane and Kathleen Miller. What the Research says about…. Spatial Variations in Factors Affecting Poverty. Rural Poverty Research Center Research Brief 2004-1 (March 2004).

Nantambu, Kwame. "Pan-Africanism versus Pan-African Nationalism: An Afrocentric Analysis," *Journal of Black Studies.* 28/5 (May 1998): 561–74.

National Convention of the Socialist Party Proceedings. 1934: 134–36; 1936: 310–13.

*New Healthy Life Expectancy Rankings Japan Number One in New 'Healthy Life' System*, Geneva, Switzerland: WHO Issues Press Release (4 June 2000).

Nixon, Ron. "Turning Back the Clock on Voting Rights," *The Nation* (15 November 1999). Www.thenation.com/article/turning-back-clock-voting-rights, accessed 30 December 2012.

Orfield, Gary, and Chungmei Lee. "Brown at 50: King's Dream or Plessy's Nightmare?" Cambridge MA: Civil Rights Project at Harvard University, 2004.

———. "Why Segregation Matters: Poverty and Educational Inequality." Cambridge, MA: The Civil Rights Project at Harvard University, 2005.

Orfield, Gary, J. Wald, and C. Swanson. 2004. *Losing Our Future: How Minority Youth Are Being Left Behind by the Graduation Rate Crisis.* Cambridge MA: The Civil Rights Project at Harvard University, 2004.

Contributors: Advocates for Children of New York, The Civil Society Institute.

Paper and Proceedings of the Sixty-third Annual Meeting of the American Economic Association, *From Hearings before Special Subcommittee on Cotton of the Committee on Agriculture, House of Representatives, 80th Congress 1st Session.* Washington, DC, Government Printing Office, 1947.

*A Path to Smarter Economic Development: Reassessing the Federal Role.* Washington, DC: National Academy of Public Administration, 1996.

Percy, Susan. "Marketing Georgia," *Georgia Trend* (April 2007) www.georgiatrend.com/April-2007/marketing-georgia/, accessed 30 December 2012.

Peter, Michael and A. C. (Tina) Besley. *Building Knowledge Cultures: Education and Development in the Age of Knowledge Capitalism.* New York: Rowman & Littlefield, 2006.

Phillips, Ulrich. "The Origin and Growth of the Southern Black Belts," *The American Historical Review.* 11/4 (July 1906): 798–816.

*Plessy v. Ferguson*, 163 US 537 (1896). *United States Supreme Court Reports.*

Poe, Janita. "Southern Group Vows to Fight Black Belt Poverty," *Atlanta Journal Constitution.* (14 October 2001).

Prager, Karen. *Community Partnerships Bring Community Revitalization.* Issue report 5. Center on Organization and Restructuring of Schools. Wisconsin Center for Education Research, University of Wisconsin-Madison.

Price, Rita. " Kids or Concrete Governors Support Focus on Highway, Water, Sewers Over Children's Program," *The Columbus* (OH) *Dispatch* (29 September 1999).

*Privilege: A Reader.* Edited by Michael Kimmel and Abby Ferber. Cambridge MA: Westview Press, 2003.

*Race Class and Gender: An Anthology.* Edited by Margaret Anderson and Patricia Hill Collins. Belmont CA: Wadsworth, 2001.

Raper, Arthur. *Preface to Peasantry.* Chapel Hill: University of North Carolina Press, 1936.

Raper, Arthur and Ira De A. Reid. "The South Adjusts—Downward," *Phylon.* 1 (1st quarter, 1940): 6–27.

Redkey, Edwin S. *Black Exodus: Black Nationalist and Back-to-Africa Movements: 1890–1910.* New Haven CT: Yale University, 1969.

Richardson, James. *A Compilation of Messages and Papers of the Presidents 1789–1897.* Washington DC: Government Printing Office, 1897.

Riepenhoff, Jill. "More Money Landing in Poorest Areas Appalachian Regional Commission," *The Columbus* (OH) *Dispatch* (11 November 1999), 01A.

Riepenhoff, Jill and Mark Ferenchik. "Champions of the Game Prosperous Counties Consume Big Slice of Appalachian Pie," *Columbus* (OH)

*Dispatch* (27 September 1999). Www.sullivan-county.com/info/dispatch/game.htm, accessed 30 December 2012.

Rolinson, Mary. *Grassroots Garveyism: The Universal Negro Improvement Association in the Rural South 1920–1927*. Chapel Hill: University of North Carolina Press, 2007.

Rosenfeld, Stuart. "The South's Rural Community Colleges in the New Millennium." In *Rural South: Preparing for the Challenges of the 21st Century*. ERIC ED438117 n3 (February 2000). Mississippi State University, Southern Rural Development Center.

———. "The Tale of Two Souths." In *The Rural South in Crisis*, edited by Lionel Beaulieu. Boulder CO: Westview Press, 1988.

———. *Vocational Education and Economic Growth Connections and Conundrums*. Occasional Paper 112, 1986. The National Center for Research in Vocational Education, Columbus, Ohio.

Satterfield, M. H. "Trends in Rural Local Government in the South," *The Journal of Politics*. 10/3 (August 1948): 510–35.

Schulman, Bruce J. *From Cotton Belt to Sunbelt: Federal Policy, Economic Development and the Transformation of the South 1938–1980*. New York: Oxford University Press, 1991.

*The Second Wave: Southern Industrialization from the 1940s to the 1970s*. Edited by Phillip Scranton. Athens: University of Georgia Press, 2001.

Sen, Amartya. "Critical Reflection, Health in development," *Bulletin of the World Health Organization*. 77/8 (1999): 619–23.

Smith, Jessie and Carrell Horton. *Historical Statistics of Black America: Media to Vital Statistics*. Volume 2 of Historical Statistics of Black America. Farmington Hills MI: Gale Research, 1995.

Smith, John David. *Black Voices from Reconstruction: 1865–1877*. Gainesville: University Press of Florida, 1998.

Smith, Kelly. "Black Farmers Have Beef with the USDA: Loan Denials Spark Legislation Proposal to Protect African American Farmers—Proposed USDA Accountability and Equity Act," *Black Enterprise Magazine* 28/6 (January 1998): 16.

Smith v. Allwright, 321 US 649 (1944). *United States Supreme Court Reports*.

Spencer, Thomas. "Politics of Color: Who Deserves to Lead," *The Birmingham* (AL) *News* (13 October 2002). Www.al.com/specialreport/birminghamnews/index.ssf?blackbelt/blackbelt 12.htm, accessed 30 December 2012.

Strong, David, Pamela Barnhouse Walters, Brian, Discoll, and Scott Rosenberg. "Leveraging the State: Private Money and the Development of Public Education for Blacks," *American Sociological Review*. 65/5 (October 2000): 658–81.

Swanson, Louis, Rosalind Harris, Jerry Skees, and Lionel Williamson. "African Americans in Southern Rural Regions: The Importance of Legacy," *The Review of Black Political Economy*. 22/4 (Spring 1994): 109–24.

Taylor, Stephanie. "Two Accused of Voter Fraud in Hale County," *The Tuscaloosa* (AL) *News* (17 August 2007).

Thomas, Miessha, Jerry Pennick, and Heather Gray. "What is African American Land Ownership?" Federation/Land Assistance Fund. 2004. http://www.federationsoutherncoop.com/aalandown04.htm, accessed 30 December 2012.

Thompson, Wilbur. *A Preface to Urban Economics*. Baltimore MD: John Hopkins Press, 1965.

Tickamyer, Ann and Cynthia Duncan. "Poverty and Opportunity Structure in Rural America," *Annual Review of Rural Sociology*. 16 (1990): 67–86.

Tolnay, Stewart. "The Great Migration Gets Underway: A Comparison of Black Southern Migrants and Non-migrants in the North, 1920," *Social Science Quarterly*. 82/2 (June 2001): 235–52.

United States General Accounting Office Report to Congressional Committees. Economic Development. Multiple Federal Programs Fund Similar Economic Development Activities. GAO/RCED/GGD-00-220. September 2000.

United States v. Cruikshank, 92 US 542 (1876). *United States Supreme Court Reports*.

United States v. Reese, 92 US 214 (1876). *United States Supreme Court Reports*.

Van Sickle, John V. "The Southeast: A Case Study in Delayed Industrialization," *The American Economic Review*. 41/2 (May 1951): 384–93.

Vina, Stephen and Tadlock Cowan. "The Pigford Case: USDA Settlement of a Discrimination Suit by Black Farmers." December 2005. CRS Report for Congress. Washington DC: Library of Congress.

Wadley, Janet K. and Everett Lee. "The Disappearance of the Black Farmer," *Phylon*. 35/3 (third quarter 1974): 276–83.

Walton, Hanes, Jr., and Robert C. Smith. *American Politics and the African American Quest for Universal Freedom*. 2nd ed. New York: Longman, 2003.

Washington, Booker T. *Up from Slavery*. New York: Doubleday, 1901.

Weinberg, Daniel. "Rural Pockets of Poverty," *Rural Sociology*. 52/3 (Fall 1987): 398–408.

Whitener, Leslie and David McGranahan. "Rural America: Opportunities and Challenges." Amber Waves. US Department of Agriculture Economic Research Service. http://ageconsearch.umn.edu/bitstream/130677/2/feature-rural%20america.pdf, accessed 20 December 2012.

Wilcox, Jerry and Wade Clark Roof. "Percent Black and Black-White Status Inequality: Southern versus Nonsouthern Patterns," *Social Science Quarterly*. 59/3 (December 1978):421–34.

Williams, Eric. *Capitalism and Slavery*. New York: Russel & Russel, 1961.

Williams, Patrick and Laura Chrisman. *Colonial Discourse and Post Colonial Theory A Reader*. New York: Columbia University Press, 1994.

Wilson, Theodore. *The Black Codes of the South*. Tuscaloosa: University of Alabama Press, 1965.

Wilson, William Julius. *The Truly Disadvantaged: The Inner City, the Underclass and Public Policy*. Chicago: University of Chicago Press, 1987.

Wimberley, Ronald and Libby Morris. *The Southern Black Belt: A National Perspective*. Lexington: University of Kentucky, 1997.

———. "The Regionalization of Poverty: Assistance for the Black Belt South," *Southern Rural Sociology*. 12/1 (2002): 294–306.

Wimberley, Ronald, Libby Morris, and Donald Woolley. *The Black Belt Databook*. Lexington: University of Kentucky, 2001.

Womack, Veronica. "Continued Abandonment in Dixie: No more Policy as Usual," *Harvard Journal of African American Public Policy*. 13 (2007): 41–53.

Wood, Philip J. *Southern Capitalism: The Political Economy of North Carolina, 1880–1980*. Durham NC: Duke University Press, 1986.

Woodard, C. Vann. *Origins of the New South 1877–1913*. Baton Rouge: Louisiana State University Press, 1995.

Wright, Gavin. *Old South New South Revolutions in the Southern Economy since the Civil War*. Baton Rouge: Louisiana State University Press, 1986.

Wright, Richard. *Black Boy*. New York: Harpers, 1945.

# INDEX

Abernathy, Rev. Ralph David 154
Absentee ballots 101, 102
African: Descent 18, 23; Slaves 204
African Americans 75; Education 73, 123; Leadership 52, 53, 55, 58, 69, 100, 110, 161; Officeholders 92, 105, 108, 109, 107; Political power 85, 110, 198, 202; Political participation 59; Population 3, 5, 7, 85, 92, 117, 118, 119, 123, 194; Poverty 110, 115, 116, 119; Self Defense 48, 70, 87; Unemployment 170, 171
African Methodist Episcopal 74
Agriculture 80; Economy 33; Owners 66; Workers 66
Agricultural Adjustment Act of 1933 171
Agricultural Adjustment Administration 172
Alabama 14, 53, 58, 87, 116, 122, 123, 177; Black Belt 43, 49, 93, 95, 99, 102, 112, 113, 134, 180; Black belt Aristocracy 14, 82; Black Belt Commission 180; Birmingham 86; Constitutional Convention of 1901 59; Economic Development 122; Education 124, 134; Emelle 93, 95; Eutaw 94 101; Greene County 101, 180; Greensboro 49; Lowndes County 60, 70, 88, 89, 101; Macon County 24, 81; Montgomery 203; Selma 86, 111; Perry County 101; Sumter County 93, 101, 121; Tallapoosa County 60; Toxic Waste 94; Wilcox County 43, 101, 124; Unemployment 134
Alabama Development Office 180
Albany Movement 86
Amendments: 13th 37; 14th 38, 40, 59; 15th 38
American Colonization Society 34
Appalachian 182, 183, 192, 202, 213
Appalachian Development Highway 168
Appalachian Regional Development Act of 1965 168
Appalachia Ohio Regional Investment Coalition 183
Appalachian Regional Commission 168, 169, 188, 192, 195, 196, 202, 215
Appointed positions 92

Appointive power structure 96, 99
Archer, William 5
Area Redevelopment Act of 1961 168
Arkansas 58, 116, 125, 166; Black Belt 125, 135; Education 125; Unemployment 135
*Atlanta Monthly* 45

Balance Agriculture with Industry program 176
Barbados 73
Bentley, Margaret 181
Black Belt 10, 22, 155-158, 213; Culture 140; Definition 7; Education 140, 141; Inequality 16, 200-201; Politics 57; Self-defense ideology 89
Black Belt Commission 180, 195
Black Belt Improvement Society 43, 44
Black Belt Initiative 194, 194
Black Belt Nation thesis 69, 70, 89
Black: Descriptive representation 52, 54, 92; Domination 50
Economic dependence 43; Farmers 144, 146, 147, 148, 149, 150, 152, 154; Labor 29; Political ideologies 75; Political participation 47, 52, 54, 57; Self-defense 47, 87; Self-sufficiency 34, 62, 72, 87, 154; Black Church 74, 86, 87
Black Codes 20, 25, 29
Black nationalism 71, 73, 74, 75, 76, 77; Race pride 77
Black panther party 87
Black power 54, 61, 67, 69, 70, 71, 87, 89
Blackness 2
Boyd, John 148
Broadband 166
*Brown v. Board* 81, 90; *Brown decision* 59
Bureau of Refugees, Freedmen and Abandoned Lands 33

Camilla Riot 54
Capitalism 71
Carmichael, Stokely 87
Carpentar, Rosie 101
Carolina coast 7
California 64

Chemical Waste Management 93
Christianity 5
Citizen's Council 82
Civil Rights Act of 1866 31, 38
Civil Rights Act of 1875 40
Civil Rights Act of 1964 83, 111, 115
Civil Rights laws 51, 82, 90, 92
Civil Rights Movement 86, 87, 91
Civil War 15, 16, 19, 20, 23, 27, 35, 36, 37, 40, 41 42, 46, 47, 48, 60, 87, 164, 174; Black Soldiers 27, 28
Civil Works Administration 173
Classism, African American 109, 110, 111, 112
Colonization 74
Colored conventions 31, 53, 54,
Colored Farmers Alliance 61, 68, 62
Communist party 70
Communists 10, 69, 70, 71
Community based organizations 193
Confederates 31, 35, 36; Pardon 35, 76
Congo 73
Congress 39, 50, 90; Black Experience 37, 55, 57, 105, 107, 108
 House 107, 108
Constitution (US) 18, 19, 37, 43, 81
Convict camps 61
Congress of Racial Equality 88, 153
Cooperatives 62, 70, 153, 154
Council-Manager government 95, 96, 97, 98, 99
Counties: Poverty 166
Cultural/institutional factors 12
Culture of Poverty 205

Davis, Artur 112, 195, 196
Deacons for Defense and Justice 87
Department of Agriculture 169
Delta Black Belt Regional Authority 195, 196; Constituency Representation Board 195, 196
Delta Regional Authority 169, 189, 195
Democracy 71
Democracy Resource Center 183
Democratic party 50, 51, 56, 57, 67, 69, 71, 77, 78, 79, 90, 106,
Dixiecrats 106
 Southern 55, 57, 77, 79, 90, 106
Denali Model 189
*Detroit Plains Dealer* 63
District of Columbia 46

Dixon Clan 60
Doctrine of black inferiority 21
*Dred Scott* 19, 20, 58
Du Bois, W.E.B., 7, 16, 22, 30, 44, 72, 73, 118, 121, 164
Durant Commercial Company 63

Eastern Carolina University 194
Economic dependency 43, 46, 63, 71, 77, 78, 79, 81, 161, 191
Economic development 160, 163, 168, 175, 182, 198, 204, 206, 210; Global 122; Incentives 178; Local development districts 197; Nationalistic approach 86, 169; Place-based development 122, 167, 202, 206; People-based development 122, 167, 206; Public investment 122
Education; Community college 209; Dual system 160; Funding, Higher education 211, 213; Inequality 117, 133; K-12 210; National priority 209
 Regional 209
Edward, Williams 43
Egypt of the Confederacy 22
Elazar, Daniel 11
Emancipation 27
Emancipation Proclamation 27
Emigration 64
Empowerment trap 198
Energy and Water Development Appropriations Act 192
Enforcement Acts 39
England 73
Entrepreneurship 182, 183
Exodusters 64

Farm Bill 151, 152, 169, 215
Farmers: Black 47, 204; Tenant 49
Farming 47
Farm Security Administration 145
Farm Services Agency 145
Federalism 19
Federal Housing Administration (FHA)173
Federal Reserve Bank of Kansas City 214
Federation of Southern Cooperatives 152, 153, 154
Filtering down theory 175
Florida 58, 104, 125; Black Belt 125, 135; Education 135; Unemployment 135
Fourteenth amendment Interstate 203, 204

# Index

Freedmen's Bureau 33, 46, 142
Freedmen 31, 32, 39, 42, 142
Freedmen's Savings and Trust Company (freedmen bank) 46

Garvey, Marcus 75, 77
Garvey movement 76
Generational wealth 65
Georgia 23, 27, 58, 61, 88, 116, 123, 126, 203; Atlanta 121; Augusta 203; Black Belt 22, 23, 54, 73, 98, 118, 119, 121, 127, 135-36; Dougherty County 22, 142; Educational attainment 119, 126, 135, 136; Foreign investment 122
Generational wealth 65; Hancock county 23, 24, 126; International offices 122; Macon 203; Milledgeville 98; Population counties 118; Poverty 118, 119, 126, 127; Quality of life 120; Unemployment 135-136
Globalization 162
*Gomillion v. Lightfoot of 1960* 81
Gordon, Spiver 101
Gore, Sr., Albert 83
Governmental Accountability Office (GAO) 186, 187
Great Depression 144
Griffin, Floyd 99

Hamer, Fannie Lou 154
Hampton College 72
Hayes, President Rutherford 55
Hayes-Tilden election 164
Haywood, Harry 10, 89
Historically Black Colleges and Universities (HBCUs) 192, 193
Hogue, Spencer 101
Holder, Eric 102
Honda, 179, 180
Howard, Oliver 33, 34
Hurricane Katrina 163
Hyundai 179, 180

Immigrants 3
Imprisonment 42
Indentured servants 3, 4
India 212, 213
Indian Institutes of Technology (IIT) 212
Industry Recruitment 121, 168,
Inequality 182
Interracial effort 71

Jamaica 73
Jim crow laws 58, 63
*John Punch Case 1640* 4
Johnson, Andrew 31, 33, 35, 36
Johnson, Bobby Joe 101
Lyndon, Johnson 33, 34, 35, 36, 37, 39, 83

Kansas 64
Kefauver, Estes 83
Kentucky 58, 177
Kentucky Economic Justice Alliance 183
Key, V.O., 50
King, Martin Luther 86
Knowledge-based economy 206, 210
Knox, John 59
Ku Klux Klan 82, 87, 88
Labor 49; Gang 49
Landownship 142, 152; Blacks 46, 47, 67; Confiscation 32; Forty acres 32
Land and politics 47, 61
Leadership 96
Legacy 9, 12, 40, 43, 36, 161
Liberia 73
Local government structure 42, 93, 95, 96, 97, 99, 159, 197, 199
Local policy making 57, 208
Local politics 57, 208
Lodge Bill 63
Louisiana 41, 58, 87, 116, 127, 136, 166, 177; Black Belt, 136-137; Bogalusa 88; Education 136-37; St. Landry Parish 62; Unemployment 136-137
Lowndes County Freedom Organization 87
Loyal leagues 48, 49, 61
Luizzo, Viola, 87
Lynching, 76

Manufacturing economy 206
Majoritarian system 106
Majority-minority districts 106
Mayors: African Americans 97
Mayor-council government 95, 97, 99
McIntyre, Mike 192, 196
Melham, Ken 107
Mercedes 179, 180
Montgomery Improvement Association 86
Migration: Black 60, 77; Great migration, 165
Military: Service, 27, 28
Militia 34, 48

233

Miller, Zell 192, 193, 196
Mississippi 29, 58, 59, 87, 88, 104, 116, 129, 137, 153, 166, 176, 177, 195, 203; Black Belt 128; Black codes 29; Delta 200; Discriminatory 200, 201; Education, 129, 137-138; Leflore county 62, 63; Meridian 203; Natchez 203; Poverty 129; Unemployment 137, 138
Missouri Compromise of 1820 20
Moseley, Jim 214

Native Americans 20
National Academy of Public Administration 186, 187
National Association for the Advancement of Colored People 86, 153
National government 37, 79, 107, 165; Discriminatory 37; Policy 171, 172, 195
New Deal 79, 80, 159, 172, 173
New Mexico 64
New South 18, 36, 59, 103
Nixon, Richard 106
Nonviolent ideologies 86
North American Free Trade Agreement (NAFTA) 183, 184
North Carolina 116, 129, 138, 150; Black Belt 129, 138; Education 138; Poverty 129; Unemployment138

Obama, Barack 112, 113, 151
*Of Mr. Booker T. Washington and Others* essay 44
Oklahoma 64
Old Economy 209
Old Testament 6, 19
Old South 1, 5, 9, 87, 30, 59, 63, 103, 118,
One party system 42, 50, 56, 71, 78
Old order 56, 64

Pace, John 60
Pan Africanism 71, 72, 73
Pan African Congress 72
Paris, Wendell, 95, 101
Peonage 60
Perry, Benjamin 31
Persistent poverty 162, 166, 192, 205; Study, 192
*Persistent Poverty in the South A Community Based Perspective* 193
Physical infrastructure 162, 209, 213

*Pigford v. Glickman* 149, 150, 151, 152
Pigford case 148
Planters 71
Plantation economy 80
*Plessy v. Ferguson (1896)* 40, 58, 59
Perry, Benjamin 31
*Policy as usual* 215
Political culture 10, 42, 71, 77, 93, 109, 198; Conservative 77
Political fraud 61
Political ideology 109
Political integration 162
Poverty 15, 116, 205; Generational 15; Regional 116; State rankings 116
Prosser, Gabriel 27
Progressive Movement 98
Poverty trap 185
Protest: Slave 27; Stono rebellion 27; Gabriel's Revolt 27; Denmark Vesey 27; Nat Turner 27
Public Private partnerships 215

Racial discrimination 160
Racism 159, 197, 202, 206
*Radio Free Dixie* 89
Readmittance into the Union 39
Raparations 74
Raper, Arthur 118, 121
Reconstruction 31, 40, 41, 43, 50, 51, 52, 55, 56, 58, 59, 105
Reconstruction Acts of 1867 38
Recession 170
Redistricting 106
Regio: Development 132, 187; Differences 117, 170; Importance of 214
Regional commission 191, 192, 194, 195, 196
Regional economies 162
Reno, Janet 102
Republicans 58, 107; African Americans 47, 54, 107; Leaders 49, 53; Organizations 47
RNC 107; Party 47, 49, 50, 51, 52, 55, 56, 78, 90, 106, 107
Right to Work 178
Riley, Bob 180
Rochester Participative governance process 213
*Rodriguez v. San Antonio* (1973),
Roosevelt, F.D. 79, 164

# Index

Rural: Economy 121; Development policy 121, 165; People 115, 116; Places 121
Rural Development Act of 1972 169
Rural Electrification Act of 1936 168

Salaam, Yusuf 111
Secretary of Agriculture 145
Segregation: Separate but equal 59
Selective Service Act of 1940 80
Seminole War 27
Sharecropper 65, 69, 71, 172
Sharecroppers Union 69, 70
*Slaughterhouse case* 39
Slavery 12, 20, 21, 22, 23, 24, 26, 74; Industrial 26
Tavis Smiley 107
*Smith v. Allwright (1944)* 81
Snow Hill Institute 43
Social: Contract 59; Control 82; Exclusion 205, 206; Order 42, 198
social/cultural factors 12
Socialists 67, 68
Social security 80
Society: Closed 7, 36; Southern 26
South 6; States 195
South Carolina 25, 27, 31, 106, 116, 130, 139, 177; Black Belt 139, 130; Education 139; Unemployment 139
Southern: Aristocracy 15; Culture 1, 41, 42; Economy 26; Development 154, 162; Mythology 1, 5, 9; Region 3, 105, 116, 195
Southern Alliance 63, 64
Southern Christian Leadership Conference 86, 153
Southeastern Crescent Authority SECA 194
*Southern Manifesto of 1956* 83
*Southern Literacy Messenger* 21
Southern Regional Council 153, 154
Southern Strategy 106
Southern Tenants Farmers Union (STFU) 68, 69, 76
Stalin 70
State competitiveness 181, 185
State constitutional convention 52, 53
State legislature expulsion of black 54
State's rights 82
Stevens, Thaddeus 31, 32
Stewart, Ken 122
Student Nonviolent Coordinating Committee 86, 87, 153

Sumner, Charles 31
Supreme Court 19, 39, 40, 210

Talmadge, Herman Eugene 173
Taxes: Tax incentives and abatements 162; Tax credits 176
Tea Party 107
Technology 214
Tennessee 58; Black Belt 131, 139; Education 139; Nashville 86; Unemployment 139
Terrorism 43, 58,
Texas 58; Houston County 61
Textile mills 174
*The Souls of Black Folk* 7
Thurmond, Strom 106
Tilden, Samuel 55
Threadgill, Thomas 101
Trumball, Lyman 31, 38
Turner, Albert 101
Turner, Henry, McNeal 73, 74, 77,
Turner, Mary: Lynching 76
Tuskegee Institute 72
Tuskegee University 192
Tydings amendment of 1942 79

Union: Membership 176, 177
Union Leagues 49, 61
Universal Negro Improvement Association UNIA 75, 76
*Up From Slavery* 7
United States Department of Agriculture (USDA) 144, 146, 148; Discrimination 144, 146, 150
*US v. Reese* 39, 40
*US v. Cruishank* 39, 40
United States Housing Authority 174
University of Georgia 192, 193

Vilsack, Tom 152
Virginia 57, 195; Black Belt 131, 140; Education 131, 140; Jamestown 3, 21; Unemployment 140
Violence 40, 42, 49, 60, 63, 64, 68
Voting Rights Act of 1965 92, 101
Voting 104
Voters 103
Voter fraud 100
Voter registration 91
Voter turnout 110, 113

War on Poverty 192
Washington, Booker T. 7, 44, 45, 72, 73
Webster, Adeline 101
White 55; Citizens 82
Elites 14, 5; Local 14; Poor 82; Southern
    race mythology 1, 2, 4, 20, 37;
    Supremacy Nationalism 6
Working class 13
Whiteness 2
Williams, Robert 89
Wimberley, Ron 9, 124-131, 131-139
Works Progress Administration (WPA) 173
World War I 76